HIGHER and INTERMEDIATE 2

# Business Management

## SECOND EDITION

Peter Hagan
Alistair B. Wylie

## Hodder Gibson

A MEMBER OF THE HODDER HEADLINE GROUP

The Publishers would like to thank the following for permission to reproduce copyright material:
**Photo credits** Page 10 © Will Burgess/Reuters/Corbis; page 15 © HBOS; page 17 © Gary I Rothstein/epa/Corbis; page18 © Jacks of London; page 22 © Alex Segre/Rex Features; page 24 © DPA/EMPICS; page 25 © Lucas Schifres/Corbis; page 26 © Stagecoach Group; page 27 © Wm Morrison Supermarkets plc; page 28 © Scottish Power Group Company; page 34 © David Pearson/Alamy; page 43 © Pat Shearman/Alamy; page 47 © Colin Cuthbert/SPL; page 48 © Chris Collins/Corbis; page 49 (left) © www.morguefile.com; page 49 (right) © Scott Camazine/Alamy; page 50 © Closon-Jacquemart/Rex Features; pages 58 and 74 © Burns Express; page 71 © Helen King/Corbis; page 72 © Mackie's of Scotland; page 75 © Frank Chmura/Alamy; page 77 © Rob Lacey/vividstock.net/Alamy; page 79 © Bernd Kammerer/AP Photo/Empics; page 87 © Yadid Levy/Alamy; page 98 © Paul Thompson Images/Alamy; page 115 © Susan Ragan/Reuters/Corbis; page 117 © Photofusion Picture Library/Alamy; page 122 © Helene Rogers/Alamy; page 123 © David Levenson/Alamy; page 125 (top) © Advertising Archives; page 125 (middle) © Quality Meat Scotland/www.qmsscotland.co.uk; page 128 © James Leynse/Corbis; page 133 © Photofusion Picture Library/Alamy; page 141 © Keith Dannemiller/ Alamy; page 150 © Alex Segre/Rex Features; page 156 © British Standards Institution; page 157 © Baxters Food Group; page 169 © Action Press/Rex Features; page 193 © Clive Dixon/Rex Features; page 196 © Photodisc; page 201 © Photodisc; page 203 © Dennis MacDonald/Alamy; page 208 © Jess Hurd/reportdigital.co.uk; page 210 © Paul Faith/PA/EMPICS; page 212 © Johnny Green/PA/EMPICS; page 215 © 2004 UPP/TopFoto; page 223 © The Royal Bank of Scotland; pages 225 and 242 © Clydesdale Bank PLC; page 226 © James Fraser/ Rex Features; page 234 © epa/Corbis
**Acknowledgements** Artworks by Tony Wilkins Design and DC Graphic Design Limited.

Every effort has been made to trace all copyright holders, but if any have been inadvertently overlooked the Publishers will be pleased to make the necessary arrangements at the first opportunity.

Although every effort has been made to ensure that website addresses are correct at time of going to press, Hodder Gibson cannot be held responsible for the content of any website mentioned in this book. It is sometimes possible to find a relocated web page by typing in the address of the home page for a website in the URL window of your browser.

Papers used in this book are natural, renewable and recyclable products. They are made from wood grown in sustainable forests. The logging and manufacturing processes conform to the environmental regulations of the country of origin.

Orders: please contact Bookpoint Ltd, 130 Milton Park, Abingdon, Oxon OX14 4SB. Telephone: (44) 01235 827720. Fax: (44) 01235 400454. Lines are open from 9.00 – 5.00, Monday to Saturday, with a 24-hour message answering service. Visit our website at www.hoddereducation.co.uk. Hodder Gibson can be contacted direct on: Tel: 0141 848 1609; Fax: 0141 889 6315; email: hoddergibson@hodder.co.uk

© Peter Hagan, Alistair Wylie 2006
First Edition Published 2002 (entitled *Higher Business Management*)
Second Edition Published 2006
This Edition Published 2006 by
Hodder Gibson, a member of the Hodder Headline Group
2a Christie Street
Paisley PA1 1NB

Impression number    10 9 8 7 6 5 4 3 2
Year                          2012 2011 2010 2009 2008 2007

Cover photo by: ImageState/Alamy

Typeset in 10.5pt ITC Century Light by DC Graphic Design Limited, Swanley Village, Kent.

Printed and bound in Great Britian by Martins The Printers, Berwick-upon-Tweed for Hodder Gibson, a division of Hodder Headline, 2A Christie Street, Paisley PA1 1NB

A catalogue record for this title is available from the British Library

ISBN 13: 978 0 340 913697

# CONTENTS

# About the Authors

### Peter Hagan

Peter Hagan entered the teaching profession in 1991 after 10 years working in the service industries. He has produced work for a number of national education bodies, specialising in Business Management. He currently works as a Principal Teacher of Business Education and is an Examiner in Business Management for the SQA.

He is the author of *How to Pass Higher Business Management* (0340 885564) and worked with Alistair Wylie and Rhona Sivewright on the Case Studies and Exam Preparation book (0340 914742), which will be the perfect companion for this textbook.

### Alistair Wylie

Alistair Wylie qualified as a teacher in 1995 and has since taught in both the secondary and further and higher education sectors. He also works regularly as a consultant for national bodies and has previously run his own business.

He has written several books and currently works in the national education sector. This is his second collaboration with Peter Hagan. Surprisingly, the two men only met face-to-face some two years after completion of the first edition.

# Introduction

Welcome to the second edition of our book which has been renamed, *Higher and Intermediate 2 Business Management*.

This book is intended as a companion to the Scottish Qualification Authority (SQA) courses in Business Management at Intermediate 2 and Higher levels as revised for first implementation in Session 2006/7.

It has been written in simple and everyday language wherever possible and is intended for use by students and teachers alike.

The book is designed to follow the course content as set by the SQA and follows on from the first edition in providing the most comprehensive coverage available with up to date examples taken from Scottish business. The book is designed with a deliberate 'Scottish flavour' to reflect the Scottish base of the course and external assessment.

The authors are both experienced educators with over 30 years of teaching experience between them gained in the secondary, further and higher education sectors, as well as the national education arena. We have drawn on the successes of the first edition and, hopefully, taken on board the praises and criticisms received to provide an even better resource in this new edition. We have opted for a single textbook and also the production of an accompanying book for Higher level: *Higher Business Management Case Studies and Exam Preparation*. This accompanying book contains 15 case studies set to the standard of Section One of the Higher external assessment; examples of questions set to the standard of Section Two of the Higher external assessment; suggested answers to case studies and all questions; useful tips for exam preparation and details of the construction of the external assessment.

Each chapter in this second edition has been structured in the same way for ease of use and comprises:

- content summary
- topics
- information points
- end of chapter revision questions
- chapter summary.

In addition, the glossary has been updated and more recent Scottish business examples have been added throughout the text.

We are indebted to our families for their patience during the writing of this second edition, and to our friends, colleagues and peers for their feedback from the first edition, advice and encouragement in the preparation of this edition. Special thanks must also go to the staff at Hodder Gibson, Paisley. In particular, John Mitchell for his unwavering support for the book and Katherine Bennett for her due diligence and patience in dealing with us and proofing the book before publication.

We, the authors, hope that you will find this a useful resource during your period of study. We have attempted to include information that is as recent as possible, including website references that have been checked prior to publication.

*Peter Hagan*
*Alistair B Wylie*

January 2006

# SECTION ONE

# Business Enterprise

# CHAPTER 1

## Business in contemporary society

This part of the course contains the following topics:

**Role of business in society**

Wealth creation, production and consumption of goods and services, satisfaction of wants, sectors of activity.

**Types of business organisations**

Self-employed, private limited company, public limited company, voluntary organisation, charity, publicly-funded organisation.

This covers firms of all sizes and the national and international aspects of their operation, including multinationals.

**Objectives**

Profit maximisation, survival, sales maximisation, growth, social responsibility, managerial objectives, provision of a service. This relates to different types of organisations.

**Role of enterprise and the entrepreneur**

Identifying business opportunities, franchising, combining factors of production, innovation and risk-taking.

**Stakeholders**

Shareholders, customers, employees, donors (for charities), management, government, suppliers, banks, other lenders, taxpayers, community as a whole, local government; influence of stakeholders on organisational objectives and behaviour.

**Methods of obtaining finance**

Internal and external sources, short- and long-term sources, shares, loans, banks, local enterprise companies (LECs) and government.

**Factors affecting the operation of business**

Sources of finance and sources of assistance – local enterprise companies (LECs), banks, local authorities, including subsidised premises, government help, such as grants and allowances, help for exporters through trade fairs, advice and courses for small businesses, European Union (EU), grants.

Methods of growth: horizontal and vertical integration, diversification, merger and takeover, demerger, divestment.

| | |
|---|---|
| **Business as a dynamic activity** | The impact of changes in demand, demographic trends, competition, regional policies, structure of the labour market, local and central government, privatisation, EU, environment, technology, ICT. |
| | The above can be grouped under headings of socio-cultural; technological; economic; environmental; political; national and international competitive environment. |
| **Changes in the business environment** | The increasing significance of multinationals, the greater business orientation of publicly-funded organisations, changes in the size of firms, e.g. the importance of small firms, downsizing and franchising. |
| | Factors which can cause change: internal and external. |
| | The importance of change to business, e.g. the need to respond to internal and external pressures, and the need to ensure survival. |

# Topic The role of business in society

## *What is a business?*

A business is *any* organisation which is set up in order to achieve a set of objectives. This includes the obvious – businesses that sell their products for profit – but also any other organisation that has been set up to achieve other objectives. This would include organisations such as charities, local and national government (including education).

It may seem odd to think of your school or college as a business, but they perform the same function as profit-making businesses in organising themselves to provide a good or service.

## *Why are businesses important?*

Businesses provide us with the goods and services that allow us to live our lives the way we do. Before we organised our society with businesses, we would all have to make our own clothes, build our own shelter, and grow or catch our own food. There would be little time for anything else, and we would be living a very basic existence.

Business has allowed us to live much better lives and continually works to improve them.

## *Wealth creation*

Businesses not only provide us with the goods and services we need, but they also provide us with the jobs that give us the wages and salaries that allow us to buy those goods and services. The more businesses there are, the more opportunities for us to earn money.

The wealth of countries is measured by how many goods and services the country can produce. The more business activity there is, the more goods and services that are produced, and the wealthier a country is. So the more we produce, the better off we can become.

BUSINESS ENTERPRISE

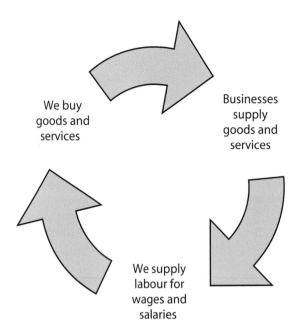

## *Cycle of business*

The cycle of business can be described as the constant production of goods and services to satisfy the wants of consumers.

In order to survive and enjoy life, there are certain things that we want or need. The needs are simple, in that we need food, clothing, shelter and warmth to survive.

### Satisfaction of wants

Our wants can be very complicated and varied depending on our individual character and interests. We all have different tastes, for example.

It is the role of business to identify these wants, and then produce goods and services to satisfy them. However, people living in a modern economy are always looking for newer, more advanced goods and services, so businesses have to identify and satisfy these new wants.

This constant creation of new wants stimulates business to supply more goods and services, and so we have this cycle of new wants and new production.

In reality, it is even more complicated than that. Most consumers do not know all that they want in the future, so business has to try to anticipate what consumers will buy in the future. For example, it can take up to five years to develop a new car, so car producers have to try to work out what it is we will want in the future from our cars. With billions of pounds being spent on developing a new car, there is a huge risk involved.

## *The production of goods and services*

What are goods and services?

### Goods

Goods are things we can see and touch such as clothes, mobile phones, i-Pods, food, etc. They are described as tangible products and are split into two categories: **durable goods** and **non-durable goods**.

- We can use durable goods again and again like computers, mobile phones, etc. They have a reasonable life span. Some will be expensive (such as cars), while others (such as pencils) will be cheap. They will not last for ever, but we would expect them to stand up to a lot of use.

- Non-durable goods are things we can normally only use once, such as food, drinks, newspapers, etc.

## Services

Services are things that are done for us. They can be described as non-tangible products. Our main traditional service industries include banking, insurance, tourism, education and health.

The service industries make up the largest part of our modern economy in Scotland, with the majority of employees working in services.

## *Resources needed for production*

In order to produce goods and services, businesses need to use resources. These resources are the **inputs** for business activity, with the goods and services that they produce being the **output** of business activity.

These resources are called the **factors of production**. These are the resources that business needs in order to produce goods and services:

### Land

This includes the natural resources such as oil, water, and the land itself. It refers to everything that can be extracted from the land and sea, grown on the land, or produced in the atmosphere. It can also include sunshine which is used with solar panels to create energy.

### Labour

All organisations need people to work for them. Some only need a few, while many, like local government, need thousands of people. Labour is the number of people required to make the organisation work. It includes all their physical and mental effort.

### Capital

These are the man-made resources. In other business areas, capital is described as the money invested in an organisation; however, here we use it as an economic term to describe factories, machines, lorries, tools, etc. They have all been created or produced from natural resources, and are necessary to produce goods and services.

### Enterprise

This could be described as the most important factor of production, because without it production would not take place. Enterprise is the human effort and will to provide goods and services. The entrepreneur is the person who brings together all the other resources and takes the risks to produce the goods or services.

BUSINESS ENTERPRISE

### Consumption of goods and services

Consumption means using up. We use up goods and services by buying them. We will look at how and why we do this in detail in Chapter 4, Marketing; however, by buying them we provide income to businesses to produce more goods and services through the profits that they make, and this in turn creates more jobs and provides more people with income.

### Sectors of industrial activity

There are three sectors of industry:

1   **Primary sector:** businesses that are involved in exploiting or extracting the natural resources (e.g. farming, mining, fishing, oil exploration).

2   **Secondary sector:** businesses that are involved in manufacturing and construction. They take the natural resources produced in the primary sector and change them into things we can use (e.g. car manufacture, building firms).

3   **Tertiary (service) sector:** businesses that are involved in providing services rather than goods, such as banking and tourism.

All economies start out in the primary sector, and as their economies grow they move through each of the sectors. This process is called **de-industrialisation**, which the Scottish economy has gone through during the last 30 years. Although Scotland still has an important primary and secondary sector, the numbers employed in these sectors has declined dramatically over this time.

Many of our manufacturing industries like ship-building, steel-making and car manufacture have been greatly reduced in size or have disappeared entirely, and service industries are now much more important to our economy. For example, there has been significant growth in employment in call-centres and also e-commerce firms.

## Topic  Types of business organisations

Organisations are made up of people working together and using resources to achieve objectives. These objectives will include producing goods and services by changing inputs into outputs. Business organisations exist to satisfy consumers' wants by making and providing goods and services.

All organisations fall into one of two categories – public sector or private sector businesses.

### Private sector organisations

These organisations are run by private individuals, not the government. For most, the basic aim or objective is to make a profit. Profits are achieved when the income from sales exceeds the expenditure on costs. The basic aim of voluntary and charity organisations is to raise money for good causes, or to provide services that would otherwise not be provided.

## *Profit-making businesses*

The most common types of profit-making private business organisations are:

- sole traders
- partnerships
- limited companies.

### Sole trader

This is a business which is owned and managed by one person (e.g. small shops, hairdressers, tradespeople).

#### Advantages

- It is very simple to set up.
- You make all the decisions.
- You can keep all the profits.

There are no legal formalities to go through to set up in business as a sole trader – you can simply start trading. As the person in charge of the business and the only owner, you have the power to make all of the business decisions, and can run it however you like. Also and very importantly, you do not have to share the profits with anyone.

#### Disadvantages

- Borrowing from the bank is more difficult, and they may charge higher rates of interest on loans to sole traders.
- The sole trader has unlimited liability, so if the business is not successful and runs up debts, the owner could lose not only the business but his/her home, car and possessions to pay off these business debts. If this still was not enough, they could be made bankrupt by the courts.
- They have to run the business without help. Taking holidays or falling ill means that there is no income, but the costs continue.

Sole trader used to be the most popular form of business, but the disadvantages make it far less attractive today. Probably the most important factor is the unlimited liability involved. The prospect of losing everything is often not worth the risk. When you consider that over 80 per cent of new businesses fail within the first year or so of operation, it is easy to see why. Because it is now much easier and cheaper to set up a limited company, most people prefer to set up a new business this way.

### Partnerships

This is a business that is owned and controlled by two or more people but less than 20 (except for solicitor and accountancy firms who are allowed more). Again it is normally a small business, but is the preferred type of organisation by the professions such as doctors, dentists, lawyers, accountants, etc.

Partnerships should have a legal agreement stating how profits are to be shared, what the responsibilities are, how much money they are allowed to draw from the business, etc.

BUSINESS ENTERPRISE

### Advantages

- The partners can share the responsibilities involved in running the business, so that taking holidays or falling ill will not be so much of a problem.

- Partners can specialise (e.g. a plumber and an electrician).

- More money can be invested in the business because there are more owners.

### Disadvantages

- They also have unlimited liability (except for certain types of sleeping partners).

- There may be arguments between the partners on how to run the business.

- Partners can leave or new partners can be taken on, which can upset the running of the business.

## Limited companies

Most new businesses now prefer to set up as a limited company rather than a sole trader or a partnership. The costs involved have decreased and it is becoming much simpler. For example, you can now set up a new limited company over the internet. As their name suggests, limited companies have limited liability. They only lose the money or capital they have invested in the business, not any of their personal possessions. The **shareholders** (a minimum of two is required by law) are those people that own a share of the business (in the form of share certificates), and so are the owners of the business.

There are two types:

1 Public limited companies – Plc

2 Private limited companies – Ltd.

To become a limited company you must register your company with the Companies Registrar and complete two legal documents – **Memorandum of Association** and **Articles of Association**. These set out the aims of the business, how they will be run and financed.

The profits are shared out in the form of **dividends**, each shareholder receiving a certain amount for each of the share certificates they own in the business.

The main difference between the two is that plcs are allowed to sell their shares to the public through the stock exchange. Private limited companies cannot, they can only sell to individuals who are invited to buy shares with the full agreement of the existing shareholders.

### Advantages

- Shareholders have **limited liability**. If the business fails, they only lose the amount of money they have invested.

- For private limited companies only, they do not have to disclose most of the information that public limited companies have to provide to the public, such as their annual reports.

- For public limited companies only, because you can buy and sell the shares at any time, people are more willing to invest; the business can raise money by selling more shares to the public for big projects, which means it may be easier to plan, develop and expand.

### Disadvantages

- All companies must be registered with the Registrar of Companies. This means they have to disclose some financial information, which the public and their competitors can see.

- Big organisations can be very difficult to manage efficiently and may experience diseconomies of scale.

- It is more difficult to keep workers happy and well-motivated in a big organisation.

- There is a cost in setting up and administrating the legal requirements placed on limited companies.

The majority of big firms are public limited companies like BP, British Airways, Stagecoach.

## *Multinationals*

These are normally very large businesses which have outlets or production facilities in a number of different countries. Many British businesses have opened facilities in other countries. There are a number of good reasons for doing so:

- Governments in other countries may offer incentives such as tax concessions or large grants to entice them to open there.

- Lower wage rates may lower the cost of production.

- Higher skilled workers may be available for the same or lower cost.

- Legislation in other countries may be more relaxed, meaning production can be much cheaper (working hours, environmental restrictions, minimum wage, building regulations, etc).

- The rate of corporation tax may be lower which means the owners can keep more of their profits.

- The business can then operate competitively in the local market.

However, there are a number of factors which may deter organisations from locating abroad:

- Legislation in the local country may be too restrictive to operate profitably.

- The local currency may be too weak to allow profits to be converted back at a good rate.

- There may be a lack of technical expertise or equipment, including poor infrastructure.

- Cultural differences may make the products unpopular for both production and sale.

- The country may be politically unstable.

## Info Point

Mars, Incorporated now operates its three core businesses – snackfood, petcare and main meal food – under the Masterfoods name in most parts of the world.

In Europe, the Americas, Asia and Australia/New Zealand, the combined core businesses are run on a regional basis, each reporting to a Regional President.

On a global basis, Mars does not have a large central headquarters because responsibility for 'getting the job done' is held by its various businesses around the world.

Because the businesses are now also integrated at the individual country level, Mars has the flexibility to operate very effectively across multiple countries, while at the same time allowing the company to leverage its combined businesses within a single country when necessary.

Outside the Masterfoods structure, Mars also operates a smaller business, MEI/Drinks Group, which makes drinks vending systems and electronic coin changers, bill acceptors, and other electronic transaction solutions for a range of industries.

Finally, Information Services International (ISI) operates globally to provide technical infrastructure and information technology support for the entire company.

*Source:* www.Mars.com

## Trading internationally

Markets for many goods and services are now global, so firms in Scotland will face competition from organisations across the world. On the other hand, this also means that the markets for Scottish goods and services are worldwide. Improvements in communications technology have made it much easier for organisations in this country to trade internationally. The internet has opened up international markets for even the smallest firms, who could not have dreamt of trading abroad before.

**Benefits of trading internationally:**

- A much larger market is available.
- You can develop an international brand.
- It allows the organisation to grow outside saturated or highly competitive markets.
- Higher profits may be available through higher market prices.

**Constraints in trading internationally:**

- There is more competition from other international and local businesses.

- There may well be additional transportation costs, either of goods or personnel.

- Legislation in different countries will affect what is produced, how it is produced, and how it is advertised. This includes artificial barriers (red-tape) to keep the level of imports low. There will be tariffs (additional taxes added to the cost of imports) and trade barriers which restrict the amount of imports that a country will allow.

- There will also be cultural differences in what local markets will buy.

- Language difficulties may reduce the success of trading internationally.

## The voluntary sector

These organisations' main aim is not to make profits but to raise money for good causes, or to provide services to the public which would otherwise not be provided at all or not to a high standard.

Any profits that charities make are used to help people. Charities are formed by people sharing similar beliefs or concerns.

Charities have to be registered with the Charity Commissioners who oversee their activities. To be recognised as a charity the organisation has to have one or more of the following as their main objectives:

- to relieve poverty

- to advance education

- to advance religion

- to carry out activities beneficial to the community.

Once they have been recognised as a charity they are given 'charitable status', which means they do not have to pay some taxes such as VAT.

## Info Point

This table shows the legal status of enterprises in Scotland, 2003:

| Legal status | Number of enterprises | Total Scottish employment |
|---|---|---|
| Companies (incl. Building Societies) | 53,495 | 1,212,430 |
| Sole proprietors | 52,990 | 152,830 |
| Partnerships | 33,400 | 192,420 |
| Public corporation/nationalised body | 25 | 29,210 |
| Central and local government | 205 | 516,680 |
| Non-profit-making bodies and mutual associations | 7,580 | 138,350 |
| **Total registered** | **147,695** | **2,241,910** |
| Unregistered enterprises | 115,055 | 133,190 |
| **Total** | **262,750** | **2,375,110** |

*Source:* Scottish Executive, ONS (IDBR)

**BUSINESS ENTERPRISE**

### *Publicly-funded organisations*

These are organisations set up and owned by the government to provide services to the public which the private sector could not provide very well or could not provide at all. Making a profit is not always important, however keeping within the budget (money allocated from the government) is very important.

## Public corporations

A public corporation is one which is owned by the public or in which the public has a substantial interest.

There used to be many more public corporations but these have been **privatised** (sold on the stock market), such as British Telecom, BP, and the gas and electricity companies.

## Government-funded service providers

The government provides us with services such as the National Health Service, Social Security and Defence. These are services which the private sector would be unlikely to offer to the public in ways that the government or the public would find acceptable.

They are financed by the government in order to carry out their policies in these areas. Each year they are given a set amount of money to spend. Each service usually has its own appointed government minister who has supervisory control and provides guidelines to managers as to how the service should be run. The managers then make many of the decisions as to how the money could be best spent to meet the government objectives.

## Local authorities

They provide us with services such as education, housing, leisure and recreation, and street lighting. They receive money from council tax, government grants and fees for using their facilities, such as sports centres.

Local authorities either set up their own departments to provide these services, or they **contract out** to private companies who receive a fee for providing these services, such as cleaning or meals for schools. The local authority has to do this, as national government legislation insists that some services have to be put out to **compulsory tendering**, where private companies are invited to bid for the work. Those who offer the best value for money are given the contract for a number of years.

# **Topic** Business objectives

All businesses must have objectives. These objectives will differ from organisation to organisation and will often depend on the type of organisation.

Objectives identify the specific goals of the organisation, how they are to be achieved and the eventual end result.

Objectives may be split in any organisation and identified as being either:

- general, or
- specific.

## Info Point

This table shows Scottish Executive and Local Authority spending (£ millions):

| | Net expenditure financed from grants, non-domestic rates, council tax and balances | | |
| --- | --- | --- | --- |
| | 2001–02 | 2002–03 | 2003–04 |
| Education | 3,001 | 3,343 | 3,659 |
| Social work | 1,352 | 1,611 | 1,766 |
| Police, fire and emergency planning | 1,008 | 1,035 | 1,133 |
| Roads and transport | 373 | 456 | 487 |
| Environmental services | 369 | 397 | 425 |
| Culture and related services | 457 | 488 | 529 |
| Planning and economic development | 126 | 137 | 148 |
| Other services | 302 | 351 | 338 |
| Loan charges | 739 | 739 | 773 |
| **Total** | **7,726** | **8,557** | **9,259** |

*Source:* www.scotland.gov.uk/stats

General objectives are those objectives which are determined by the top layer of management in the organisation. They outline the general goals and aims of the organisation, and may not necessarily identify how these are to be achieved at a departmental level.

Specific objectives are made in the light of general objectives and are more focused in their nature. They identify how the general objectives of the organisation can be achieved through the performance of each department within the organisation.

Business objectives will differ according to the organisation in question. However, the main business objectives can be identified as:

- profit maximisation
- survival
- sales maximisation
- growth
- social responsibility
- managerial objectives
- provision of a service.

Each of these objectives is fundamental to the continued existence of an organisation. For many organisations, the objective of maximising profits will be their primary goal, but this does not apply to all organisations. For example, a charity does not have profit as its main objective. Charities exist to provide a service to those in need, and the provision of the services required would be among their main objectives.

## Profit maximisation

Commercial organisations are all concerned with making profits. A profitable business means money for its owners and stakeholders.

Profit maximisation is not enough for the continued success of the business. The growth and development of the business as a whole is also important.

## Survival

All businesses, given a choice, would like to survive into the future. Survival is one of the main business objectives but it is dependent upon and related to the business objectives of profit (maximisation) and growth.

## Sales maximisation

Commercial organisations which offer goods or services for sale are concerned with making money. Profit maximisation can be achieved through sales maximisation, e.g. increased sales mean increased revenue, which can lead to increased profits.

## Growth

While it is not a pre-requisite for survival that a business should grow, it is necessary for all businesses to develop if they wish to survive.

It is unrealistic for a business to expect that its products and customer base need never be altered. Any business that adopts this attitude to the market will not survive in the long term. Survival is dependent on the development of the business and its staff, and the re-invention and evolution of its products.

## Social responsibility

Many businesses nowadays are concerned with how the public perceives them and how they treat the environment. This is called **social responsibility**, and can cover the following areas:

- working conditions
- treatment of the environment
- business associations.

Businesses that are not socially responsible may find that they attract the interest of pressure groups, have their products boycotted by consumers and are not an attractive proposition for investors.

## Managerial objectives

Managerial objectives exist in an organisation where managers have their own objectives which may operate alongside or contrary to the main business objectives; e.g. they may wish to increase their own salary or position within the company.

## Provision of a service

Most businesses provide some type of product or service, but there are some types of organisations for which the provision of a service is their main concern. That is to say, they may not be concerned with profits or growth but only in providing a service to their customers.

The typical type of organisation that is concerned with providing a service is a charity.

Other business objectives which may be identified include:

- innovation
- market position
- management performance and development
- productivity
- physical and financial resources
- public responsibility
- employee performance and relations
- environmental concerns
- maximise use of available resources
- public profile.

## Info Point: HBOS

'The job of management is to run businesses for the long term. Real success is measured by the increased value created for shareholders. Companies that prosper also remember that they have no right to the loyalty of customers – they earn it through the best strategies, products and service, delivered by outstanding people. HBOS is that sort of business.

The financial services industry is hugely competitive and fast-moving, with new ways of doing business and new channels opening up all the time. An era of substantial value creation for shareholders derived primarily from customer inertia is rapidly being replaced by one of consumer-led competition. In everything we do we seek to take our business closer to that consumer.

In many areas we act as a new entrant in other people's markets. We are aggressive and bold with new products and make no apology for striving to deliver better value to our competitors' customers than they are prepared to do. The strategy for HBOS is therefore, to use our strengths and focus on making sure we deliver the best performance of any in our peer group.

It is comparatively simple:

Everywhere we drive existing businesses much harder and seek to realise their full potential. We seek to be more productive, sell more, and hold on to our customers by giving them real value and superb service.

The UK's most comprehensive new channel strategy is seeing HBOS make major investments in the new ways in which customers will want to trade with us. Business

*continued* ➢

**BUSINESS ENTERPRISE**

by phone and on the net is now a substantial part of our distribution mix and HBOS has advanced product capability in these growth areas.

Knowing what to do and having the resource to do it is the easiest part of most strategies. Being better than anyone else at what you do requires outstanding management. Everywhere in the HBOS group, external management talent has been added to strengthen the HBOS team. I believe this team will win. This business is about growth.'

*Source:* www.insider.co.uk

### Question

Identify two business objectives of HBOS from the information.

### Activity

How do the business objectives of an organisation like the BBC (a publicly funded organisation) differ from an organisation like the Scottish Media Group (a commercial television company)?

Your answer should aim for 100 words.

## Topic  The role of enterprise and the entrepreneur

### *What is enterprise?*

Enterprise is economic activity. It is about finding new and better ways of providing goods and services, or providing new goods and services. It is important because:

- it increases the wealth of our country
- it increases employment opportunities
- it provides profit for investment
- it should mean that resources are used more efficiently
- this should in turn increase our standard of living.

At the centre of enterprise is the role of the entrepreneur. The entrepreneur is the person who combines the factors of production to produce goods or services. Or to put it another way, the entrepreneur is the person who brings together the workers, the natural and man-made resources and organises them to produce goods and services which we need or want.

Without someone taking on the role of the entrepreneur, nothing would be produced. He or she will identify an opportunity to provide new goods or services, or to provide existing goods or services cheaper, or in a better format.

Business enterprise

In all cases they use their own money or borrow money to put all the necessary resources together. They are **risk-takers** – they can stand to lose everything if the idea does not work.

Entrepreneurs can set up any type of business, but the safest for the risk-taker would be a private limited company. One way to get a better chance of success is to buy a franchise.

## *Franchising*

Franchises are business arrangements where one firm pays for the right to run under the trading name of another.

The person or firm who owns and runs the business is called the **franchisee**. The firm that owns the name is called the **franchiser**.

The franchisee buys the right to trade as the franchising business, but has to run the business in a way agreed with the franchiser.

### Advantages for the franchiser

- The franchise can expand relatively quickly without having to buy additional premises or recruit, train and pay staff.

- They will receive a share of the profit and/or a percentage of the sales revenue of the firm.

- Product innovation can be shared among all the franchisees.

- The franchiser can protect themselves from competition by allowing others to open as franchises rather than as direct competition.

- The business will grow as the franchiser wants, as it can set strict guidelines on things like suppliers used, products sold, layout and image of the franchise.

- Growth will allow them to become a recognised brand or organisation.

### Advantages for the franchisee

- The new business gets the existing well-established name and reputation of the franchise with all their brand products, and will have a good chance of attracting a lot of customers immediately. The chance of success will therefore be higher.

- The new business will be helped and supported by the franchiser including benefiting from their advertising and their established processes for quality.

- The franchiser may offer full training in the running of the business.

- A large number of entrepreneurs in the organisation will make successful innovation more likely.

### Disadvantages for the franchiser

- The franchiser's reputation depends upon how good the franchisees are. If there is one piece of bad publicity about a single product or branch, it will affect all the branches.

BUSINESS ENTERPRISE

## Disadvantages for the franchisee

- The franchise agreement allows the franchiser to tell the franchisee exactly how to run the business, and the franchisee may have to buy all their supplies from them.

- The franchisee has to pay part of his/her profits or a percentage of sales to the franchiser.

### Info Point

When Sue Whitehead found she could count the number of male customers coming into her salon on one hand, she knew she'd found a gap in the market.

So she drew a deep breath, gathered all her savings and started **Jacks of London** – an upmarket hairdresser's with a modern twist. It is a modern barber's shop where men can hang out with other men, watch football and have a beer with their salon-style haircut.

Patrick Allen is a marketing consultant and outlines some of these crucial steps. "First, there should be some kind of market research taking place to identify consumer needs," says Patrick.

"If you find these and can provide a solution, there will be some kind of genuine marketable proposition. Most companies try to identify a need or what people are asking for. Consumers don't always realise there is a need for something and so don't ask for it. You should then quickly get your products replicated in the market place.

Going down the franchising route or offering consumers a better experience through websites gives you a word-of-mouth element into the marketing mix. That quickly gets your brand established. Once that is established the next top tip is to think about how you are going to defend it from competitors. They'll be hungry to take your market share away from you so you must build some kind of barrier to prevent competitors stealing your market share," adds Patrick.

Sue and her team are always looking for new ways to stay one step ahead of the competition. They have installed a webcam so customers can click onto the salon's website and find out if there's a queue. Another hit with the punters is that they can have their hair cut in the morning before they go to work, or well into the evening.

And Sue's well thought-out selling points have brought in a steady stream of regular clients – among them premiership footballers and film stars.

"We have 10,000 on our database and we've only been running it for a year. We're now looking to franchise," says Sue.

And Sue hopes that by going down the franchise route, she can expand her business quickly, giving her the best possible chance of keeping copycats at bay.

continued ➤

Sue had realised that her new salon needed to be quite distinctive, so Jacks of London looks very different from the average hairdresser's. It has plasma screens, internet access, free beer and the right sort of magazines. However, just one feature is not enough to make a business stand out. Anyone can quickly take on staff to open twelve hours a day or order in some beer. It takes much longer to copy a product with a clear identity. That is why Sue made Jacks of London so special.

She captured a market before anyone could catch up with her. The niche she has found has a lot of potential: half the population is male! She might not catch them all but there is certainly a big potential market.

*Source:* BBC lunch lessons, November 2004

# Topic Stakeholders

Stakeholders in business are those people who have a key interest in the business. Their interest as a stakeholder will differ according to the type of business in which they have an interest.

Stakeholders in business may include:

- shareholders
- customers
- employees
- donors
- management
- government
- suppliers
- banks
- other lenders
- tax payers
- community
- local government
- investors
- members
- committees.

Stakeholders have an effect on all businesses as they may be able to exert control or influence decisions which have to be made. The degree to which they are able to exercise their influence will be determined by their involvement or interest in the company.

For example, within a public limited company, a shareholder in possession of 35 per cent of the shares in a company will be regarded as a greater stakeholder when compared to an employee holding one per cent of the shares.

The amount of influence that a stakeholder can exert on a company will also be determined by the circumstances under which the influence is exerted. For example, a company may normally regard its owners as the key stakeholders in the business. However, imagine the scenario where a company is polluting the local environment. In this case, the local community may be able to exert a great deal of pressure and hold greater influence compared to the owners even although the local community is not a major stakeholder.

BUSINESS ENTERPRISE

Examples of the different aims that stakeholders have in an organisation include:

- customers interested in obtaining the best prices and the highest quality
- employees concerned about job security and future prospects
- suppliers wishing to receive payment for their goods as soon as possible.

Examples of the influence that stakeholders can exert on organisations include:

- lending institutions having the power to grant or refuse applications for loans
- managers making decisions on a day-to-day basis
- the community as a whole persuading business to carry out its wishes
- shareholders exerting their right to vote at the Annual General Meeting of a limited company.

# **Topic** Financing an organisation

Organisations need money in order to carry out their business. They need money to start up, and to grow or make changes within the organisation. There are a number of different sources of finance available, and the organisation must decide which would be best for them.

All sources come with costs and benefits, e.g. a plc may decide to raise capital through selling shares on the stock market. The benefits are that a large amount of money can be raised relatively quickly, and it does not have to be paid back. The costs are that the profits of the plc will now be split between more shareholders, meaning less for each. Also the new shareholders now have a say about how the business should be run, which could mean loss of control for the directors.

Sole traders, partnerships, voluntary organisations, and publicly funded organisations cannot sell shares to raise money, and of course private limited companies cannot sell shares on the stock market, so they have to look elsewhere.

Sole traders usually start up with the owner's own money being invested, and possibly some borrowing from the bank. The benefit of using your own money is that you do not have to pay it back. Even plcs can use retained profits from previous years. The major drawback of doing this is the opportunity cost involved. What else could you have used the money for? Could it have earned you more money if invested elsewhere?

The table below shows the costs and benefits for each type of organisation, and which is available to each type of organisation:

| Source of finance | Available to | Advantages | Disadvantages |
|---|---|---|---|
| **A loan from a bank** with fixed or variable monthly repayments | All | • quickly arranged<br>• can be repaid over a number of years | • interest will have to be paid<br>• small businesses may find it harder to obtain and may pay higher rates of interest |
| **Mortgage** – a large sum of money borrowed from a bank or building society secured on a property | All | • can be paid back over a long period, e.g. 25 years<br>• can be arranged quickly<br>• interest rate is often lower than a bank | • interest will have to be paid<br>• can lose the property if payments are not kept up |
| **Leasing** – renting vehicles or equipment | All | • can get the asset quickly<br>• do not have to pay out a large sum of money<br>• the asset is replaced when it becomes obsolete | • in the long run it is more expensive than buying<br>• you never own the asset |
| **Selling shares in the business** | Plcs and ltds | • a large amount of money can be raised<br>• do not have to pay the money back | • dividends have to be paid to shareholders<br>• new shareholders will have a say in how the business is run |
| **Debentures** – long-term loan certificates which can be bought and sold on the stock market | Plcs | • you pay interest only until the redemption date<br>• interest payments are fixed<br>• you do not give up any control of your business | • on the redemption date the full amount of the loan must be repaid<br>• interest still has to be paid |
| **Hire purchase** – where you pay a deposit for the asset you are buying and make monthly payments until it is fully paid for | All | • you do not need to pay out the full sum straight away | • the finance company owns the asset until it is fully paid for<br>• it is more expensive in the long run as interest will have to be paid |
| **Grants** – money given by the government | All | • it does not have to be repaid under normal circumstances | • only given if the business can meet certain criteria, e.g. creating jobs in a depressed area |
| **Selling assets** – selling something that you no longer need, or selling it to a finance company and leasing it back | All | • you can get money that does not need to be repaid | • if you lease it back, you will end up paying back more than you received for it |

*continued* ➤

| Source of finance | Available to | Advantages | Disadvantages |
|---|---|---|---|
| **Retained profits –** using money from previous years' profits that has not been spent | All | • you do not have to pay anyone | • you could use the money for something else |
| **Government funding** | Publicly funded organisation | • The money does not have to be repaid | • must stick within the budget set<br>• you have to spend the money as the government says |

# Topic Factors affecting the operation of business

## Sources of finance and assistance

### Local enterprise companies (LECs)

Local enterprise companies have existed for many years and they are a valuable source of information for new companies in the process of starting up, as well as providing information to established companies.

They have access to a wide range of expertise and information including sources of finance, e.g. grants that can be applied for by businesses.

### Activity

If you have access to the internet, visit the website of Scottish Enterprise (www.scottish-enterprise.co.uk) and write a short report (200 words) on the services that they are able to offer to local businesses.

### Banks

Banks (high street and commercial) are a valuable source of information and finance to businesses.

Banks have access to the latest information and many years of expertise in dealing with the individual needs of businesses. They are not only able to offer finance solutions to business but can also assist in the planning process and give general financial advice.

Banks are able to provide both short- and long-term sources of finance. For example, an overdraft facility may be required to overcome a short-term cashflow crisis, or a long-term loan may be required to finance the purchase of new assets for the business.

> ### Activity
>
> If you have access to the internet, visit the website of some of the better known banks and compile a short report on the services that they offer to business customers. Is there a difference between the banks and the services that they offer? Is there one bank that is clearly better than all the others? Your report should be in the region of 250 words.

You may wish to use the following sites:

- www.bankofscotland.co.uk

- www.rbs.co.uk

- www.cbonline.co.uk

## Local authorities

Local authorities can be a source of assistance to businesses, although they would not normally be in the field of finance.

Local authorities may be keen to help businesses set up in their area if there is an existing need for that particular type of business. Assistance may be in the form of a grant (this may or may not need to be repaid at a later date) or in the form of subsidised accommodation.

> ### Activity
>
> If you have access to the internet, visit your local authority's website and see if they have information on assistance available to companies setting up in their area.
>
> For example, the website for Glasgow City Council is www.glasgow.gov.uk

## Grants and allowances

Financial assistance may be available from either central or local government in the form of grants and allowances.

There are typically two areas that attract grants and allowances:

- the setting up of a new business

- the relocation of an existing business to an area of need.

Grants may or may not have to be repaid by the business at a later date. It is usual for an allowance not to have to be repaid. Where grants have to be repaid at a later date, this will usually be at a very favourable rate of interest. Areas of need are identified by central and local government and will include areas of regeneration and high unemployment.

## Trade fairs

Trade fairs are often organised at a local level by enterprise companies, and at a national level by other national organisations or even by central government departments themselves.

BUSINESS ENTERPRISE

They are a useful way of bringing together businesses from different areas of one country or from different countries, enabling agreements for exports and imports to be agreed.

## Advice and courses for small businesses

Small businesses are not usually able to take advantage of the kind of staff training that is available in larger organisations, due to reasons such as a lack of expertise and small staff numbers.

Local enterprise companies, central and local government and other businesses are a vital source of advice for small businesses.

The areas of information technology, employment and European law and accounting are all essential areas where knowledge and advice is often required by small businesses.

Local enterprise companies often run business seminars to share good practice and disseminate information. Specialised training companies are able to offer training sessions and consultancy on many other areas of business operation.

## European Union (EU) Grants

EU grants are available to businesses that meet specific criteria for application. The amounts and types of grants available change, depending on identified areas of need within the European Union countries.

## Retained profits

Some businesses may opt to use profits from previous years to self-finance their business. The benefit of this method of finance is that there is no associated cost. However, organisations that use retained profits often do not have sufficient levels of finance in order to grow quickly.

## Small Business Gateway (www.bgateway.com)

The Small Business Gateway is a partnership with Scottish Enterprise, Scottish Executive and local authorities to assist small businesses with their start-up and development.

## The Prince's Trust (www.princes-trust.org.uk)

The Prince's Trust offers advice, training and grants to young people (aged 14–30) who are starting their own business.

## Inland Revenue (www.inlandrevenue.co.uk)

The Inland Revenue are in charge of tax affairs in the UK and are able to give advice on all taxation matters to individuals and businesses.

## *Methods of growth*

### Horizontal and vertical integration

Companies may grow and develop in different ways and this can have an effect on their operation. Integration of companies occurs when organisations combine to become larger and more powerful.

**Horizontal** integration occurs when two companies which operate at the same stage of production merge into one. Reasons for this include:

- an attempt to dominate the market in which they operate
- a desire to become stronger and therefore more resistant to future takeover
- more efficient operation.

**Vertical** integration occurs when two companies which operate at different stage of production in the same industry decide to merge into one. Advantages to be gained here include:

- more efficient operation
- acquisition of production process at a different stage, reducing the need to 'contract out' work.

**Forward** vertical integration occurs when an organisation takes over a customer, thereby allowing control to be exercised over the chain of distribution and supply.

**Backward** vertical integration occurs when an organisation takes over a supplier, thereby giving a guaranteed source of stock. There may also be financial gains as stock may be cheaper.

**Diversification** is often a business's response to a change in its market, or may be used as an opportunity to enter new markets. Richard Branson's company, Virgin, is a good example of a company which has successfully diversified. Virgin operates businesses as diverse as aeroplanes, trains, personal investment, soft drinks and alcoholic drinks, and music stores all over the world.

Diversification is the result of the takeover or merger of different firms operating in different markets.

The reasons for this include:

- growth and development
- spread of risk in case one area of the business fails
- acquisition of assets
- collection of new knowledge and experience.

Stagecoach is a good example of a Scottish company which has diversified and continued to grow very rapidly over the past 25 years.

BUSINESS ENTERPRISE

## Info Point

Stagecoach, founded in Perth, Scotland, in 1980 with just two buses, is now one of the world's biggest rail and bus groups, operating around 13,000 vehicles and more than 30,000 employees worldwide, and revenues last year approaching £2 billion.

**STAGECOACH** GROUP

With its headquarters still in Scotland, Stagecoach Group plc has four main divisions: Stagecoach UK Bus, Coach USA, Stagecoach Rail, and Overseas Bus. About half of the Group's employees are in Britain and half overseas, and a quarter of the company is American.

In Britain, Stagecoach UK Bus operates more than 8000 buses and coaches from the Highlands of Scotland to South-West England and is made up of 20 regional companies.

Stagecoach also runs the biggest UK rail franchise, with 1,600 trains per day on South West Trains out of London Waterloo, and the smallest, with Island Line on the Isle of Wight.

Stagecoach holds 49 per cent of shares in Virgin Rail which runs the key West Coast and CrossCountry long distance rail routes, and it runs Sheffield Supertram (a light rail network).

The company's acquisition of Coach USA in the summer of 1999 made Stagecoach Group the second-largest coach and bus operator in the vast North American market, with businesses in 38 US States and Canada. With its headquarters in Houston, Texas, Coach USA runs commuters into Manhattan, cruise passengers from airport to ship in Florida, and tourists around the streets of New York and San Francisco, as well as a host of tour and charter, sightseeing, airport shuttle, convention and taxi services.

Stagecoach Group is also the largest bus operator in New Zealand where it also operates ferry services, the second-largest bus operator in Hong Kong with Citybus; and also runs buses in mainland China and Australia.

In April 1993 the company was floated on the London Stock Exchange. Stagecoach's businesses provide a broad portfolio of transport interests with a good exposure to both the UK and international transport markets. Other investments include a 23.3 per cent stake in Road King, a toll operating company in China, and thetrainline.com, a joint venture with Virgin Group.

Stagecoach is committed to building a substantial international transport business and is encouraged by the UK Government's commitment to public transport and greater usage.

Stagecoach owns National Transport Tokens, working with more than 150 local authorities and education agencies in the UK to deliver concessionary travel systems.

(adapted from www.stagecoachplc.com)

## Mergers and takeovers

Mergers and takeovers can often lead to a combination of both negative and positive factors affecting the operation of a business.

A merger occurs when two businesses **agree** to join forces and act as one business.

A takeover, however, arises from one business buying another business. This purchase often occurs under duress and in a predatory manner.

Mergers are generally viewed as being good for both companies involved as well as the customers that they serve. Sometimes they do have a negative effect in that they can lead to down-sizing and job losses.

Takeovers are usually viewed as being bad for the company being taken over and good for customers. They are normally regarded as a cause of job losses and having a negative impact on the company which has been taken over.

### Info Point

**Morrisons Supermarkets**

**Familiar name:** Morrisons can trace its roots back to the start of the last century, when egg and butter merchant William Morrison, the father of current chairman Sir Ken Morrison opened a stall in Bradford Market. The first town-centre shop opened in 1958 and the first supermarket three years later. In 1967, Morrisons became a public company. The share offer was 174 times over-subscribed as more than 80,000 investors applied.

**Watershed year:** In February 2004, the group opened its first store in Scotland, at Kilmarnock. A month later Morrisons completed the multi-billion-pound **takeover** of Safeway. The move created the UK's fourth-largest supermarket group. The enlarged company's share of the UK's grocery market sits at more than 15 per cent, and the firm employs some 150,000 members of staff in stores, factories, distribution centres and head office administrative functions.

*Source*: www.business.scotsman.com, October 2005

**BUSINESS ENTERPRISE**

## Info Point

**Takeover talk continues to power Scottish energy giant**

'Shares in ScottishPower continue to rise on speculation that a takeover bid is brooding in the electrical wings.

As reported in The Scotsman a few weeks back, two of the main contenders thought to be running the numbers over the Glasgow-based utility are E.ON of Germany, which runs Powergen in Britain, and homegrown Centrica.

Both have the cash and the ambition to do a deal for ScottishPower, perceived as weakened by the announcement of the $9.4 billion sale of its US subsidiary Pacificorp after a less than happy foray in America.

To E.ON and Centrica, says the latest market buzz, however, must be added another German utility giant, RWE.

Scottish & Southern Energy remains an outsider bet, if not a rank one.'

*Source*: www.business.scotsman.com, October 2005

## Demerger

Demerger occurs when two companies which have previously joined forces decide to part company and operate individually once more. This kind of situation will have an impact on how the businesses are operated.

## Divestment

Divestment involves selling off one or more subsidiary company originally belonging to the parent company. This is usually done to raise money.

## Asset stripping

Asset stripping involves buying up other businesses and then selling off the profitable parts of that business bit by bit, while closing down the loss-making sections. This often happens after a hostile takeover by another organisation.

## *Contracting out or outsourcing*

Outsourcing has become a very popular business method in the modern business world and many profitable businesses exist to provide this service to other businesses. It is common practice where an organisation is either unable to make a particular good/part or provide a particular service, or where it is more cost-effective to have another business provide the good or service. Outsourcing enables organisations to grow quickly and move rapidly into new market areas where they do not necessarily have the expertise to produce a good or service themselves.

## Info Point

**Oiling the wheels of industry**

As the leading companies across industry sectors become increasingly global in their reach, and, by the same token, find themselves facing global competition even in their home markets, they have had to look for ways of cutting costs and improving efficiencies. One obvious way of achieving this is to outsource non-core activities to a specialist provider.

Craig Anderson, KPMG's senior partner in Scotland, notes whether the task is dealing with simple commodity processes, which are relatively straightforward to outsource, or more complex processes, such as running a company's back office processes (sales order processing, for example), or taking over an entire IT department, the basic idea is the same. "Identify business processes and activities that have to be done but don't really add value to the business. These are all candidates for outsourcing on the grounds that organisations specialising in each of these activities should be able to do the work more efficiently and cheaply," he said.

But cost is by no means the sole benefit of outsourcing.

As Kirk Smith, outsourcing strategist for LogicaCMG, notes, there is an increasing awareness among top companies that outsourcing can do more than simply cut costs. There is a growing sense that there should be other positive effects accruing from outsourcing, and that these effects should make a measurable and positive impact on corporate performance.

Indeed the logical assumption is that the very least one would expect is that by releasing a chunk of senior executive time (since they no longer have to manage the outsourced service day to day) the company should see some benefit from this redeployment of executive effort.

"One senior executive rather memorably summed this up in a recent conversation with us by saying: the shareholders are going to be pretty disappointed if we can't achieve something significant with all this additional time!" Smith says.

*Source*: www.business.scotsman.com, October 2005

## Management buy-out and management buy-in

Management **buy-out** occurs when the top layer of management in an organisation buy the business they work for from the owners. The managers then run and own their own business. The main reasons that this happens are:

- a desire to keep their jobs
- because the current owners wish to sell
- a desire to make the organisation more efficient
- a desire to make the business grow and benefit more directly from the rewards of increased growth and, hopefully, increased profits.

Management **buy-in** occurs when managers from outside the organisation take over the business from its current owners and run it.

> ### Info Point
>
> **Docuserve sells print division**
>
> The Edinburgh-based outsourcing business Docuserve has sold off its specialist digital print division in a management buy-out to expand its core business.
>
> The division, with a mix of blue-chip financial, pharmaceutical and property customers, has been bought by managing director Jim Rae and his team for an undisclosed sum.
>
> **Woodlands MBO**
>
> Scottish Woodlands, the country's largest forestry management company, has had a management buy-out. SWL Ltd, the buy-out vehicle, is now 90 per cent owned by Scottish Woodlands' management and staff, with a 10 per cent stake held as an investment by James Jones, Scotland's largest saw-milling company.
>
> *Source*: www.business.scotsman.com, October 2005

### Competitive environment

Finally, it should be remembered that the competitive environment acts as both a positive and negative influence on the operation of business. A *positive* influence can be seen in the example of a business sector where healthy competition results in the production of new products which benefit the consumer. Conversely, a *negative* influence is demonstrated by the example of the effect that new companies entering an existing market can have on the companies already established in that particular sector. As an example, consider the effect that Camelot's operation of the National Lottery has had on companies such as Littlewood's Pools: huge redundancies and site closures. There is also added pressure on companies as the United Kingdom is part of the European Union. Organisations may not only be under threat from competition from within their own country, but also from other countries within the EU.

## Topic External factors affecting the operation of business

Several factors exist which can affect the operation of any organisation. Factors which come from the external environment are generally outside the control of the organisation. Generally, the majority of factors may be seen as negative but several can be identified as being positive.

Changes in the external environment are sometimes referred to by the acronym PESTEC:

- P – political
- E – economic
- S – social
- T – technological
- E – environmental
- C – competitive.

## Political factors

Political factors which could affect the operation of business include the implementation of government policies. For example, the government has strict policies on the sale of weapons and arms to certain countries. This acts as a restriction on the size of market that a weapon-manufacturing company is able to target.

## Economic factors

Economic factors affecting the operation of businesses may take several forms. One economic factor which is outside the control of any organisation is the state of the economy. This is a factor which greatly affects the operation of the business and over which the business has no control.

The national and international competitive environment is an area over which the organisation can exert some control. This could be in the form of an advertising campaign or through competitive pricing policy.

Another economic factor which may impact on an organisation is pressure groups. Pressure groups can exert a negative influence on organisations to the extent that the organisation may have to alter its plans or change a course of action in order to meet the demands of its consumers. An example of an environmental pressure group is Greenpeace.

## Socio-cultural factors

Socio-cultural factors acknowledge the fickleness of the consumer and changes in the needs and wants of the population. Items that are 'in fashion' one year are rarely still 'in fashion' the following year. Consumers are generally regarded as being fickle and prone to impulsive buying. Tastes change quickly and consumers are rarely loyal to one particular brand or product. They tend to be influenced to a much greater extent by special offers or new features.

Furthermore, changes in the population lead to changes in items that are purchased by consumers. The population trend for most of the developed countries shows that over the next few decades there will be a greater proportion of elderly and retired people in the general population because of advances in medicine and the fact that we are all living longer. This means that there will be a knock-on effect to organisations as their products and services may have to alter to suit the needs of this changing population.

## Technological factors

Technological factors are especially relevant today as most organisations rely heavily on the use of information technology in their everyday operation.

Information technology has evolved into information and communication technology and the pace of change is phenomenal. The majority of businesses are investing heavily in information and communication technology to improve their operations. However, there is a downside to the use of modern technology. The pace of change is such that hardware and software that was up to date just last year is now already out of date. This means that there is a great cost involved for businesses. Money which did not require to be spent a decade ago is now dominating the buying decisions of many businesses.

The increase in the use of technology is not an option for many companies as they could easily go out of business as their competitors race ahead through the use of new technologies. Maintaining a competitive advantage is essential to stay ahead of the competition. All of these factors place an added strain on the business.

In most cases however, it can be said that the benefits to be gained far outweigh the costs.

### *Environmental factors*

Environmental factors are not usually controllable by organisations. The weather and man-made pollution are just two examples that may have an impact of business.

### *Competitive factors*

All businesses face competition and this, in turn, influences the way in which they operate. Sometimes this may mean changes to the way in which their products and services are marketed and in other cases it may mean completely redesigning their product range or changing the way in which they market and sell products.

## Topic  Business as a dynamic activity

Businesses must be dynamic (i.e. be able to react to changes in the environment) if they are to survive and develop. Pressure to change may come from within or outside the business.

Examples of internal pressures include:

- a change of management

- the introduction of new technology

- a change in the company's financial position.

Examples of external pressures include:

- **Political/legal:** changes in the government may bring about changes in legislation that adversely affect the operation of the business. This is especially relevant within the EU where all member countries are subject to Europe-wide legislation.

- **Economic:** within the EU, companies are subject to economic competition not only from rivals within their own country but also from companies across Europe.

- **Social:** business must try to anticipate the future needs and wants of the consumer and thereby stay ahead of the competition. Mistakes in anticipating what the customer wants or unexpected contributory factors can have negative effects on the success of the business.

- **Technological:** changes in technology such as the continuing development of the internet and e-business are costly to business. There may be a reluctance for businesses to get involved where the benefits of the technology are unproven or the financial cost is high.

## Info Point

**CuriousOranj**

'Creative thinking isn't limited to concept and creation; creativity runs throughout every aspect of CuriousOranj. Whether it's in strategic market planning, brand development meetings or time spent with the expanding and reputable client list; as one of the UK's leading marketing agencies, CuriousOranj ensure that the serious side of operations are kept up-to-date with the most creative thinking in the field. Occasionally this means luring young raw talent onboard with our various shiny industry awards, however we do as we must to deliver results. Welcome to CuriousOranj, where strategic and creative thinking ignite … to sell stuff.'

*Source*: www.curiousoranj.com

# Topic  Changes in the business environment

Business is constantly evolving and changing. In fact, all organisations must change and adapt in order to survive in the modern business environment.

In this section we will consider the importance of different types of organisations, and how internal and external changes can influence these different organisations.

## *The increasing significance of multinationals*

A multinational is a company that operates in more than two countries. Such companies are becoming increasingly important, particularly where they bring investment to developing countries. This investment may be monetary or may be in the form of employment. When multinationals choose to invest in developing countries, they also contribute to the economy of that country and may also help to up-skill their workforce.

Multinationals may also view developing countries as a good place in which to invest. This may be due to several factors:

- availability of cheap labour
- economic incentives provided by the government
- availability of purpose-built premises
- availability of land.

## *The greater business orientation of publicly-funded organisations*

Publicly-funded organisations are organisations which are paid for by the public. For example, the British Broadcasting Corporation (BBC) is funded by the public through the collection of the television licence fee from all people in the country who have a television.

Increasingly, publicly-funded organisations have become more business-orientated. In other words, they have become more aware and more reactive to the environment in which they exist and operate.

This means that they may change their mode of operation. Publicly-funded organisations exist to serve the needs of the public. Commercial organisations, however, will typically exist for other reasons, e.g. to maximise profits, be the market leader, diversify into other markets. Recent behaviour of publicly-funded organisations, such as the BBC, supports the idea that they have become much more 'business aware'.

## Info Point

The BBC website (www.bbc.co.uk) lists some of the business services provided by the BBC which include:

- BBC Worldwide Limited
- BBC Ventures Group
- BBC Resources
- BBC Broadcast
- BBC Monitoring
- BBC Research Central
- BBC Training
- BBC International
- beeb.net
- bbcshop.com
- bbccanadashop.com
- bbcamericashop.com

The BBC is a worldwide organisation and acts as a commercial business, in addition to fulfilling its duty to the UK public who fund its existence.

## Changes in the size of firms

Business organisations may increase or decrease in size over a period of time to suit their needs, or in reaction to the market in which they operate.

In the modern economy, there is much emphasis placed on the importance of large organisations and their ability to meet the needs of consumers in the right location and at the right price etc. This is often to the detriment of smaller businesses. However, the UK Government has invested heavily in the promotion of small businesses and to aid their creation.

In recent years the UK Government has sought to increase the number of small businesses starting up in the UK. It has done this by offering start-up loans/grants and offering free advice from local centres dedicated to the needs of small business. It has also given tax incentives to small business and reduced the amount of corporation tax that they may be liable to pay by creating a reduced rate of taxation.

## Info Point

Companies with annual profits below £1.5m are taxed as follows (in 2003/04):

- up to £10,000 at 0 per cent

- between £10,001 and £50,000, at a marginal rate, calculated according to a formula designed to bring the rate up gradually from 0 per cent to 19 per cent

- between £50,001 and £300,000, at 19 per cent

- between £300,000 and £1.5m, at a marginal rate, calculated according to a formula designed to bring the rate up gradually from 19 per cent to 30 per cent.

No matter how successful a company might become or how many employees it has, there is always room for resizing in an organisation that grows very quickly. This does not necessarily mean that employees will lose their jobs, but they should prepare for the worst possible scenario.

A company cannot achieve constant growth without proper management. Companies must self-assess and rationalise the number of employees.

Despite the fact that you may be an excellent employee, there is never a guarantee that you can make it past the downsizing. You may not lose your job but you may become responsible for double your original remit. The reorganisation of a company's employees does not simply involve firing employees; it also opens up opportunities that can benefit employees with increased responsibility, salary and prospects for future advancement.

## Info Point

'Scottish Opera chief executive Chris Barron has admitted that more than a third of its full-time staff are facing redundancy as the company pays back a £4 million loan.

Barron's bleak appraisal of the company's current cash crisis was contained in a letter to its 240 full-time employees. In it he said that SO was currently working under "intolerable circumstances" and that he was frustrated by the "slow and torturous" progress of discussions with the Scottish Arts Council [SAC] and the Scottish Executive.

It is understood that Scottish Opera has submitted two plans to the two bodies. The first of these involves the repayment of a £4 million loan over the next two years – effectively cutting the annual grant of £7.5 million to £5.5 million a year – which would lead to "far more than 80" job losses at the company, according to industry sources. The second plan involves repaying the loan over a longer period, with fewer resultant job cuts.

Barron explained to staff that the manner in which the SAC and Scottish Executive expected the company to repay the loan of £4 million was the critical factor in determining how many staff would lose their jobs.

"Crucially, it is the resolution of the advanced cash issue which will dictate the severity of the downsizing needed during the next two years, rather than the ability to work within the 'known funding' of £7.5 million," he wrote.

*continued* ➤

BUSINESS ENTERPRISE

> The need for job cuts had been determined by two factors. The first is that the company is the same size as it was in 1999/2000 when it was saved from certain closure by extra cash aid from the Scottish Executive.'
>
> *Source:* www.thestage.co.uk, 20 April 2004

## Franchising

As we have already seen in this chapter, franchising is an area of business that has grown considerably over the past few decades. It is a convenient way for many people to get into business with an established company and brand name without a large initial investment of capital.

The benefits to the person running the franchise are that they are able to use another business's name and sell the other business's products or services.

The main advantages to the franchiser are:

- increased market share with little investment

- reliable source of income

- does not have to bear all of the risk.

## Factors which can cause change

There are many factors which influence the continuing operation of business. Some of these factors are internal and the organisation may be able to predict, plan or influence these changes to minimise disruption to the business. Other factors may be external and the organisation may not be able to plan in advance for the impact that such factors will have on its business.

Change, and the management of change, are essential to the continuing success of every business. Let us now consider some of the factors which can cause change.

### Internal change

Examples of internal change include changes in costs and the development of new products. Changes in costs can usually be predicted, planned for and budgeted when they occur internally within an organisation. This means that there can be good management of the change to lessen the impact on staff and other areas of the business. Likewise, the development costs and associated time of developing new products can be planned by the organisation. It is usually the case that internal change can be controlled by the organisation, thereby lessening its impact.

### External change

External change is more difficult for organisations to manage as they may not always be able to predict and plan for the changes in advance of them happening. Here are some examples of external change:

- Changes in demand for the business's products or services. This may be an increase or a decrease in demand, both of which may be good or bad for the business. An unexpected increase in demand may, at first, appear to be a good thing for business. However, if the demand cannot be met to provide customers with the product or service, they may take

their business elsewhere and the organisation may build up a bad reputation. Unexpected falls in demand may also be bad for business, as organisations which produce perishable stock may have to write off stock which has gone past its sell-by date.

- Changes in technology are commonplace nowadays, and many organisations may struggle to keep up to date. This may be due to inexperience, cost or the inability to react quickly to changes. A good example of this is the recent move by many businesses to trade online and make their goods and services available for customers to buy via the Internet. Where this is commonplace in a particular industry, businesses who do not offer this service may be losing a vital market share.

- Changes in taxation are decided by the Government, and businesses have no control over the level that is decided. Businesses will usually have about one year's notice of changes in taxation.

- Changes to the competitive market mean that businesses may face stiffer competition from their existing competitors or from new businesses entering the market.

- Changes to UK and EU legislation cannot be controlled by individual organisations, and such changes may have either a positive or negative impact on business. For example, import restrictions on certain goods or services to other EU countries may mean that a UK business is not able to carry out business in another EU country. Conversely, where there is a shortage of a particular good or service in another EU country, a UK business may be able to capitalise on this in the short term.

All changes that are taking place, whether internal or external, have to be evaluated by the organisation. Failure to properly evaluate change and its likely impact on the organisation may lead to lost business and missed opportunities in both the short and long term. Businesses must be responsive to internal and external pressures in order to survive, grow and develop. The basic business objective is survival. Businesses that do not survive are not able to compete, develop and grow.

# End of chapter revision questions

1 Discuss the role of business in modern society with reference to wealth creation, production and consumption and the satisfaction of human wants.

2 Identify and describe three different types of business organisations.

3 List three advantages and three disadvantages of running a public limited company compared to running a private limited company.

4 What do objectives help to identify?

5 Identify and explain three different business objectives.

6 Define the term 'entrepreneur'.

7 What is a stakeholder in business?

8 Give three examples of stakeholders in business.

9 What kind of influence may stakeholders be able to exert on business?

10 Complete the following table by inserting an example for each type of business. The first row has been completed as an example.

| Type of organisation | Example of stakeholder | Example of influence |
|---|---|---|
| sole trader | owner | owner's motivation to succeed |
| partnership | | |
| private limited company | | |
| public limited company | | |
| voluntary organisation | | |
| charity | | |
| public corporation | | |
| government-funded service provider | | |
| local government-funded provider | | |

**11** Identify and explain at least three sources of finance and advice to business.

**12** Explain why different methods of finance may be available to a public limited company compared to a private limited company.

**13** State three factors which can affect the operation of business.

**14** Give one example of a socio-cultural factor.

**15** Give one example of an economic factor.

**16** Give one example of a political factor.

**17** Explain the terms 'merger' and 'demerger'.

**18** What is divestment?

**19** Explain the term 'multinational'.

**20** What is downsizing and how does it affect an organisation and its employees?

**21** Identify and explain one factor that can cause internal change.

**22** Identify and explain one factor that can cause external change.

**23** Explain why it is important for organisations to respond to internal and external pressures.

**24** Identify as many different types of business organisations as you can which would be involved in producing a new music CD.

**25** Explain why there has been a growth in employment in call centres in Scotland, and state the reasons why it is important that Scotland continues to attract these jobs.

**26** Identify a local business organisation and describe each of the factors of production it uses in order to operate.

**27** Identify three local businesses that operate in *each* sector of industry.

**28** For each of the following examples, identify which would be the best type of business organisation. Justify your decision for each.
   a) firm of solicitors
   b) window cleaner
   c) garage repair and sales.

29 Which of the following services are provided by government and publicly funded? You should also identify if they are provided by local or national (Scottish or UK) government.
a) university education
b) local bus service
c) water supply
d) sheltered housing
e) letter postal service.

## Chapter Summary

At the end of this chapter you should know the following:

★ Business activity is the production of goods and services to satisfy consumer needs.

★ The factors of production are land (natural resources), labour (the mental and physical effort of people), capital (man-made resources), and enterprise (the activity of entrepreneurs).

★ Wealth creation is achieved through the production of goods and services – the more a country produces, the wealthier it will be.

★ The cycle of business identifies the production of goods and services to satisfy peoples' wants and needs, only for them to dream up new wants for business to satisfy.

★ The sectors of industry are primary (extraction and agricultural industries), secondary (manufacturing industries) and tertiary (service industries).

★ Private sector organisations are profit-making, and include sole-traders, partnerships, private and public limited companies.

★ Public sector organisations are government-funded, either nationally such as the Benefits Agency, or locally such as education.

★ The voluntary sector is made up of organisations producing goods and services for the benefit of their members or for the benefit of society, such as charities.

★ The entrepreneur brings together the factors of production to produce goods and services. They are risk-takers, and think of new ideas.

You should be able to:

★ list and describe the main business objectives – profit maximisation, survival, sale maximisation, growth, social responsibility, managerial objectives, provision of a service.

★ identify different groups of stakeholders

★ discuss the influence of different groups of stakeholders on business

★ list different sources of finance and assistance available to business at a local and national level

★ identify the factors affecting the operation of business in relation to the impact on the organisation

★ explain the increasing significance of multinationals

★ discuss the increasing business orientation of publicly-funded organisations

★ discuss changes in the size of firms

*continued* ➤

BUSINESS ENTERPRISE

★ identify and explain factors which can cause change

★ discuss the importance of change

★ discuss the competitive environment in which business operates.

# CHAPTER 2

## Business Information and ICT

This part of the course contains the following topics:

| | |
|---|---|
| **Sources of information** | Primary, secondary, internal, external. |
| **Types of information** | Written, oral, pictorial, graphical, numerical, qualitative, quantitative. |
| **Value of information** | Accuracy, timeliness, completeness, appropriateness, availability, cost, objectivity, conciseness. |
| **Uses of information in business** | Monitoring and control, decision-making, measuring performance, identifying new business opportunities. |
| **ICT in business** | Uses of ICT – hardware and software, costs and benefits of ICT, e.g. speed, flexibility, handling of complex information, financial outlay, staff training, data corruption. |
| | Awareness of current legislation. |

## Topic  Sources of information

All businesses rely on information in order to operate effectively and efficiently, and to make good business decisions.

Information can come from four different sources:

- primary
- secondary
- internal
- external.

### Primary information

Primary information is usually information which has been collected by the business itself. This type of information is very important. The characteristics of primary information are that it should be free from bias or distortion, and must be able to be traced to its original source. Businesses use primary information as a basis for making informed decisions on the running of the business.

Examples of primary information include market research, customer complaints, financial data, customer questionnaires and feedback and other statistics prepared by the business. Another characteristic of primary information is that it is usually quite expensive to obtain. However, it is the most reliable and useful source of information available to a business.

## Secondary information

Secondary information is a cheaper source of information than primary. The reason that it is cheaper is because it is more general, and may not be ideally suited to the purpose required by the business. It may also be less reliable and may have been skewed to meet a particular need. It may not be possible to trace the original source of this information, and for this reason alone, secondary information may not be a suitable basis from which a business can make important decisions.

Examples of secondary information include any kind of published information, market surveys published by third parties, newspapers, magazines, journals, reports from analysts, financial reports and information collected from the internet.

## Internal information

Internal information is information that is sourced from within the business. This could be financial data or information on customers. All internal information should be verifiable and reliable.

## External information

External information is information that is sourced from outside the business. This could be government statistics, market research by third parties, consumer test reports, income statistics and demographics. This gives useful information on the operating environment for the business, and can provide information on the business's direct competitors. The only downside to this type of information is that it is not generally verifiable.

## Strengths and weaknesses of different sources of information

The following table provides a useful summary of some of the strengths and weaknesses of different sources of information.

| Type of information | Strengths | Weaknesses |
|---|---|---|
| Primary | Reliable, verifiable | Expensive to obtain, difficult to collect |
| Secondary | Gives a wider view than primary information since it takes into account external influences; wider variety of sources compared to primary; cheap to obtain | May not be 100 per cent relevant; may be biased or out of date; the same information is also available to competitors |
| Internal | Reliable, verifiable | Accurate records must be kept for this information to be useful |
| External | More sources available compared to primary | May have a financial cost; can be time-consuming to gather; information is also available to competitors |

# Topic Types of information

Information can be presented in a variety of different formats:

- written
- oral
- pictorial
- graphical
- numerical.

**Written** information may be presented on paper or on computer screen, e.g. via email or on the internet. Written communication of information remains one of the most popular forms of presenting information.

**Oral** information is information communicated by voice. Where this information is not recorded for future use, its value may be diminished and its reliability called into question.

**Pictorial** information means information displayed in the form of a photograph or picture. Sometimes a picture or sign can communicate information more quickly and effectively than written information, e.g. road signs.

**Graphical** information is often used to display complex data in a format which is easy to understand and pleasing to the eye. It is of particular use where comparisons have to be made or where there is a comparison over a period of time. An example of a company's sales performance forecast for the current year is given in Figure 2.2.

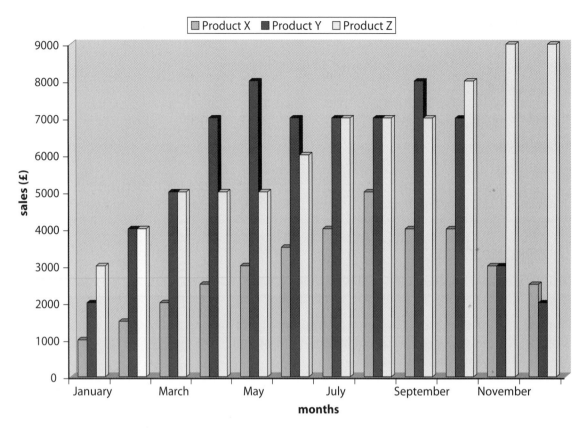

**Figure 2.2** Product X, Y, Z Sales

**Numerical** information is any form of information that is presented as numbers rather than text; e.g. the financial results of the business.

There are two types of information that can be used by businesses in the decision-making process:

● qualitative

● quantitative.

**Qualitative** information is descriptive in nature and may also include people's personal judgements or opinions.

**Quantitative** information is both definable and measurable, and is normally expressed numerically. It is often used for the purposes of comparison, e.g. to compare the performance of one business with another, or to compare the performance of the business over a period of time.

# Topic  The value of information

Any information that is to be used by business as part of its operation and decision-making must be of actual value to the business. Good and reliable information is required to make correct and informed decisions. The value of information to any business cannot be underestimated, and it is important to remember that not all information will be of use to a business.

Many business decisions are affected by the quality of the information available in order to make the decision. Large quantities of information are useless if the information contained is not of a suitable quality. It is preferable to have a small amount of reliable, high quality and verifiable information, than a large quantity of unreliable, poor quality and non-verifiable information.

High quality information should display the following characteristics:

- **Accuracy** – this is important because decisions which are based on inaccurate information will lead to the incorrect outcome.

- **Timeliness** – information for decision-making must be available when it is required by the business, and must be up to date and reliable. Late and out-of-date information will lead to the wrong decisions being made.

- **Completeness** – any information that is to be used for decision-making in the business must be complete. The use of incomplete information will not provide a true picture, and will lead to inaccurate decisions being made.

- **Appropriateness** – the information used by the business must be appropriate to the situation to which it is being applied. If irrelevant or inappropriate information is used, there is an increased risk that the wrong decision will be made.

- **Availability** – information required by the business for decision-making must be readily available. In certain instances, it may be necessary to use substitute information of a lower quality. This may be preferable to having access to no information at all.

- **Cost** – the collection and storage of information for the business must be cost-effective. Where the purchase or gathering of information is not cost-effective, its collection and use must be called into question.

- **Objectivity** – all information used in the decision-making process should be objective, i.e. free from bias. It should not contain subjective and personal opinions.

- **Conciseness** – information used for decision-making should be concise and straight to the point. Fussy presentation or giving too much information may hide the key points.

All good quality information should meet each of the eight criteria listed. Fast access to high quality, concise information is of greater importance to business than access to huge quantities of lower quality information, which also may have to be sorted.

The value of information that is collected by the business will also be influenced by the purpose for which the information is to be used. For example, a business will be more willing to pay more money for important information that it requires to make an important decision which could potentially make it a lot of money in the future, compared to, say, information about the latest tax regulations relating to its particular business sector.

## Activity

'Most information is useless regardless of its source, type or value. In fact, it is usually out of date by the time I receive it!'

Discuss the above quote in the context of sources, types and values of information. Your answer should be in the region of 250 words.

BUSINESS ENTERPRISE

# Topic Uses of information in business

There are a variety of different purposes for which information may be used by a business. The main categories to be considered are:

- monitoring and control
- decision-making
- measuring performance
- identifying new business opportunities.

## Monitoring and control

Businesses must monitor and control different aspects of their operations in order to succeed. One of the most important areas that requires monitoring and control in any business is the finance function. The use of accounting information in this area is crucial to the continued success of the business, and this type of information is used by management to make decisions about the future of the business.

Financial information is often computerised and many companies make use of financial monitoring software such as Sage, Pegasus and Quickbooks.

## Decisions

The provision of information is not enough. Management must have access to the correct type of information so that they can make informed decisions. Sometimes, decisions will be easy to make based on the available information. The information used to make decisions may be financial (quantitative) or it may be in the form of a written report with recommendations (qualitative).

## Measuring performance

Businesses also use information to measure their performance. Business performance may be measured using different criteria:

- financial performance
- meeting output targets
- meeting targets for staff
- individual department targets.

Whatever criteria are adopted, all successful businesses depend on a variety of information to measure their performance. It is useful for management to compare internal reports on their performance with reports produced by third parties. Any reports produced by third parties will usually take the form of qualitative reporting since it is unlikely that they would have access to sensitive quantitative data.

## Opportunities

Business managers also make use of information (usually available in the public domain) to identify new business opportunities. For example, by studying economic statistics, it is possible to identify potential areas of growth in the economy and then develop a business idea to meet the need in that area.

# Topic ICT in business

Computers are used throughout business today and most businesses would not be able to operate without them. They are used to collect, store, process, retrieve and display data and information to be used in decision-making processes.

Information technology used in business today is changing rapidly; some current examples include:

- mainframe computers
- desktop computers
- laptop computers
- handheld computers/Personal Digital Assistant (PDA)
- networks:
  a) local area network (LAN)
  b) wide area network (WAN)
- information communication technology (ICT) – including email and the internet
- multi-media – including CD-ROMs.

Let us take each of these in turn to explain more about them and how they are used in business.

## *Mainframe computers*

Mainframe computers are large computers which can deal with millions of operations at the same time. They are extremely powerful and expensive. Several decades ago, a mainframe computer would have occupied a large room in an office building, and would have to have been kept in a temperature-controlled environment. They were seen as the pinnacle of computer technology and only people who had been trained in their use and operation were allowed to use them. In fact, their use was strictly limited.

Nowadays, the advances in computer technology mean that the computer that sits on your desk is likely to be as powerful, if not more powerful, than the mainframe computers of the 1970s. This demonstrates the huge advances in the development of computer technology. Mainframe computers are still used nowadays and are often referred to as **supercomputers**. Their use is restricted to very specialised tasks, and they remain the most powerful, fastest and most expensive computers in the world. They are much smaller than their predecessors and are mainly used by government agencies and large companies for scientific and engineering purposes. One of the

most prolific users of supercomputers in the world is the American military and NASA (the National Agency for Space Administration) of America.

## Mini computers

Mini computers is the term given to a whole range of computers which are smaller in size than mainframe computers. Nowadays, we are most likely to use this term when describing a **desktop** machine, but it can be extended to include portable machines, laptops, notebooks and handheld computers. We will consider some of these later.

The birth of the mini computer began back in the 1980s. The market for mini computers was borne out of the need for a variety of people within organisations to have access to computer facilities. Very few organisations actually had computers, and those that did were restricted to the use of one mainframe. As more and more people within the organisation wanted to be able to use the computer facility, there was more pressure put upon the time available on the mainframe. At the same time, IBM (International Business Machines) was developing the personal computer, as they identified a gap in the market for a small computer that could be used in the workplace by the individual.

Little did they realise that their invention of the personal computer in the 1980s would create such great wealth and success for the company. The success of the personal desktop computer went beyond all expectations, and throughout the 1980s and 1990s the personal computer continued to develop; it increased in power and reduced in size while continuing its migration from the office and into the home. Nowadays, almost every home and office has a computer, and the increase in power of the desktop machine means that there is no requirement for more powerful machines such as the mainframe computer.

## Laptop and handheld computers

Laptop computers are a product of the late 1980s and early 1990s, and the Japanese obsession with miniaturisation. They differ from desktop computers mainly because they are smaller and are often referred to as portable computers. As well as laptop computers, recent times have seen the introduction of so-called notebooks and handheld computers, often referred to as Personal Digital Assistants (PDAs). Notebooks differ from laptops in the respect that they will not usually have a 'footprint' (the space taken up by the piece of equipment) of more than the size of a piece of A4 paper.

Handheld computers (PDAs) are smaller again and are able to be held in the palm of your hand. Typically, these small computers are much less powerful and have fewer functions when compared to their larger family members.

Laptop computers have the following characteristics:

- small size, making them portable
- hinged screen to allow closure for transport
- LCD (liquid crystal display) screen which is light and has low power consumption

- battery-powered (typical battery endurance is three to five hours, although many powerful laptops require more energy)

- trackpad device to replace the mouse

- all the other features that you would expect to find on a desktop machine, including built-in modem, connections for USB and parallel ports, CD/DVD drive, CD/DVD burner, network capability (often wireless).

The most highly specified laptops nowadays have evolved in size and weight, but this is at a cost. As size and weight have reduced while processor speed and screen size have increased, this has led to greater power consumption and more dependence on mains power. There is also the financial consideration to be made. A top-of-the-range laptop costs in the region of $2,500, whereas a similarly specified desktop machine can be purchased for half the price. PDAs are now available for as little as $100, although a top-of-the-range model may cost up to $1,000. How much do you value reduced size and style?

## Computer networks

The use and development of computer network technology is relatively recent in the history of computing. Much of the technology in operation today is based on client–server technology. This is a relatively inexpensive and flexible way of harnessing the power of many computers connected together. A computer network is where several computers are connected together using special hardware and software.

The main advantage of the latest computer networks based on client–server technology is that they are all connected to a central computer, or server. The server is just a normal computer that acts like a traffic warden on the network, directing information and messages across the network. It operates and controls the network using special software. Each user that is connected to the network has their own login name and password to access network facilities and maintain security.

Computer networks can be 'wired' in two different ways. The traditional method of connection for machines on a computer network is by using cables or wires. This has the instant disadvantage of meaning that every computer connected to the network must have a cable connecting it to the server that operates the network. Imagine, for example, a computer network of 500 machines in an office building, with 500 individual cables throughout the building eventually terminating at

the server. On a large network, cabled networks can get very messy.

The latest alternative to the traditional cabled network is the 'wireless' network. This type of network operates in the same way as a traditional network, but instead of relying on cables to connect the computers on the network, it uses radio communication technology. This removes the need for cables, and the technology can operate easily within the confines of an office building up to a range of about 150 metres. There have, however, recently been concerns raised about the security of wireless networks, and the ease with which information can be stolen from them using relatively simple telecommunications equipment. However, many businesses are setting up wireless networks as they are now more cost-effective than 'wired' networks.

## Local area networks (LAN)

Local area networks or LANs are a common feature in business today. They are most often used where several (a few or even several hundred) computers have to be connected over a small common area, e.g. an office or a building.

They possess the following characteristics:

- computers are linked using cables or by radio communication
- network covers a small geographical area
- the main use of the network is to share information and peripheral devices
- there is a low error rate
- it is easy to set up and maintain
- detailed technical knowledge is often not required
- relatively cheap
- secure
- peripheral devices can be shared
- internet access can be shared across the network.

## Wide area networks (WAN)

Wide area networks or WANs are networks that operate over a geographically dispersed area. They are unlike LANs because the computers that are connected to the network may be in a different town, city or country, and are not in the same office or building.

The method connection used in a WAN is, therefore, not the same as that used in a LAN. It would be impractical to suggest that a computer operating in Glasgow could be connected on a network to a computer operating in Aberdeen via a cable such as that used in a LAN. The method of connection for a WAN utilises telephone lines, dedicated high speed cable connections and even satellite links. Sometimes where a company operates a WAN, say

between offices in different towns or cities in the same country, they use a method of connection called a **leased line** – a dedicated high speed line which is leased from a communications company for the sole use of the company. This means that no one else has access to the line, and only the company can use it for communication purposes. The downside to this is that leased lines are usually very expensive.

The main characteristics of WANs are:

- computers linked via telephone lines or dedicated leased lines, or even satellite link
- many different world locations can be attached to the network at any one time
- network coverage is over a wide geographical area and may even be global
- there is a higher risk of error when compared to LANs
- the main use of the network is communication
- many owners and organisations can be connected to the network
- more expensive to set up, maintain and operate compared to a LAN
- more likely to require technical expertise to operate and maintain compared to a LAN
- greater chance of data being intercepted by third parties
- the network may not be permanently 'live'.

WANs are usually used by global organisations, such as IBM and Apple Computer.

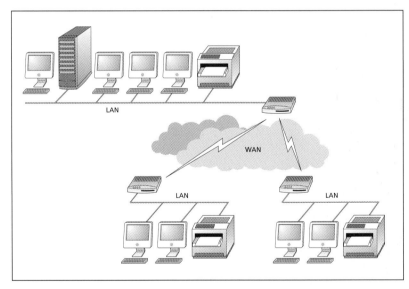

**Fig 2.7** Diagram of WAN

## Information Communication Technology (ICT)

Information Technology or IT is a phrase with which you should be familiar. It is the term used to describe the use of computers and computer technology.

Information Communication Technology (ICT) is the term used to describe all the different technologies that exist in the field of IT, as well as the emerging technologies that involve both IT and communication technology. The internet is at the forefront of communication technologies, and is probably the most easily recognised piece of information communication technology in the current time.

Recent developments in telecommunications technology have utilised the telephone network, e.g. the Internet. The telecommunication companies have been eager to expand their networks and improve the services that they are able to offer. As the Internet has developed, it has started to outgrow the current telephone network which was never originally designed with its current use in mind. The existing telephone network in the United Kingdom is constantly being replaced and updated.

Internet access speeds can be improved dramatically through the use of digital telephone lines such as ISDN (Integrated Services Digital Network) and ADSL (Advanced Digital Services Line), which offer much faster communication when compared to the normal telephone network. The cost to consumers continues to fall, and high speed internet access is now available to many residents in the UK at a reasonable cost.

The telecommunications network spanning the United Kingdom and beyond is used for a wide variety of different purposes. The most common are as follows:

- the Internet
- email
- Telnet
- Prestel
- FTP
- JANET (Joint Academic NETwork)
- internet banking.

We will consider each of these applications in turn.

## The Internet

The Internet is a good example of a Wide Area Network (WAN), and is an easy way of sharing information cheaply across the world. The most commonly used part of the Internet is the world wide web (WWW).

Many people think that the world wide web *is* the Internet, but it is in fact only a small part of it. The Internet comprises three main areas: email, newsgroups and sharing information (i.e. the world wide web). The chart in Figure 2.8 demonstrates the increase in the use of the Internet in recent years.

Email is the communication tool of the Internet (we will consider it later in this chapter). Newsgroups are sometimes referred to as discussion groups or bulletin boards, and provide forums for people to post messages and respond to messages from other people.

The final part of the Internet is where information is shared, stored and retrieved, the fastest growing part of which is the world wide web. Information can also be shared using a facility called File Transfer Protocol (FTP). This is basically a set of computer rules for sending and receiving information. Before the advent and development of the world wide web in the mid-1990s, FTP was the main method for sharing information on the Internet.

The Internet has actually been in existence since 1969, but it was only in the mid-1990s that it became available to the wider public. Within a very short space of time, the Internet has been recognised and developed as a major tool for communication and a valuable source of information, which can be used by individuals and businesses alike.

The Internet makes use of existing telephone lines and other faster means of communication to connect computers throughout the world. The main reason for connecting computers is so that they can share information and communicate with each other.

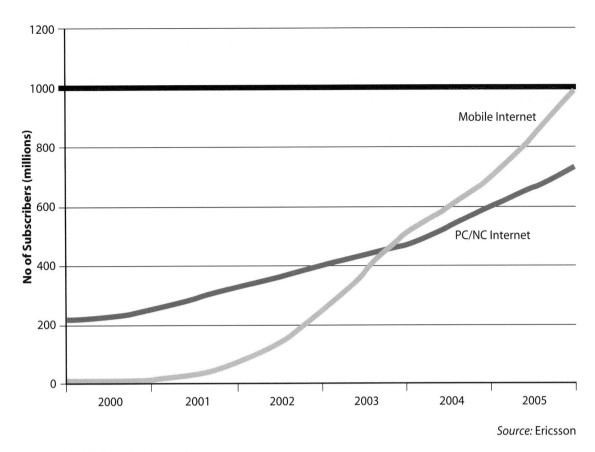

Source: Ericsson

**Figure 2.8** Worldwide Internet Users

Internet availability and use has mushroomed in the past few years as the cost of computers has fallen and it has become easier to get connected to the Internet. The main prerequisites for connection to the internet are:

- fast, modern computer
- up-to-date Internet browser software
- ethernet connection/connection to wireless network
- telephone/cable line
- subscription to an Internet Service Provider (ISP).

The ISP provides individuals and businesses with a connection to the Internet routed through their powerful network of computers, which are connected directly to the Internet. There is now a wide variety of deals available from many different ISPs. Many ISPs offer 24 hours' access, seven days a week, for as little as £15 per month with no other charges. Other deals are often bundled with free local telephone calls.

The importance of the Internet to business cannot be underestimated in the current economic climate. Most businesses now have an Internet presence and often offer their products and services for sale via their websites. The Internet has become as important a tool for business as it has for the person using it for leisure or personal interest.

The scope and content of this course cannot significantly address the changing phenomenon that is the Internet. If you are interested in learning more about this subject, a good source of reference is *The Rough Guide to the Internet* by Angus J Kennedy, published by Penguin. The book is updated every year.

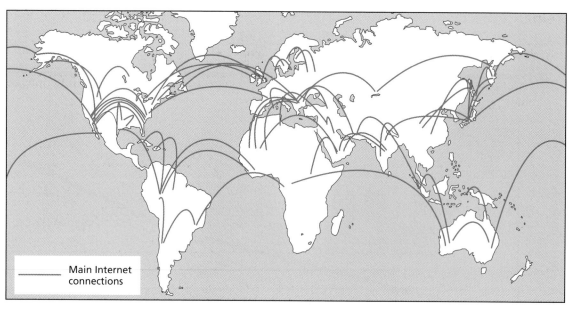

**Figure 2.9** A basic topology of the Internet

## Email

Email is the electronic worldwide postal service supported by the Internet. It is a very fast and efficient way of communicating, and does not depend on time zones. Information can be communicated across the world in a matter of seconds.

In order to send email, you require a connection to the internet and a valid email address. There is little restriction on the type of information that can be communicated via email. Different files can also be attached, e.g. pictures, spreadsheets.

The advantages of using email include:

- fast and efficient communication
- cheap compared to normal post
- messages can be easily filed and tracked
- messages can be sent at any time of the day or night.

The disadvantages of using email are:

- it is only useful if people know how to use it properly
- people's reactions and responses are different when communicating via email, so there is a need for the rules of 'netiquette' to be followed
- receipt and successful delivery of email requires the person receiving the email to check their account
- immediate communication on your part does not always guarantee an immediate response
- junk mail (spam) can become a problem and mean that more important messages are lost among the junk.

## Telnet

Telnet is one of the original uses of the Internet. It allows remote access by one computer network to another computer network via a standard telephone line connection.

For example, many libraries operate a Telnet facility to allow users to access basic functions at the remote site, e.g. search the library catalogue.

## FTP

File Transfer Protocol is a set of computer rules which allows the transfer of files between computers via a network, e.g. the Internet.

Using an FTP program, the user is able to send information from his computer to the host computer (upload) and copy information from the host computer to his own computer (download).

## JANET

The **J**oint **A**cademic **NET**work is a computer network covering the United Kingdom which links all of the universities and colleges of further and higher education.

## Internet banking

Increased competition within the banking sector has meant that the High Street banks have had to think of new ways to attract new customers and retain their existing customers. The ability to access account details and carry out account maintenance and transactions online increases the usefulness to customers who have a computer and access to the Internet.

Most banks now offer an online service for their customers. This has two distinct advantages: as far as the bank is concerned, it stops people from going to the branch thereby reducing congestion, and as far as the customer is concerned, it is much more convenient to carry out bank business at any hour of the day or night and not be restricted by the normal opening hours of the bank.

## Info Point

**Minola Smoked Products, Abergavenny**

'As one of the most progressive traditional smokers of oak smoked Scottish salmon, fish, game, poultry and cheeses in the UK, we supply many of the best hotels, restaurants and gourmets worldwide via the internet.

Internet banking from Bank of Scotland offers us a free means to manage our funds.

Payments are available instantly, and account reconciliation is much tidier now. The problem of unpresented cheques becomes a thing of the past, as we no longer handle then due to enhanced safety of online transactions.

Our cash management has also been made easier due to the consistency provided by regular scheduled payments. Suppliers also respond positively to our use of internet banking – telling them that we make payments by BACs inspires confidence, and they see it as a more proactive and business-like service.'

*Source*: Hugh and Jane Forestier-Waker, www.bankofscotland.co.uk

## Questions

1   List two ways in which using Internet banking services has benefited Minola Smoked Products.

2   How does the use of internet banking facilities make Minola Smoked Products able to operate in a global market?

## Multi-media systems

Multi-media systems utilise a variety of different media, primarily for the purpose of presentation. Typically, this involves the use of:

- text
- text and sound
- text, sound and pictures
- text, sound and video
- video and sound
- interactive elements:
  a) voice
  b) mouse
  c) keyboard
  d) touch screen
  e) live participation.

Common uses of multi-media include:

- interactive training videos
- video conferencing
- CD-ROMs
- DVDs.

Interactive videos are used for training staff, as they can easily demonstrate simulations of the workplace environment. Employees can then be tested on their reactions to these and learn from the scenarios.

Video conferencing is a multi-media facility which was developed many years ago, but it has never really been utilised to its full potential, except by big business. The use of video and audio links enable a 'virtual' meeting to take place where the participants are in different locations, sometimes in different countries. There is obviously a cost- and time-saving aspect to be made, compared to the situation where people have to travel a great distance at cost to meet in a common place. More recent advances using internet technology mean that video-conferencing technology has been superceded to some extent; the use of a cheap webcam and an internet connection can achieve very similar results. Another reason for the lack of success of video conferencing can be attributed to the fact that humans like face-to-face contact in person, something that video conferencing could never achieve.

CDs and DVDs (higher storage capacity) are a convenient way of storing, sharing and recording electronic information. They can be used to store both computer data and music files. CD-ROM means 'read only memory' – the media can only be read from and not written to (i.e. nothing can be saved on the CD). It is, however, also possible to buy CDs which can be recorded. These are called CD-Rs and permit only one recording to be made. CD-RWs are CDs which allow multiple writes to be made, although these tend to be more expensive.

DVDs are the new standard in video technology. DVD stands for Digital Versatile Disc, and a DVD looks just like a CD. The difference is that an entire movie can be stored on a single DVD, and then played back on either a DVD player or a computer equipped with a DVD drive. Most new computers come with a DVD drive which will also read/burn CDs. DVD-R discs are also available which allow the user to 'burn' their own movies to disc. There is a great improvement in quality when watching and listening to a movie from a DVD compared to a video cassette.

## Other information technology used in business

### Facsimile (FAX)

The fax machine was one of the great inventions of the twentieth century. It allows documents to be sent from one fax machine to another using the normal telephone network. Nowadays, they are cheap to buy and offer relatively fast transmission times. The main form of competition comes from the use of email.

### Telex

Telex is now a relatively old means of communication which has been virtually replaced by the advent of email. It uses the telephone network to transmit information which is read and converted to text by the receiving machine.

## EPOS and EFTPOS

Electronic Point of Sale (EPOS) and Electronic Funds Transfer at Point Of Sale (EFTPOS) are two systems which are in common use in the retail industry.

These systems allow an electronic record to be kept of all purchases and returns, and assist in the control of stock and ordering. In the case of EFTPOS, this system also encompasses payment in the form of a debit card such as Switch or Delta.

These systems are attractive both to the retailer and the customer for different reasons. The retailer usually receives payment more quickly than payment by cheque, and the customer does not have to carry cash or a cheque book to carry out transactions.

## Satellite technology

Many businesses now make use of satellite technology to track vehicles and for navigation purposes. Recent developments in the use of this technology mean that it is now much more financially accessible and portable.

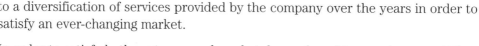

### Info Point

**Burns Express**

Burns Express Freight Ltd is a leading provider of logistical solutions based near Glasgow Airport, and has expanded rapidly since formation in 1993.

The main focus of the company has always been customer service. This has led  to a diversification of services provided by the company over the years in order to satisfy an ever-changing market.

In order to satisfy both customer and market demand, and to remain competitive, new technology has been embraced in the form of satellite tracking of vehicles and computerised traffic management systems. Costs can be monitored using both these systems, ensuring that the company can provide a cost-effective service to its customers and still maintain a realistic level of profitability. There are added benefits to the customer, e.g. freight can be tracked from A to B removing concerns over loss, and this again helps the company to retain a competitive edge.

Due to the growth in turnover and also as a result of the diversification of services within the company (i.e. provision of new services like Parcel deliveries and an Irish Groupage Service), there has also been a requirement to recruit additional drivers and administrative staff. The company has changed its structure and created new departments, in order to split the workload and appoint dedicated staff as the main point of contact for each area. This ensures that any customer enquiry or query can be directed to the correct department and dealt with more efficiently.

Even the purchase of certain vehicles within the company is usually a customer-led decision, in that certain criteria have to be met for certain customers. This can range

*continued* ➤

from the size of vehicle to how much the vehicle can transport, i.e. volume and weight. In certain cases, there is a limit to the age of vehicle that can be used. In order to keep within these limits, the company has an age policy on vehicles and renews its fleet every three years. As all vehicles are liveried with the company logo and contact details, this also ensures that the company is presenting a good image to customers and also acts as 'advertising on wheels'.

This investment in technology, equipment and human resources over the past few years is an ongoing project, and the company is continually looking at new developments such as hand-held scanners and enhanced traffic software, to ascertain if they will be an added benefit now, or in the future. As the company continues to grow, it will invest in all these areas as a necessary requirement, rather than class them as a luxury. This will ensure that standards are maintained and the company is able to continue as a market leader in its field.

*Source*: Derek and Carolyn Burns (owners)

## *Using ICT for decision-making*

IT and ICT in business are powerful tools which can provide management with the ability to handle large amounts of data and information. The effective control, management and processing of this information means that management are able to make more informed decisions.

The decision-making process is aided by the provision of more high quality, relevant and up-to-date information from a wider variety of sources, thereby allowing good decisions to be taken in a short space of time.

The use of the internet as a main source of business communication has removed time delays and the restrictions of time zones, so that businesses can operate for 24 hours a day around the world if the need arises.

Developments in the use of IT have also led to great benefits in the production processes for manufacturing business. A good example where the use of new technology has had a very positive impact is the car industry. There is great reliance placed on the use of computer-aided design (CAD). Product research, development, design, production and testing are all integrated and computerised so that the time taken from design to availability to the consumer has been greatly reduced. This has also led to huge cost savings.

Many manufacturing processes are highly automated, and computers are used to control armies of robots who all carry out different tasks. The use of computers and robots can often achieve better results than the use of human labour.

B U S I N E S S   E N T E R P R I S E

## Info Point

**Innovative use of the Internet**

Scotland is first to see interactive online recruitment advertising.

www.ScottishAppointments.com, Scotland's market leader in online recruitment, is the first UK service to offer interactive job adverts online.

This pioneering application of interactive advertising takes online recruitment advertising to new heights, at a time when recruitment giants Stepstone and TopJobs are pulling out of Scotland, leaving the niche market to specialist companies like ScottishAppointments.com.

ScottishAppointments.com users are the first to benefit fully from the potential of new internet technology. The software behind the adverts has been created inhouse, here at Scotland On Line, enabling companies to advertise cost-effectively with sound, video and still images.

Johanna Cordery, Editor of Online Recruitment magazine confirms Scotland On Line's claim of an industry first:

"Online Recruitment magazine concurs with Scotland On Line's statement that it is the first online recruitment site in the UK to use this kind of advertising."

ScottishAppointments.com is a recruitment website devoted exclusively to Scotland and has already built up a substantial audience since its launch in April 2001, doubling visits to the site and exceeding its traffic targets.

Since launch, the site has had 160,000 unique users visiting 1.5 million pages. Even more staggering is the 31.4 per cent level of repeat visits, each lasting an average of seven minutes. Users from as far afield as America, Australia and Europe have registered with the service, finding it a valuable method of looking for a job in Scotland.

*Source*: www.insider.co.uk

## Info Point

**Join the Internet banking revolution**

Internet banking, as we know it, has been around for about eight years now, and many of us can barely imagine banking in any other way. However, the concept has been around for a lot longer.

Corporate customers of the Bank of Scotland will probably remember its innovative Home and Office Banking Service (HOBS). Launched all the way back in 1986, this service allowed customers to access their accounts directly on a television screen via a Prestel telephone network, and was essentially an early application of Internet technology!

*continued* ➤

Being able to bank online has certainly become more popular in recent years, and a report from Lloyds TSB has revealed that eight in ten Internet users now feel confident, or very confident in banking online.

Unsurprisingly, younger people feel happiest banking from home, with over half (51 per cent) of those aged between 25–34 saying they feel confident, and over a third (34 per cent) stating they feel very confident. Those aged over 55 admitted to being least confident.

And when it comes to the sexes, men lead hands down. A whopping 84 per cent feel fairly or very confident to bank online, compared to 76 per cent of women. And it seems that the recent spate of phishing scams has done little to affect our usage, as 20 per cent of us believe our confidence in the safety of banking online has grown significantly over the past few years, and nearly half of us (48 per cent) say that our confidence has improved slightly. However this does not mean that we take security lightly. The biggest concern for 30 per cent of us would be accidentally divulging a password, or piece of security information.

There can be little doubt as to the usefulness of Internet banking. For those of us who use it regularly, it is a fantastic way to keep track of your finances without the need to queue up in a bank in your lunch hour. Online banking is also a great way to spot problems early, as it allows us to check credit and debit card transactions daily, rather than just via our monthly printed statement (where dubious entries may not even be spotted). And should you experience any type of fraud, provided you have taken reasonable steps to protect your security information, most banks will fully refund you for any losses.

And by reasonable steps, this generally means:

- not writing down, storing or informing others of your security information

- taking immediate steps to change your password etc. should you believe that someone else knows it

- never giving away security information in reply to an email/phone call (it is likely to be from a fraudster)

- choosing a strong password containing letters and numbers and changing it regularly

- not logging into your Internet banking from a publicly accessible computer (such as in an Internet café) as it may not be secure; if you must use one, ensure that no one is watching what you type

- checking your account regularly for fraudulent transactions

- making sure web pages are secure before logging in, by checking for the locked padlock symbol and that http has changed to https

- always ensuring you 'log out' when you have finished banking (do not just close the browser window)

- ensuring that your computer is properly protected. Always make sure that patches for your operating system and browser are applied promptly when they are issued (you can find the latest versions by going to their website, e.g. Microsoft, Apple)

- you should also install anti-virus software and consider also installing anti-spyware software and a firewall. They do not have to be expensive; you can find sites to download them from for free. Ensure that they are regularly updated.

As you can see, you do need to be aware to bank online, and take some responsibility for yourself.

Those who are particularly concerned about fraud will worry that their details are never completely secure. However, this is the case even for those that use a branch-based banking system, and at least with online banking you have the ability to take a quick look at your account whenever you like, and thus spot any problems quickly.

So if you have not signed up for internet banking yet, why not find out more about what your bank offers? You may just find it is exactly what you need.

*Source*: www.fool.co.uk

## Info Point

**New communication technology**

Invsat Limited, the Aberdeenshire headquartered maritime telecommunications systems integrator, has launched its new £1million C and Ku Band Teleport facilities, providing two principal services: end-to-end broadband satellite communication services, and terrestrial connections to fibre optic and microwave circuits for voice, data traffic, multimedia and video conferencing.

Michael Salmon, General Manager of Invsat Limited, said that the new Teleport would strengthen Invsat's communications capabilities, and broaden the range of options for its customers to access the increasing array of communications services on offer.

"Broadband satellite delivery is a rapidly expanding service, and it is characterised by a very high demand for communications and entertainment services."

Invsat Limited is a wholly owned subsidiary of Inmarsat Ventures plc. The company project-manages and delivers VSAT solutions, satellite and broadband networks and VPNs to a global client base, incorporating the maritime, oil and gas, government and emergency services sectors. Further information is available from the Invsat website at www.invsat.com.

*Source*: www.insider.co.uk

## Costs and benefits of IT and ICT

The use of IT and ICT gives rise to a series of trade-offs. Generally speaking, businesses are happy to spend money on IT and ICT where it can be demonstrated that the overall benefits to be gained from implementation outweigh the associated costs.

The main costs and benefits of business information systems are shown below. Please note that this is not intended to be an exhaustive list.

## Costs of using IT:

- initial and recurring costs of hardware and equipment
- on-going costs of replacing and upgrading obsolete systems
- installation costs, e.g. the costs of installing a network infrastructure can be quite high
- new furniture to house equipment
- staff training – this will inevitably lead to a loss of working time
- losses in efficiency as even staff who have been trained to use the new system will be unfamiliar with it for a period of time, and more likely to make mistakes
- teething problems will also contribute to inefficiencies
- possibility of losing information
- computer viruses
- increased risk of commercial espionage and hacking
- health and safety issues for staff, e.g. repetitive strain injury, backache
- the continued use of IT leads to a dependency culture which becomes more and more difficult to escape.

## Benefits of using IT:

- increased efficiency
- increased flexibility
- increase in the amount of data and information that can be handled
- increased customer satisfaction
- competitive edge – at least until rivals catch up
- possibility of reduced staffing costs
- creation of home workers
- access to new markets and customers.

---

### Activity

Can you think of any more costs and benefits of using IT?

## *Legislation*

The increased use of computers as a medium for the electronic storage of information has brought many advantages to business. However, it also carries additional risks. For example, there may be instances where the information held by a business about an individual is incorrect, or the use of the information held on the individual may be questionable.

### The Data Protection Act 1998

The Data Protection Act 1998 aims to protect the rights of the individual by providing legislation to govern the collection, storage and use of information that is held in electronic or paper file systems.

The Data Protection Registrar holds a list of businesses that are registered under the Data Protection Act, and it is the responsibility of the individual business to register their interest with the Registrar. This means that if you are running a business and you hold information on third parties, it is your responsibility to register your business under the Act and follow the rules of the law.

There are eight basic Data Protection Principles which organisations must follow:

1  Obtain and process data fairly and lawfully.

2  Register the purpose for which the information is held.

3  Do not disclose the information in any way that is different from those purposes.

4  Only hold information that is adequate, relevant and not excessive for the purposes you require.

5  Only hold accurate information, and keep it up to date where necessary.

6  Do not hold the information any longer than necessary.

7  Take appropriate security measures to keep the information safe.

8  Give individuals copies of the information held about themselves if they request it and, where appropriate, correct or erase the information.

The Data Protection Principles apply to organisations in both the public and private sectors and also information held about children.

The main job of the Data Protection Registrar is to oversee the enforcement and application of the rules of the Act. He or she also has the power to correct and erase inaccurate records. The Registrar also deals with complaints by members of the public. A complaint may be raised by an individual where there is a failure to allow access to records, or where there has been a breach of one of the Data Protection Principles.

In cases where there has been a serious breach, the individual concerned may be entitled to compensation if it can be successfully proven that they have suffered a loss or damage as a direct result of incorrect information being held by the organisation.

The Data Protection Register is a list of all companies who are registered with the Data Protection Registrar. It is a public record and can be viewed on the internet at www.dataprotectionregister.gov.uk.

The information that appears on the register includes:

- the name of the organisation

- the type of information it holds

- the type of individuals that the organisation holds information about

- what the information is used for

- where the information was obtained from

- any other party that the information has been disclosed to

- the name and address of the person that the individual should write to if they wish to obtain information.

There are certain circumstances in which the individual does not have a right to access information. Specific examples are where the information is held for the purpose of:

- preventing or detecting a crime

- catching or prosecuting offenders

- accessing or collecting taxes or duty

- restrictions relating to information held by the government departments of health and social work.

The rules of the Data Protection Act also state that where an individual writes to an organisation and requests a copy of the information that is held about them, the organisation must reply within 28 days and provide the information to the individual. Some organisations may charge a minimal administration fee for this service, but it is an offence under the terms of the Act not to reply within the 28-day period.

In summary, the Data Protection Act 1998 is a piece of legislation that aims to protect the rights of the individual with regard to the storage of their personal information by third parties. The burden of responsibility is placed with the organisations that hold the information and penalises them where the information held is incorrect or causes damage or loss.

## The Computer Misuse Act 1990

The Computer Misuse Act 1990 was passed to deal with the problem of hacking of computer systems. In the early days of hacking, the problem was not taken very seriously – it was seen as mischievous behaviour, rather than as something which could cause serious loss or problems to companies, organisations and individuals. Before 1990, it was difficult to prosecute people for hacking – existing laws were not written with that in mind. However, it became increasingly clear that hacking should be against the law, and that the laws should be effective and enforceable. As a result, the Computer Misuse Act was passed in 1990.

The Act created three new offences:

1 unauthorised access to computer material

2 unauthorised access with intent to commit or facilitate commission of further offences

3 unauthorised modification of computer material.

It is generally accepted as good business practice nowadays to issue IT Guidelines or an Acceptable Use Policy to all employees. This document should make reference to the provisions of the Computer Misuse Act 1990.

### The Freedom of Information Act 2000

The Freedom of Information Act 2000 is 'challenged with the task of reversing the working premise that everything is secret, unless otherwise stated, to a position where everything is public unless it falls into specified excepted cases' (Lord Chancellor's first Annual Report on the implementation of the Freedom of Information Act 2000, November 2001).

The Freedom of Information (Scotland) Act 2002 gives everyone two specific separate rights:

1  the right to know whether information exists

2  the right to access that information (subject to exemptions).

The individual right of access was introduced on 1 January 2005. The main features of this are:

1.  Every written request for information including emails will be considered to be an access request under the Freedom of Information Act. There is no set format, nor is there any requirement to justify the request. There are no citizenship or residency restrictions, and the only requirement is that applicants provide a name and address.

2.  Access requests must be dealt with within 20 working days.

3.  If the information is not available or the information is not supplied the applicant must be told why.

4.  In cases where either the precise information covered by the request is unclear or where the scope is so wide as to make it likely that the request would be refused on the grounds of cost, public bodies are encouraged to discuss with the applicant the nature of their request to see whether it can be redefined to lead to a positive outcome.

5.  The Act requires public bodies to set up an appeals procedure to review refusals at the request of the applicants, and if the applicant remains unhappy at the refusal, there is an avenue of recourse to the Information Commissioner.

It is hoped that the Freedom of Information Act will encourage transparency in decision-making, leading to a re-establishment of the trust between national and local public bodies and the people they serve.

# End of Chapter Revision Questions

1  What is primary information?

2  What is secondary information?

3  What is internal information?

4  What is external information?

5  Choose two different sources of information. Describe these sources and give an example of each one.

6  Identify at least one cost and one benefit of the sources of information chosen in your answer to question 5.

**7** List at least three different types of information.

**8** Identify at least five characteristics of good information.

**9** Complete the table below by answering whether the source of information linked to the purpose required is either high or low value, and give a reason for your answer. The first one has been completed for you.

| Source | Purpose | High/Low? | Reason |
|---|---|---|---|
| Personal Computing Magazine | To decide which computer to buy | High | Information source is specific to the need and is from a reliable source |
| The internet | To find the latest weather forecast | | |
| *The Scotsman* newspaper | To decide how to cast your vote at the next election | | |
| Magazine advert for a new snack food | To decide whether or not to buy it | | |
| Conversation overheard on the bus | To predict the winner of the Snooker World Championships | | |
| Scottish Qualifications Authority | To find out students' exam results from last year | | |
| Telephone banking service | To find out the balance on your account | | |
| Horoscope in a magazine | To find out what will happen to you in the future | | |
| Person standing next to you on the train station platform | To find out when the next train is due to arrive | | |

**10.** Identify at least three examples of information technology in use today.

**11.** What is a mainframe computer, and why is its use in modern business less widespread?

**12.** Define the terms LAN and WAN, and explain how they are different.

**13** How might a modern business make use of different types of computers? Mention at least two different types.

**14** Define and explain the term 'ICT'.

**15** Identify and explain at least three examples of modern use of the telecommunications network.

**16** Give at least one advantage and one disadvantage of email.

**17** How might a business make use of developments in IT and ICT to expand its operations? You may wish to focus on an example of a modern business that obviously used these developments to its advantage. As a guide, your answer should be in the region of 150–200 words.

**18** What is the scope of the Data Protection Act 1998?

**19** List at least five Data Protection Principles.

**20** What is the maximum time limit that an organisation has to respond to a request for information?

21  List at least two circumstances where an individual could be refused access to information held about themselves under the Data Protection Act 1998.

22  Describe the implications of the Freedom of Information (Scotland) Act 2002.

23  Discuss the importance of the Computer Misuse Act 1990.

## Chapter Summary

At the end of this chapter you should know the following:

★ Information is important to all businesses, particularly for decision-making.

★ Primary information is collected by the business and is verifiable.

★ Secondary information is collected from third parties and is not usually traceable to source.

★ Internal information is collected from within the business.

★ External information is collected from sources outside the business.

★ Generally, the more expensive the information, the more reliable and verifiable it should be.

★ Sources of information include primary, secondary, internal, external.

★ Types of information include qualitative, quantitative, written, oral, pictorial, graphical and numerical.

★ There are various costs and benefits which can be associated with each type and source of information.

★ High quality information should have the following characteristics:
   a) accuracy
   b) timeliness
   c) completeness
   d) appropriateness
   e) availability
   f) cost
   g) objectivity
   h) conciseness.

★ Computers that are in common use today may be one of the following types:
   a) mainframe
   b) desktop
   c) laptop
   d) notebook
   e) handheld/PDA.

★ The use of networks has transformed the way in which we use computers in modern business and society.

★ A LAN is a local area network typically used in an office.

★ A WAN is a wide area network, e.g. the internet.

★ Information Communication Technology (ICT) has transformed the way that we use computers to communicate, and makes extensive use of the telephone network.

★ Email is the preferred form of business communication; fast and cheap to use.

★ The internet has revolutionised business and the way in which business communicates.

★ Use of the internet continues to expand, and new internet technologies and uses are being developed.

*continued* ➤

★ Other examples of IT include multi-media, CDs and DVDs.

You should be able to:

★ recognise the different uses of information technology in business

★ state the different costs and benefits of using IT

★ analyse and describe accurately different sources of information, in terms of their reliability and value for a particular business

★ analyse accurately the main types of information technology used in modern business

★ discuss the main costs and benefits of information technology to business

★ discuss the main principles of the Data Protection Act 1998

★ discuss the main principles of the Freedom of Information (Scotland) Act 2002

★ discuss the main principles of the Computer Misuse Act 1990.

BUSINESS ENTERPRISE

# CHAPTER 3

## ●● Decision-making in business

This part of the course contains the following topics.

| | |
|---|---|
| **Decision-making** | The nature of decisions; types of decision: strategic, tactical and operational; role of managers. |
| **A structured decision-making model** | Identify the problem, identify the objectives, gather information, analyse information, devise alternative solutions, select from alternatives, communicate the decision, implement the decision, evaluate the influence of ICT on decision-making. |
| **Strengths, weaknesses, opportunities, threats (SWOT) analysis** | Development of SWOT analysis, drawing conclusions from a SWOT analysis, justification of conclusions. |
| **Problems of structured models** | Time, ability to collect all information; problems of generating alternatives, lack of creativity. |

## Topic  The nature of decisions

If we did not have to make decisions in business, we probably would not need managers. You could say that management is about making decisions.

A decision is the process of making the choice between different options to achieve an aim or goal.

In order to make good decisions, there are processes that managers should go through to make sure that they are making the best decision to achieve the organisation's goals.

Some decisions are very easy to make. For example, we all make decisions everyday about what to eat, what to wear, what music to listen to, etc. These are routine decisions that we normally do not have to spend a long time thinking about, and are usually easy to make.

Some decisions take a little longer to make. For example, if one of your long-term aims was to go on holiday next year, you then have to decide how you are going to pay for it. This will involve some budgeting decisions, such as how much you can save. Your normal monthly expenditure on clothes, entertainment etc will all now be influenced by your aim to go on holiday.

Other decisions may be about what we want to do in the future, our life goals, such as what career we want. These decisions may take some time to make, and we do not make them very often.

It is the same in business. Managers have to make routine decisions that are easy to make, but can still be very important. For example, whether or not to recruit more staff: if they do, it will cost the business money, but if they do not, they could end up not being able to supply their customers, and so lose business.

They also have to make decisions that affect the long-term prospects of the business. For example, should they develop a new product: they have to decide whether the cost of development will be too high, balanced against the risk of losing customers in the long run, by not developing a new product.

A decision is the choice made from a number of different options. Effective decisions are those which achieve the desired goal or aim of the organisation.

## Types of decision

### Strategic decisions

- These are the long-term decisions about where the organisation wants to be in the future.

- They are often (but not always) made by the most senior managers and the owners of the organisation.

- They do not go into great detail about how these decisions will be achieved.

- Major policy statements represent strategic decisions.

- There are a large number of variables to consider about the future of the organisation, and as such are non-routine decisions.

**Examples:**

- what products the firm will produce in the future

- to increase market share by 10 per cent within five years

- to maximise sales

- to have 100 per cent customer satisfaction.

Strategic decisions define the aims or objectives of the organisation. All businesses have objectives, and the managers of the organisation will be judged on their effectiveness in setting and achieving these objectives.

Businesses have to define their objectives to give direction to the organisation. They often capture the essence of the company through a **mission statement** which will tie employers and employees to a single set of goals or values, in order to motivate the business. It is also a legal requirement for many organisations.

These decisions influence the direction of the organisation. An example could be, 'providing 100 per cent customer satisfaction'. This statement will then influence all other decisions that are made within the organisation. No real thought has gone into how it will be achieved, nor does it say what the customer satisfaction level is at the moment; it simply states that this is one of the main objectives of the business.

To plan a long-term strategy for the organisation, you will have to consider:

- Where are we now?

- Where do we want to be in five, ten, twenty years' time?

- What resources will we need to achieve this?

- What changes do we have to make in order to achieve our new goals?

- How can we do better than the competition?

## Info Point

### Mackie's ice cream

'Mackie's vision is to be a global brand from the greenest company in Britain created by people having fun. Mackie's today is the outcome of the effort and foresight of four generations of Mackie's and their staff. Ice cream is currently the main focus of the business – employing 70 people and producing over five million litres of luxury ice cream a year.'

The first strategic decision here is to establish a global brand. There is no indication in the statement about how this is going to be achieved. However, it provides a goal for the business that they can work towards. The second decision was to focus on ice cream. Previously the main focus was farming, providing milk and other dairy products via 80 roundsmen. Due to an increased demand for skimmed milk, the farming business was left with excess cream, and a decision to produce ice cream with it was taken. Once ice cream was identified as a business opportunity, they gave up their involvement in milk retail, and began to use all their milk for ice cream production, not just their excess cream.

*Source*: www.mackies.co.uk

## Activity

Discuss the decisions which Mackie's could take to achieve their aim of becoming a global brand.

### Tactical decisions

- These are generally shorter-term decisions about how the strategic decisions are going to be achieved, but are likely to have long-term consequences for the organisation.
- They are often made by middle managers within the organisation, in finance, operations, human resources and marketing.
- They are based on achieving the goals or the aims of the organisation.
- They go into detail about what resources will be needed and how they will be used to achieve the aims.
- They will be subject to change as political, economic, socio-cultural, competitive and technological factors change.

**Examples:**

- to increase the number of staff employed
- to rename the business
- to issue more shares on the stock market in order to fund a new factory

- to merge with a competitor
- to increase the selling price
- to reduce costs.

> ## Info Point
>
> Mackie's move away from pig farming and milk retailing were tactical decisions in order to achieve the strategic aim of making ice cream production the focus of their activities.
>
> Their objective of becoming a global brand is becoming a reality. They began as official ice cream suppliers to the 2002 World Cup in Korea, and now supply Mackie's Asia who aspire to extend their franchise model throughout Asia.
>
> 'Norway and Saudi Arabia are new markets for Mackie's but most important is South Korea where Mackie's Asia now have 35 fully branded ice cream parlours. Mackie's ice creams are viewed in Korea as a healthy indulgence with important values of an organic range plus Scottish imagery from a "plough to plate" enterprise in Aberdeenshire.'
>
> *Source*: www.mackies.co.uk

## Operational decisions

- These are the day-to-day, routine decisions.
- They can be made by all levels of management, but mostly by lower level managers and supervisors.
- They are made in response to relatively minor but sometimes important problems that arise each day or week, so they are routine and repetitive.

**Examples:**

- arranging work rotas
- dealing with customer complaints
- ordering materials from suppliers.

> ## Info Point
>
> All organisations face day-to-day problems or unforeseen events which require some action. There should be established procedures on what to do but the decisions still have to be made.
>
> 'Cow welfare is very important, as an unhappy cow does not produce any milk. When the cows are housed during the winter, each cow has its own lying space complete with mattress. They have feed available at all times, with fresh food added twice per day. Our vet comes on a routine visit once a week and any sick animals are moved to a hospital area.'
>
> Here the operational decision would be to remove the sick animal to the hospital area. It may be the obvious thing to do, but is still a decision that has to be made.
>
> *Source*: www.mackies.co.uk

BUSINESS ENTERPRISE

Some people would argue that for most organisations, the only real strategic decision is to survive. All other decisions are made simply to achieve this objective, and are therefore tactical decisions. Even an organisation that is 'safe' would ensure that any other decisions that are made will not affect this position of safety, and therefore will be based on the organisation continuing to survive.

It can be argued that you do not need to make a profit to survive. Many businesses can survive for years without making profits – just look at most of the major football clubs. However, this ignores the human element. Entrepreneurs are risk-takers. Just continuing to survive will not satisfy them: they will have ambitions for their businesses to become bigger and better, to become the market leader, to demonstrate social responsibility, etc. Those who do not take risks are not 'safe', as competition will always defeat them.

## Info Point

Burns Express Freight Ltd is a leading provider of logistical solutions based near Glasgow Airport and has expanded rapidly since formation in 1993.

The main focus of the company has always been customer service. This has led to a diversification of services provided by the company over the years in order to satisfy an ever-changing market.

In order to satisfy both customer and market demand, and to remain competitive, new technology has been embraced in the form of satellite tracking of vehicles and computerised traffic management systems. Costs can be monitored using both these systems, ensuring that the company can provide a cost-effective service to its customers and still maintain a realistic level of profitability. There are added benefits to the customer e.g. freight can be tracked from A to B removing concerns over loss and this again helps the company to retain a competitive edge.

Due to the growth in turnover and also as a result of the diversification of services within the company (i.e. provision of new services like Parcel deliveries and an Irish Groupage Service) there has also been a requirement to recruit additional drivers and administrative staff. The company has changed its structure and created new departments to split the workload and create dedicated staff as the main point of contact for each area. This ensures that any customer enquiry or query can be directed to the correct department and dealt with more efficiently.

Even the purchase of certain vehicles within the company is usually a customer-led decision in that certain criteria have to be met for certain customers. This can range from the size of vehicle to how much the vehicle can transport i.e. volume and weight. In certain cases there is a limit to the age of vehicle that can be used. In order to keep within these limits the company has an age policy on vehicles and renews its fleet every three years. As all vehicles are liveried with the company logo and contact details, this also ensures that we are presenting a good image to customers and also acts as our 'advertising on wheels'.

*continued* ➤

This investment in both technology, equipment and human resources over the past few years is an ongoing project and the company is continually looking at new developments like hand held scanners and enhanced traffic software to ascertain if they will be an immediate added benefit or indeed in the future. As the company continues to grow it will continue to invest in all these areas as a necessary requirement rather than class it as a luxury. This will ensure that standards are maintained and will allow the company to continue to be a market leader in its field.

*Source:* Derek and Carolyn Burns (owners)

## Who needs to know about the decisions?

Everyone who is affected by these decisions has to be informed about the aims and objectives of the organisation. All the stakeholders have an interest in what decisions have been made.

### Employees

Employees should all know where the business is heading and what it is working towards, otherwise they may see no point in changes that have been made and become suspicious. This leads to resistance to change and in some cases sabotage may occur. It is very important that the changes are explained clearly to employees, and that any fears they may have are properly addressed. The organisation depends heavily on its workforce, especially during times of change.

### Investors

Investors are important because the business relies on their investment to finance the decisions that it takes. For example, they may become worried that the business has no overall direction, and then look for other places to put their money. They may not see the benefit of decisions, particularly long-term ones which could affect the amount of dividend they receive. If they are very unhappy, they could seek to replace the managing director, chairperson, or even members of the board of directors. This would leave the business weakened and prone to takeover.

One way to avoid these problems is to issue a mission statement. This could be included in the business's annual report to shareholders.

It can be released to the press to help market the business and its products, and issued to all employees and other stakeholders. It will show that the business has plans for the future, and how those plans will affect the stakeholders.

## Constraints on decision-making

It is one thing to decide that your company should be the market leader in five years' time; however, the senior managers have to be realistic about what they can actually achieve. There will be a number of constraints that businesses face, and these can be split into two categories: internal and external.

BUSINESS ENTERPRISE

## Internal constraints

### Finance available

Just as we never have quite enough money to do all that we want to do, so it is with business. They have to work with the finance that they have available in the form of retained profits, available borrowing, or investment from shareholders. Becoming market leader could involve a huge amount of investment, and if the business cannot get hold of the funds needed, then the target will never be achieved.

### Company policy

The push for growth that is necessary for the business to become market leader may lead to conflict with the company's own policy. For some businesses this would run contrary to their stated policy of keeping production in the UK.

### The employees' abilities/attitudes

How the employees react to the proposed decisions, and how able they are to achieve the objectives will have a great influence on whether or not these decisions are successful. Are they motivated for the changes? Are they capable of the tasks that will be expected of them?

## External constraints

### Government and EU legislation

Whatever actions the business may wish to take, they will have to be legal. For example, any actions which are deemed to be anti-competitive will be subject to investigation and possible prosecution by the Department of Trade and Industry and Monopolies Commission. Anti-competitive actions include any actions which prevent other businesses from entering the market, which would not be in the best interests of consumers. It could involve price-fixing, where prices are kept artificially low for a time to keep other firms out of the market.

To find out more, visit: www.dti.gov.uk.

### Competitors' behaviour

No matter what decisions the business makes, other firms will be making other decisions which will affect the original decision. More than one firm in the market may have the same objective, and so cancel out much of each other's work to achieve this aim.

### Lack of new technology

Dyson, makers of the bag-free vacuum cleaner, relies heavily on the development of new technology for its success. Where that technology is not available, it will be difficult to enter or develop new markets.

### Economic environment

During boom periods when the economy is growing quickly, it is much easier to increase sales and market share, as the market itself is usually growing. However, in times of recession, growth in the economy slows and markets shrink, making it much more difficult to achieve any increase. Some firms may benefit from a recession as they are more able to weather the bad times; when the market recovers they will survive, and gain a larger share of the growing market while others have gone out of business.

## *The outcome of decisions*

Along with the responsibility for making decisions, managers also have responsibility for monitoring and investigating the outcome of these decisions. During the process of implementing the decisions, they have to check that they are working as planned.

They must constantly:

- **Review** – what was actually achieved?
- **Evaluate** – was this what was expected?
- **Alter** – are changes required?

Something that is of great benefit during times of change is flexibility. The more flexible the organisation is, the more easily it can react to changes as their environment changes.

Evaluation is an important part of decision-making:

- Were the objectives of the decision met?
- What happened that was not expected?

If things did not go to plan, some changes may be needed. Decisions may not be successful for a number of reasons. This could be due to internal factors such as poor employee relations, or external factors such as changes in the economy. It is important that managers evaluate their decisions and make adjustments if necessary. Quality decision-making depends on checking at all stages, so any necessary changes can be made and the organisation can best meet its objectives.

## *The role of managers*

Sir John Harvey Jones, in his television series *Troubleshooter* (where he helped organisations to overcome problems), described management as an art. He said that there is not one solution that will solve the problems in all businesses, rather that it is the manager's role to identify those bits of management theory that fit best with that organisation's problems. The aim must be to encourage constant change at a speed that the organisation can best cope with.

Management theorists describe the role of managers in different ways:

' … a manager is one who is responsible for getting things done through people instead of doing the job himself'
W F Coventry

'The quality and performance of the managers determine the success of a business, indeed they determine survival'
Peter F Drucker

These two statements summarise the theoretical role which management plays within an organisation. They are a unifying resource, bringing together the people, materials, machines and money in order to solve problems, make decisions and make sure that the business gets the best possible return from its resources.

In 1973 Henry Mintzberg published his book *The Nature of Managerial Work*, containing his study of what managers actually do as opposed to what they ought to do. He found that managers perform a wide variety of roles which can be broadly grouped into three areas:

1 **Interpersonal role** – the relationships which a manager has with others.

2 **Informational role** – the collecting and passing on of information.

3 **Decisional role** – the making of different kinds of decisions.

BUSINESS ENTERPRISE

Henri Fayol, who in the early part of the last century spent some time researching what managers do, identified what he called the five functions of management:

| Function | Description |
|---|---|
| **Plan** | Looking ahead, seeing potential opportunities or problems and devising solutions, setting targets, and setting aims and strategies. |
| **Organise** | Arranging the resources of the organisation to be there when people need them, and acquiring additional resources if required. |
| **Command** | This involves the issuing of instructions, motivating staff and displaying leadership. |
| **Co-ordinate** | Making sure everyone is working towards the same goals, that all the work being done fits together, and people are not duplicating work or working against each other. |
| **Control** | Looks at what is being done, checks it against what was expected, and makes any necessary adjustments. This is the monitoring and evaluating role of management. |

Modern managers are likely to include:

- **Delegate** – give subordinates the authority to carry out tasks. This helps with motivation and reduces the manager's workload. The overall responsibility will still lie with the manager who delegated the authority.

- **Motivate** – rather than simply telling workers to work harder, which is not likely to be successful, you encourage them by helping them to enjoy their tasks through team-working, participation in decision-making, and by giving them some powers.

Decisions are often made by groups of managers in teams. This allows for a wider variety of ideas and experience to be used when making the decision. The number of people within the group and the different roles they play is important in effective decision-making.

### Info Point

A study by Professor Simon Garrod of Glasgow University suggests that group size is vital for decision-making. One or two dominant speakers can sway the discussion in larger groups of ten or more, making it a poor size for gaining a true consensus. Smaller groups of up to seven people are much more successful in coming to an agreement between the group members.

Professor Garrod suggests that companies seeking an innovative, creative solution to a business problem should limit group sizes to up to seven people.

## Organisational objectives

Whether the decisions are strategic, operational or tactical, they must fit with the organisation's objectives. For example, if social responsibility is an objective of the organisation, the organisation's decision-makers at the various levels of management must ensure that they do not make decisions which clash with this objective, such as giving up recycling materials to reduce costs, or buying from countries which have a poor human rights record. To do so, they could face criticism from pressure groups such as Amnesty International, who work to reduce human rights abuse around the world.

## Info Point

'Managing the environment is an important objective for the farm. We have planted 120 acres of deciduous trees around the farm. These areas have been designed to provide habitats for wildlife, to encourage native species to breed in this area. We have sown grass strips around some of our fields to create wildlife corridors to link the areas of woodland together. These grass strips also protect any waterways from chemicals and fertiliser, which we may apply to the land. We have created wetland areas and a pond to encourage as diverse a wildlife population as possible.

Farm waste (muck and slurry) is always a potential risk to the environment – quite apart from the smell! We therefore analyse all our waste and apply to each crop only the amount that can be utilised by that crop at that time of year in order to minimise leakage of any nitrates into waterways. We also carry out a nutrient budget each year to ensure we are balancing everything correctly.'

Mackie's have their own wind turbine which supplies enough electricity for their business and means that the ice cream is 'made from renewable energy'. The wind turbine is connected directly to the farm business where staff can instantly monitor their use. Any excess energy is added to the grid and sold to consumers by a renewable energy provider.

*Source*: www.mackies.co.uk

Each stakeholder in the organisation will have some influence on the decisions made. Shareholders can vote at the Annual General Meeting (AGM) to change decisions, or force different courses of action on the managers of the organisation.

The objectives of the organisation, the stakeholders and the ways that they can influence the organisation are dealt with in Chapter 1. You should refer back to them at this stage to see how each will influence the types of decisions that are made.

## Topic A structured decision-making model

Effective decisions can be made on the spur of the moment by managers using their experience or 'gut feeling'. However, success is not easily guaranteed, and many other good options could be ignored or missed. In practice, managers should go through a proven process in order to give the best possible chance of success.

Whatever the decision that has to be made, it is always best to follow nine simple steps. This way you have the best opportunity of making the right decision.

## Step 1 – Identify the problem

Set the aims.

- Where do we want to go?

- What do we want to achieve?

- What do we need to do to be the best?

- What exactly is wrong?

It is not always obvious what the actual problem is. For example, when a famous brand shampoo found that its sales were falling, it tried various promotions and advertising to try to boost sales with little effect. It was not until they carried out market research that they found that the problem was that they had not increased their prices in line with their competitors, and so it had become one of the cheaper well-known brands. Consumers viewed this low price as an indication of poor quality. The solution was very simple and effective; they simply increased the price and quickly regained market share.

## Step 2 – Identify the objectives

- What is it we want to achieve?

Managers have to decide on exactly what it is they want to achieve. In most cases, business organisations will not use the structured model when they are looking for a simple quick fix. If the organisation is going to go through the process of implementing major changes, there will be a variety of objectives that can be achieved at the same time.

## Step 3 – Gather information

Good information leads to good decision-making. The more information that can be gathered, the better the chance of success. Extensive use of internal and external information is required.

## Step 4 – Analyse information

Study the information you have collected. Much of the information gathered will not be of direct use in the decision-making; this will have to be sorted, and then a decision made as to what information is relevant and what is not.

- What can you do, and what can't you do?

- What will help, and what will not?

## Step 5 – Devise alternative solutions

Using the information you have collected, decide on a number of different courses of action you can take that will meet the aims. Having a range of options will make the process much more flexible should you have to change things later on due to changes in the business environment.

## Step 6 – Select from alternative solutions

From the alternative courses of action that you have devised, select the one which you think will be mostly likely to meet the aims of the organisation under present circumstances.

## Step 7 – Communicate the decision

This is a very important stage. All those involved must know exactly what is going to happen, what effects these changes will have, and why you have decided on this course of action. Failing to inform all those concerned properly will result in a less effective implementation. If everybody knows what they are doing and why, they will be far more motivated to succeed.

## Step 8 – Implement the decision

Arrange for the resources to be put into place. Changes will need to be adequately resourced if they are to be successful. Issue appropriate instructions, and ask for feedback on how things progress.

## Step 9 – Evaluate

Using the information you are collecting on how the process is going, compare this to what was expected to happen. This will ensure that everything is on target and will allow you to make further changes as necessary to ensure that the final goal will be achieved in the most effective manner.

## The influence of ICT on decision-making

As we saw in Chapter 2, developments in computer hardware and software have allowed them to become more and more sophisticated. This will allow the decision-making process to be completed more quickly and efficiently, as the information available can then be analysed more easily.

Products such as 'Automatic Decision Trees' and 'MindManager X5' provide businesses and individuals with ICT-based decision-making tools.

Records held on database can be accessed, sorted and processed into a structure that helps decision-making. Spreadsheets can run 'what if' analyses to compare the outcomes of different courses of action. Management decision-making software can also help identify the best solution from a number of alternatives. The internet can provide huge amounts of up-to-date information on any number of topics, including market information such as trends and competitors' products.

All this means that decisions can be made more accurately than before, with increased speed. The only major drawback, apart from the costs involved, is information overload, with many managers finding that there is too much information being received, and time will have to be spent in selecting the relevant information.

This is a particular problem with email, where it is just as easy to send an email to one person as it is to send it to everyone on your mailing list. In fact it takes longer to select a few recipients, so there is a tendency to send an email to anyone who might be interested within the organisation, rather than only those who need the information.

# Topic SWOT analysis

One other tool that management can use to help with decision-making is SWOT analysis. It is used to evaluate where the organisation is now and where it should be in the future. It helps with planning, deciding the way forward for the organisation, and looking at strategies which could be used.

It looks at all internal and external factors. Internal factors are the resources within the organisation. External factors are those things within the organisation's environment that are happening now or are likely to happen in the future.

SWOT stands for:

- **S**trengths
- **W**eaknesses
- **O**pportunities
- **T**hreats.

SWOT analysis is a tool that can be effectively used for any decision-making. However, it is often used when making **strategic** decisions and **marketing** decisions.

## Strengths

- What advantages do you have?
- What do you do well?
- What relevant resources do you have access to?
- What do other people regard as your strengths?

This should be considered from the organisation's own point of view and from the point of view of the people they deal with. It is important not to be modest but to be realistic.

In looking at strengths, the organisation should think about them in relation to its competitors. For example, if all the competitors provide high quality products, then a high quality production process is not a strength in the market, it is a necessity.

## Weaknesses

- What could you improve?
- What do you do badly?
- What should you avoid?

Again, this should be considered from an internal and external basis: do other people seem to perceive weaknesses that the organisation does not see? Are competitors doing better business? It is best to be realistic now, and face any unpleasant truths as soon as possible.

## Opportunities

- Where are the good opportunities facing you?
- What are the current interesting trends?

Useful opportunities can come from such things as:

- changes in technology and markets on both a broad and narrow scale

- changes in government policy related to your field

- changes in social patterns, population profiles, lifestyle changes, etc.

- local events.

A useful approach to looking at opportunities is to look at the strengths and ask whether these open up any opportunities. Alternatively, look at weaknesses and ask whether the organisation could open up opportunities by eliminating them.

## Threats

- What obstacles do you face?

- What is your competition doing?

- Are the required specifications for your job, products or services changing?

- Is changing technology threatening your position?

- Do you have bad debt or cashflow problems?

- Could any of your weaknesses seriously threaten your business?

Strengths and weaknesses are **internal** factors. Opportunities and threats are **external** influences.

SWOT analysis is most often laid out in a grid form as below.

| **S**trengths | **W**eaknesses |
|---|---|
| **O**pportunities | **T**hreats |

In each box a list is made, and this provides a snapshot of where the organisation is at this time and what the possibilities are for the future. Going through the physical process of writing it down is thought-provoking and will generate discussion of items not previously considered.

SWOT analysis can be used to cover the first four steps in the structured decision-making process, and at the end to help decide if the decisions made were successful. SWOT analysis should not be seen as a one-off exercise. It should be part of the continuing process of evaluating how the organisation is doing now and what it should be doing in the future.

It is common for a number of people to work on the SWOT, with others adding to it during the process. It is probable that different managers will have different views on each of the

BUSINESS ENTERPRISE

elements. Some threats may also be opportunities, depending on how the organisation reacts to them. Strengths may become weaknesses very quickly, and vice versa.

Not all organisations would find it useful to carry out SWOT analysis. For example, the owner of a small corner shop would keep much of this information in his head, and would be well aware of all internal and most external factors.

## Internal factors – strengths and weaknesses

These are the things that the organisation can control, and refer to the resources of the organisation or the factors of production. The skills of workforce and management, including its entrepreneurial skills, will be included in the study. How well the capital is being used to provide efficient production and distribution will be examined, as will its financial performance and the range of products. These can be compared to the market leader to analyse how successful the organisation is in these areas.

The strengths and weaknesses reflect the current position of the organisation. These strengths and weaknesses are often obvious, but may be rarely considered; it is only when management decides to spend time looking at them that they will be dealt with appropriately. The organisation can build on its strengths, using them to their best advantage, and work to reduce or get rid of its weaknesses.

When making strategic decisions the organisation will look at all aspects of the organisation including:

### Human resources

The workforce, including all levels of management, represent an investment by the organisation. It is also a resource which will have strengths or weaknesses in the quality of the management team, the level of entrepreneurial skills, and the numbers and skills of the workers.

### Capital

A major strength of an organisation will be its financial performance. A profitable business will have money available to carry out the changes it needs to make to respond to changes in the market. It will also have the ability to attract investment from shareholders or lending from the bank for major changes.

Assets represent investment in the organisation by the owners. The higher the level of this investment, the more attractive it is to potential investors and banks.

### Marketing

- the product range
- its marketing mix
- its distribution network
- the production process.

The business should decide which function it does well and which it could improve upon, in order to gain an edge over the competition.

# External influences – opportunities and threats

The organisation cannot directly control these factors. However, they will be able to take advantage of any opportunities that come along, and try to avoid or take steps to overcome threats.

The external influences will come from the business environment in which the organisation operates. Evaluation of these opportunities and threats is critical to the success or failure of the business.

## Info Point

**Sony**

Sony managed to get their Playstation 2 on to the market in November 2000, well in advance of Microsoft's Xbox (March 2002) and Nintendo's GameCube (May 2002). In doing so, they were able to capture a large section of the games market.

Now Microsoft wants to sell ten million units of the Xbox 360 within 12 to 16 months of the launch of its next generation games console. The 360 went on sale before Christmas 2005 in the US, Europe, and Japan.

Sony's PlayStation 3 is due out in spring 2006 (although it is not clear if this is just in Japan, or whether the release date also includes the US and Europe). Nintendo's Revolution is due later in 2006. Microsoft is counting on being first with its Xbox 360. It wants to take an early lead in the battle to dominate the next generation of consoles.

The software giant was a year behind Sony's PlayStation 2 in launching the original Xbox, and it never managed to make up the time in sales.

The external influences can be grouped under the headings:

- political
- economic
- socio-cultural
- technological
- competitive.

Looking at these areas is also known as **PEST Analysis**. Organisations often carry out this analysis in conjunction with the SWOT analysis, as it allows for a better view of the business environment.

Using these headings, the organisation can look more closely at the areas.

## Political

- government type and stability
- freedom of press, rule of law and levels of bureaucracy and corruption
- regulation and deregulation trends
- social and employment legislation

- tax policy, and trade and tariff controls

- environmental and consumer-protection legislation

- likely changes in the political environment.

The major source of potential threats or opportunities politically is when the government decides to introduce new laws, or alter taxation rates. For example, increases in the taxation on petrol are a threat to car sales, so manufacturers produce cars with more fuel-efficient engines. The introduction of the minimum wage was seen as a major threat to many small businesses, however, this did not result in the large scale unemployment that was predicted.

## Economic

- stage of business cycle

- current and projected economic growth, inflation and interest rates

- unemployment and labour supply

- labour costs

- levels of disposable income and income distribution

- impact of globalisation

- likely impact of technological or other change on the economy

- likely changes in the economic environment.

How the economy is performing has a major influence on the level of success of a business. Those organisations which are very dependant on borrowing will find their costs rising and falling with the interest rate, and so therefore will their profits. This makes businesses less likely to borrow money for major projects when rates are high.

Interest rates also affect consumer spending. When rates are low, consumers are much more likely to borrow and spend money, which in turn creates more sales for business. However, it is also true that when rates are high, they will borrow and spend less, decreasing the level of sales.

The exchange rate affects the prices of imported and exported goods. When the pound is valued highly against other currencies, the price of British imports becomes cheaper; however, exports then become much more expensive for other countries making them less attractive and reducing sales levels.

### Info Point

According to a report by the food policy charity Sustain, supermarket chains such as Tesco, Sainsbury's and Asda import up to a quarter of their groceries. Once proud-to-be British companies like Marks and Spencer, Reebok and Kangol boasted that their clothing lines were UK-made; now they buy from cheaper foreign suppliers. Today, tens of thousands of British jobs have disappeared in the clothing and textiles industry, as production shifts overseas in order to cut costs.          (February 2005)

During a recession people have less money to spend on luxury goods, so manufacturers will produce cheaper alternatives until the economy comes out of recession.

## Socio-cultural

- population growth rate and age profile

- population health, education and social mobility, and attitudes to these

- population employment patterns, job market freedom and attitudes to work

- press attitudes, public opinion, social attitudes and social taboos

- lifestyle choices and attitudes to these

- socio-cultural changes.

Organisations have to take account of changes in the tastes, lifestyles and attitudes of consumers. Tastes in fashions change from season to season and from year to year, so clothing manufacturers have to ensure that their latest products meet the consumers' tastes. More women are working than ever before, and this has had two effects:

1 Women have a far greater influence on what is bought within the household.

2 Working women's lifestyles changed, with less time to spend on shopping and preparing food, looking after children and daily household chores. This led to the growth in a wide variety of family convenience foods and fast food outlets, a growth in childcare facilities and nurseries, and a growth in small house cleaning companies and ironing services.

### Info Point

Women have discovered the same aptitude for Internet shopping that some have for hitting the high street. According to a new survey, women are now spending more money online than men for the first ever time.

Although surfing the net has long been seen as a man-thing, the study found the amount spent online by a typical woman rose 71.4 per cent in 2003. Among online shoppers of both sexes, the over-55s were the biggest spenders according to the report.

But back in the gender divide, the average bill for a female Internet shopper is now £495, compared to £470 for their male counterparts.

'Though surfing the net has long been seen as a male-orientated activity, this is no longer the case for e-retail, and women's inclination to shop has become the main driver of online sales growth,' said analyst group Verdict, the author of the report.

The average over-55-year-old who shopped via a website last year bought more than £527 worth of goods and services – more than any other age group.

'They have a disposable income and are able to accept deliveries during the day,' said the report.

'Many more affluent pensioners have adopted the internet as a hobby and enjoy surfing the net for cheap prices and good deals.'

*Source:* www.bbc.co.uk/news, November 2004

## Activity

Discuss how the changes in shopping habits of UK consumers described above will affect how a business operates, and what opportunities and threats may arise.

Consumers are far more aware of social issues such as third world poverty, health issues and environmental concerns. Organisations have adapted their products, image and processes to take account of consumers' concerns. For example, most supermarkets now carry a range of organic produce and 'fair trade' goods, label the contents of their products, and offer recycling facilities.

## Technological environment

- impact of emerging technologies
- impact of Internet, reduction in communications costs and increased remote working
- research and development activity
- impact of technology transfer.

The introduction of new technologies forces change on organisations. Mass production techniques allow capital-intensive automated processes, which are more efficient than labour-intensive production. The production of 'hi-tech' consumer goods such as computers uses very sophisticated robotics. As new developments in computer components are introduced, this requires new automated machinery. Firms have to keep up to date to survive.

As these new computers are introduced to some businesses, their competitors will then need to update their systems to avoid potentially losing market share.

## Competitive

Probably the biggest concern for most businesses is (rightly or wrongly) the actions of their competitors. Businesses look at how their product competes in terms of what it can do, what it looks like, what price it is or what offers are being made, and what after-sales service is available.

## Info Point

**Competition hits Somerfield sales**

Somerfield, the UK supermarket chain being stalked by potential bidders, has reported weakening sales as it faces intense competition and subdued demand.

Like-for-like sales fell 0.4 per cent in the year to 30 April, and were down 2.7 per cent in the nine weeks to 2 July.

Despite waning demand, the firm posted post-exceptional annual profits of £60.9m ($107m), up from £45.2m in 2004.

The main drag on the Somerfield group's sales came from its Kwik Save chain, where like-for-like sales were 6.4 per cent lower in the nine weeks to 2 July. Sales at Somerfield stores were down 0.7 per cent.

*Source*: www.bbc.co.uk/news, February 2005

## Drawing conclusions from a SWOT analysis

The purpose of SWOT analysis is to help make decisions about what needs to be done now and what is likely to happen in the future. The conclusions will be the basis for the future of the organisation, so it is important that the SWOT is correctly interpreted.

The strengths will identify areas where the business is doing well at this present time, and where possibilities for the future exist. For example, having new products in the development stages ready for launch will provide a very good platform for the business to progress.

The weaknesses will highlight the areas where attention needs to be paid now in order to ensure survival. For example, having a high level of borrowing will make the business vulnerable to changes in the economy, and as part of the strategic plan, steps should be taken to reduce borrowing.

Opportunities have to be carefully measured to make sure that the business makes the best of them. These opportunities could come about from any of the factors mentioned in the PEST analysis. To take advantage of these opportunities, the business must include them in their strategic planning.

## Info Point

Alcohol could be on sale 24-hours-a-day in supermarkets across England and Wales as they aim to take advantage of changes to the country's drinking laws.

Sainsbury's, Tesco and Asda confirmed a number of their stores have applied for licences allowing them to sell alcohol around the clock. Current laws limit the sale of alcohol to between 8am and 11pm.

But Alcohol Concern has urged retailers to be responsible, warning the move may lead to a rise in 'problem drinking'. The charity urged supermarkets to ensure that they did not offer cheap drink promotions or sell to customers who were underage or drunk.

*continued* ➤

Sainsbury's said it had applied for 24-hour licences for 'the majority' of its 727 stores. Asda, owned by US giant Wal-Mart, added it was trying to get permits for more than 100 outlets. The licences would be extended to match the opening hours of its stores. Meanwhile, Tesco said the 'majority' of its stores would be applying for the extension, in order to offer its customers greater convenience.

The new rules allowing 24-hour drinking in England and Wales come into force in November 2005.

*Source*: www.bbc.co.uk/news, February 2005

As with opportunities, threats come from the political, economic, socio-cultural, technological, and competitive forces. It is necessary for the business to take action to deal with these threats, to ensure survival.

### Info Point

Manchester United fans angry at the recent takeover of their football club by Malcolm Glazer have been urging shirt sponsor Vodafone to 'hang up' on the US tycoon.

Fans have been calling for a boycott of major club sponsors, such as Vodafone.

But Vodafone said it did not see any reason why it should not continue to benefit from Manchester United links.

However, Vodafone has not renewed its sponsorship agreement with ex-United star David Beckham, which was signed in 2002, and renewed in 2004 for a further 12 months. Shareholders United warned that Vodafone's public image may suffer if Mr Glazer's stewardship of the club was not successful.

In December 2003 Vodafone and Manchester United signed a £36m four-year shirt sponsorship deal. With so many fans unhappy with Mr Glazer's takeover, it is possible that many fans will cancel their Vodafone contracts.

They may also be 'reluctant' to buy Vodafone's Manchester United Mobile products and services, a key aspect of the strategic tie-up between the two companies.

As well as Vodafone, boycotts could also potentially affect sales at Nike, Pepsi and Budweiser.

*Source*: www.bbc.co.uk/news, July 2005

Evaluation of the conclusions drawn should take place to ensure that decisions were accurate. Carrying out another SWOT analysis will allow the business to see if their conclusions were correct.

# **Topic** Problems of structured model

## *Time*

The structured model does not go for the 'quick fix'. If a solution is needed in a hurry then the structured model will add too much time to the process, and so the response may come too late to solve the problem. It takes time to go through all the steps involved, and in taking that time, more thought will go into coming up with the best solution. Some decisions are easier to make than others. The amount and the detail of the information, and the greater the options available, the longer it will take to decide the correct course of action.

## *The ability to collect all the information needed*

It is not always possible to get hold of all the good information required to make the best decisions. Some information will be hard to get hold of. On the other hand, you may receive great amounts of information but have to search to find the parts that are relevant.

## *Problems of generating alternative solutions*

It may be difficult to come up with alternatives. People can be reluctant to make hard decisions, and may not favour solutions which will affect them badly even though that solution is the best for the organisation. It is almost impossible to realise all the consequences of different decisions.

## *Lack of creativity*

Some good managers will feel they already know what to do based on past experience. The process will put them off making decisions which are riskier but could be more beneficial. Managers may not be able to come up with imaginative alternatives, and stick with what they know best.

## *The benefits of using a structured process of decision-making*

### **The time taken**

Because the process of going through each of the steps takes some considerable time, decisions will not be rushed. Managers will have had sufficient time to put time and thought into the process. They will have had time to see what needs to be done and how best to do it, and to evaluate all possible outcomes from the various alternatives.

### **The quality and quantity of information used**

Care is taken in gathering, checking and analysing information. Using the best information available gives the best chance of the decision being successful.

### **Alternative solutions**

Generating alternatives will allow for some creativity to be included in the decision. It also allows for 'fall back' plans should the original preferred solution turn out to be wrong. Time will be available to assess the consequences of each possible alternative.

BUSINESS ENTERPRISE

### *Aids to decision-making*

There are a number of tried and trusted ways of helping managers come to generate new ideas, to co-operate, and finally to arrive at what are hoped to be the best decisions.

## Brainstorming

The step-by-step process of the decision-making model may make it difficult to be creative in finding alternative solutions. Brainstorming is when a group meet to try to think of as many alternative solutions as possible. Each member of the group thinks of as many ideas as they can, no matter how daft they might appear, and all the ideas are written down as they are suggested.

Once everyone has finished, the group works their way through each of the ideas in turn, discussing the possibilities contained in each. This way they can often come up with the most creative ideas because it encourages everyone to participate in an informal setting, without the members of the group feeling that they are in some way being judged.

## Benchmarking

This involves comparing what you do with what the very best organisations do. You could for example look at what the market leader does and then try to copy them. In this case the market leader is the 'benchmark' or ideal standard that you want to achieve. Benchmarking is used widely in operations to ensure quality, but it is equally valid as a method to aid decision-making in any of the organisation's functional areas.

# End of chapter revision questions

1   Explain why it is important for managers to communicate their decisions to stakeholders.

2   Identify the main constraints that are placed on managers when making decisions.

3   What are the main characteristics of strategic decisions?

4   What are the main characteristics of tactical decisions?

5   What are the main characteristics of operational decisions?

6   Identify Mintzberg's three main roles of management.

7   Describe Fayol's five functions of management, and identify two other functions which modern managers would employ.

8   Identify five possible objectives for an organisation.

9   Identify three stakeholders and describe at least two ways they could influence decision-making within an organisation.

10   Describe the nine steps involved in the structured decision-making model.

11   Identify the main internal influences (strengths and weaknesses) on an organisation.

12   Briefly describe the main external influences (opportunities and threats) on an organisation.

13   Identify the main problems in using a structured decision-making model.

14   What are the main benefits of using a structured decision-making model?

## Chapter Summary

At the end of this chapter you should be able to:

★ identify and describe the three main types of decision – strategic, tactical, and operational

★ describe and analyse the role of managers in the decision-making process

★ assess the influence which stakeholders have on decision-making

★ identify and describe how the organisation's objectives will influence the managers' decision-making

★ describe and use effectively a structured decision-making model

★ describe and use effectively a SWOT analysis

★ identify the costs/drawbacks of using a decision-making model or SWOT analysis.

BUSINESS ENTERPRISE

# SECTION TWO

# Business Decision Areas

# Marketing

This part of the course contains the following topics.

| | |
|---|---|
| **Marketing** | Role and importance of marketing in organisations. |
| **The marketing concept** | Marketing as a strategic activity, marketing of products and services. |
| **The marketing mix** | Place, including distribution channels; pricing strategies; product/service; promotional strategies. |
| **Target markets** | Market segmentation; methods of segmenting markets; niche marketing, market share, market growth. |
| **Market research** | Primary and secondary information. Costs and benefits. Techniques – desk research, survey, questionnaire, interview, test marketing, sampling, the assessment of customer requirements. Collection of consumer data. |

## Topic  Role and importance of marketing in organisations

Marketing is the way in which the organisation communicates with the consumer. Individual organisations will have different marketing needs: organisations in the private sector use marketing to make profits on what they sell, whereas organisations in the public sector, such as the local council, use marketing in order to try to provide the best services they can to the local community.

It is not only the private sector that needs to carry out marketing.

- How does a charity persuade people to make donations?

- How does the local council convince local people that their council taxes are well spent?

- How does the government let people know about changes in the law, or the result of research in areas like health?

All organisations in the private, public or voluntary sector need to carry out marketing activities to meet their objectives.

### *Marketing for the public sector*

They may use market research to find out what the community needs are; they will advertise their services through their own publications, at their various offices and sometimes at local post offices. They will develop new services if market research shows that the community wants them. The council will be driven by the councillors' need to satisfy their voters and the need to meet the legal requirements of national government.

## Marketing for the private sector

Small businesses' marketing needs are very different from those of big businesses. For example, the local corner shop would not need to worry too much about marketing because it continually meets its customers face-to-face, and so has direct communication with them. It may offer promotions or discounts from time to time in order to keep customers, or it may advertise its opening times in the local paper, but generally its marketing will be very limited.

Big businesses are unlikely to meet their customers, so they rely heavily on marketing to keep communicating with their customers.

Marketing needs also depend on how many customers a business has. For example, an organisation operating in the industrial markets may have only a few big customers, so they will keep in close contact with them.

## Marketing in the voluntary sector

The competition for donations is highly competitive. The number of charities is growing and one of the symptoms of this increased competition is that aggressive street fundraising is becoming more common in our towns and cities. Charities spend large sums of money on marketing, from television campaigns to visiting schools, to raise awareness.

### Info Point

Charities have to convince people that giving money for nothing in return is a good idea. The Royal Scottish Society for the Prevention of Cruelty to Children can trace its origins back to 1889. It now operates under the name 'Children 1ST' which gives the public a better idea of its activities as it no longer investigates cases of child abuse. The change of name was a marketing decision. It lets the public know that it works with children who need support and their families.

Last year it spent £748,920 on fundraising. This represents 13 per cent of its total income which could have been spent on services to children. However, if it did not spend this money on what are mainly marketing activities, it is unlikely that it would have managed to spend £4.8 million on services to children and their families. In contrast, it only spent £20,555 on administration.

Even the website where this information was made freely available is a form of marketing, as it allows the public to access the information they need in order to decide to make a donation.

*Source*: Children 1st, 2005

## What is marketing?

Marketing is one of the main functional areas of an organisation. It is an important part of any business, whether in the private or public sector. What the activity of marketing means to a business depends very much on its size and type. It is one of the main strategic areas of the business, and how successful the marketing is directly influences the success of the business.

To understand what marketing is, we first have to understand what a market is. A market is a place where buyers and sellers meet to exchange goods and services for money. The simplest form of market is the town market where local producers bring their produce to sell. Your city or town may have a weekly or monthly market, like the farmers' market in Perth where

farmers can bring their produce to sell directly to the public.

At this market the farmers can quickly find out what sells best, and by talking to customers they can find out what else they like, and what else they would like to buy at the market. Here the buyers and sellers are meeting face-to-face, talking about products. The information which the farmers gather can be used by them to meet the needs of their consumers.

Large manufacturers rarely have the chance to meet their customers face-to-face, to discuss what products they would like to see, or what changes they would like in their products. This problem led to the introduction of marketing as a function of modern business.

Marketing is communication between the producers and the consumers who under normal circumstances would never meet face-to-face. Modern marketing has been described by the Chartered Institute of Marketing as the process involved in identifying, anticipating and satisfying consumer requirements profitably:

## Identifying

What does the consumer want from a good or service in terms of price, features, quality, colours, delivery, packaging, image, after-sales service, etc? This involves communicating with the consumer in order to best meet their needs. If the company gets it right, a sale will take place; if it gets it wrong, there will be no sale.

## Anticipating

Products can take a number of years to develop, so meeting the customer's needs now is no guarantee of success in the future. Businesses have to try to anticipate what consumers will want in one, two, three, four or five years' time, depending on how long it takes to develop the new product. A new model of a car can take five years and billions of pounds to develop, so it is essential that the car is one that will meet customers' needs. Again, this involves communicating with the consumer.

However, sometimes the consumer is totally unaware of what they will be buying in the future. Who could have guessed that teenagers would see a mobile phone as an essential survival item five years ago? The marketing departments of the mobile phone manufacturers and network operators did.

## Satisfying

The business must produce the right product, at the right price and the right time, otherwise the customer will simply buy a competitor's product. There are always alternatives that the customer can buy if your product is not available, or at the wrong price. So if you get it wrong, you lose sales.

## Info Point

**High costs deter hi-tech dreams**

The high price of gadgets to create homes where TV, computer, hi-fi, phone and net connect is a big barrier, found a report produced by Accenture.

Of those questioned, 70 per cent would be happy to sign up with a single firm if they solved all these problems. The survey of 2,600 people plumbed attitudes to homes where information was happily swapped between computers, fixed and mobile phones, digital images and movies, music and any other form of digital device. While many people liked the idea of such a home, 80 per cent thought it would simply be too expensive to go shopping for all the gadgets to make it a reality.

Analyst Al Delattre, from Accenture's Communications and Hi-tech practice, said most firms only offered a small part of the full digital home package that consumers were seeking. He said hardware firms, media makers and suppliers had to work much closer together if they were to meet consumer demands. The Accenture survey described four different types of hi-tech home to those taking part.

The home entertainment system described proved most popular, with 42 per cent saying they wanted one.

A home healthcare system was popular with 37 per cent and least enticing, 28 per cent, was the idea of a digital home that doubled as a virtual office or one that helped people manage their life better.

When asked why they wanted more gadgets in the home most of those questioned (56 per cent) said it would help them save money. Others (46 per cent) said it would make their lives easier or (34 per cent) simply make home life more enjoyable.

*Source*: BBC technology, July 2005

## Info Point

**Is this the end of the telephone?**

Broadband is still growing, the mobile phone market is saturated, but consumers are still looking for new technologies at a low price to improve the way they live and communicate. The latest online technology, known as Voice over Internet Protocol (VoIP), is the next innovation set to overhaul the telecoms industry.

VoIP allows people to make calls over the internet for a fraction of the cost of fixed-line connections, and this threatens the fixed-line revenues of traditional carriers such as British Telecom. However, mobile operators will also face a challenge from VoIP providers and could lose their place at the front of technological innovation as cheap internet phone calls attract more business.

In anticipating future consumer demand, internet giant Google is the latest to jump on the VoIP bandwagon with the launch of Google Talk, a free down-load giving an internet-based instant message and voice service. All you need is the software, a

*continued* ➢

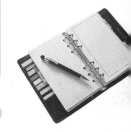

BUSINESS DECISION AREAS

**BUSINESS DECISION AREAS**

broadband connection and a headset. The VoIP market has been led by Skype, one of the first companies to offer internet phone calls. VoIP telephony revenues look set to nearly double to almost $8bn ($4.4bn).

It is expected that the growing popularity of downloading video from the internet will reduce the time people spend watching free-to-air TV, driving down audience share and advertising revenue for broadcasters.

*Source*: BBC News, July 2005

# **Topic** The marketing concept

## *Marketing as a strategic activity*

Strategic decisions usually involve marketing, so it can be described as a strategic activity of the organisation. For example, to increase market share you have to persuade customers to buy more of your product and to buy less of your competitors' product. Marketing is the tool that will be used to achieve this.

Using marketing, organisations hope to achieve a number of objectives which are essential for success:

- **To increase sales revenue and profitability** – sales revenue is the money that the business receives from the sales that it makes. Using marketing to increase sales can increase the profitability of the business.

- **To increase or maintain market share** – successful marketing will not only increase or maintain your market share but may also increase the size of the market, attracting new customers, rather than just taking existing buyers from your competitors. So market share and growth must both be considered.

- **To maintain or improve the image of the business, its brand or its product** – marketing can be used to convince consumers of the quality of a product.

- **To target a new market or a new segment of the market** – marketing can be used to enter new markets with their products, or to enter new segments of the market.

- **To develop new and improved products** – this is vital for the success of many businesses. Pencil-makers may not need to spend a huge amount of time and effort in product development, however businesses like Sony put a great deal of emphasis on developing new ideas and products.

# **Topic** The marketing of products and services

## *Types of markets*

There are two main types of market:

- **consumer** markets, which we all operate in and are familiar with

- **industrial** markets, where organisations purchase goods and services in order to produce other goods and services.

Consumer markets are made up of individuals who buy goods or services for their own personal or domestic use. The products that they buy can be classified into three major types.

1  **Convenience goods** – non-durable goods are products that we normally use only once, and then have to replace on a regular basis, such as newspapers and magazines, foodstuffs and toiletries.

2  **Shopping goods** – durable goods are longer-lasting and need to be replaced only after a number of years. Cars, washing machines and televisions are examples of durable goods.

3  **Speciality goods** – things like cosmetics, fashion items and speciality cars.

The goods and services bought on the industrial market can be similar to those in the consumer markets. For example, consumers use banking services and so do businesses; however, industrial goods also include plant and machinery, raw materials, consumable supplies and business services.

## *Product orientation*

A product-orientated business is one that concentrates on the production process and the product itself, rather than trying to establish what it is that the consumer wants. For example, it may focus on trying to improve the efficiency of its production or to produce goods which are far more advanced in terms of their technology.

A basic idea or novelty value of the product can sell it. When home computer systems were first produced in the UK, it was the technical wonder of the product that sold them. There were few companies to compete against each other, and there was a growing domestic market. There were also few overseas competitors. The product sold itself.

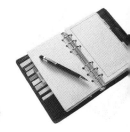

**BUSINESS DECISION AREAS**

Some industries are still product-orientated. A firm operating at the edge of innovation, such as bio-technology, pharmaceuticals or electronics, must innovate to survive. Although businesses may have a final product in mind in anticipation of consumer demand, the research is often 'pure' research – the researcher does not have a specific end product in mind. The research is being done to find out what is possible. Many of the most modern products on the market today are the result of research carried out for the US space programme.

Concorde is a good example of a product-orientated product. The development of the aircraft was carried out between the UK and France to see if it was technically possible and for political co-operation between the two countries. Although Concorde achieved its aim of being the first and only successful large civilian passenger plane capable of supersonic flight, it did not sell. Only British Airways and Air France, both of which were government-owned at the time, bought them, so it never recovered the development costs. The same could be said for the Channel Tunnel which is unlikely ever to pay off its development and construction costs.

## Market orientation

A market-orientated business continually identifies, reviews and analyses consumers' needs. Consumers are central to the firm's decision-making. They are also sometimes known as customer-orientated businesses. Products are developed in response to changing consumer needs.

### Info Point

Recent research by the Consumer Electronics Association, organiser of CES, has suggested that women make up 57 per cent of the consumer electronics market.

Women want good performance, no fuss and stylish design in their products, research suggests, and also like to be able to personalise and customise their gadgets to fit in with their lives.

'Women are an important customer of computers and electronics today, yet very few companies directly address their needs head-on,' said Rex Wong, MSI chief.

MSI's Mega View is a lightweight Linux-based device which plays and records in MPEG4 from any video source.

It also plays MP3/Windows Media music files and stores photos, plays DivX video, and claims to be the first portable media centre that is certified for the video format.

It comes with 20GB on-board, and has an SD card slot. The display is a good-sized 3.5-inch (8.9 cm) TFT LCD.

The face plates can be removed and swapped from grey to pink, red, and other colours.

January 2005

## PRODUCTS

There are two main types of product that an organisation can produce – goods and services.

## Goods

These are products that we can see and touch. They may be durable (such as mobile phones, televisions and motor cars), i.e. things that we can use again and again, or they may be non-durable (such as burgers, stamps or a newspaper).

## Services

These are things that are done for us. We cannot see them but we should feel some benefit for having used them. Banking and finance, tourism, insurance and education are some of Scotland's biggest employers, and these are all services.

Some goods come with services. Using the examples from the goods above, mobile phones need the services of a network operator to be useful; Sky provides satellite and digital services so that we can be entertained; burgers are produced using the services of a fast food outlet, and Royal Mail will deliver your letters.

# The marketing environment

The marketing environment is made up of the following:

- the government
- competition
- technology
- the economy
- consumer trends and behaviour.

These factors must be taken into account and considered when making any marketing decisions.

### *Influence of the government on marketing*

Like most areas of business, marketing is subject to government legislation, and this has to be taken into consideration when making marketing decisions. You would be unhappy if you spent money on a product that did not work, or did not do what it was supposed to do, or was unsafe. You would also be unhappy if you felt you were 'conned' by the advertising that made you buy the product in the first place.

### The Trade Descriptions Act

The goods or services which consumers buy must do what the advertising claims they can do. For example, cosmetics and medicines must be clinically proven to achieve what is claimed of them.

### The Monopolies and Mergers Act

A monopoly is in theory a market where only one firm exists to serve the whole market. This would give the firm tremendous market power to charge what it liked and provide minimal services.

For example, until the market was opened to competition, BT was the only national telephone company in the UK. It had complete monopoly power. The government put legislation in place

to make sure that BT was controlled in terms of pricing and services, until national competitors arrived.

Although there are no real monopolies left, some businesses are so big that they dominate the market and so have some monopoly powers in terms of pricing, and in terms of what is sold on the market. The Act works to limit the power of these businesses for the benefit of consumers.

## Fair Trading and Competition Acts

These Acts try to ensure that no businesses work to prevent competition in the market. Competition is thought of as being healthy for the market and for consumers, driving down prices and giving consumers a wider choice.

### Info Point

The Office of Fair Trading has ruled that there is no need for UK supermarkets to change how they deal with suppliers.

Farmers' groups, organic organisations and aid agencies had asked the Office of Fair Trading (OFT) to investigate the existing voluntary code accusing supermarkets of being slow to pay suppliers, and having a stranglehold on the supply chain.

As well as expressing shock at the decision, Breaking The Armlock – a consortium of farmers' groups and organic producers – renewed calls for OFT action.

'What we need is an independent watchdog and a moratorium on further takeovers by the big four supermarkets,' it said. 'What we have got is a supermarket-friendly report which leaves farmers and independent shops hanging out to dry.'

However, the OFT rejected calls for an independent ombudsman to deal with suppliers' complaints, adding that the current way of doing business was 'not designed to shield suppliers from hard bargaining driven by supermarket competition'.

'Consumers are benefiting from competition in grocery retailing, and evidence has not come forward that the code is being breached,' said the OFT.

It had asked auditors to examine whether the big four of Tesco, Asda, Sainsbury's and Safeway (now taken over by Morrisons) were violating the code, which was set up in 2002 to clarify the way they dealt with suppliers. No disputes between suppliers and supermarkets have gone to mediation since the code was established three years ago, with critics saying this is because suppliers risk having their contracts cancelled if they complain.

But the British Retail Consortium, which represents supermarkets, said 'supermarkets (are) observing the code, but suppliers are not making use of it'.

However charity Action Aid said the OFT ruling 'made a mockery' of its claim that it ensures fair dealing between the UK's biggest food retailers and their suppliers.

'There is nothing fair about the decision to ignore the concerns of farmers, consumer groups, environmental organisations and development agencies,' it said.

Action Aid has tried to highlight what it says are the poor conditions of casual farm workers at some supermarket suppliers overseas.

*Source*: BBC News, August 2005

## Consumer Protection Laws

Consumer protection Acts work to ensure that the products that we buy are safe. They set minimum standards of safety for things like cars and electrical goods. They also ensure that a business is liable for any damage which its defective goods may cause to a consumer.

## Code of Advertising Practice

Any business undertaking advertising must conform to the British Code of Advertising Practice. This states that adverts must be legal, honest and truthful and not cause offence. The Independent Television Commission (ITC) controls advertising on television and radio.

## The Advertising Standards Authority

This is a voluntary body set up by advertisers and marketing companies to monitor advertising in the UK.

### Info Point

There are hundreds of products claiming to be the answer to tackling cellulite. Do they work?

Creams, jeans and even tights. Like the secret to eternal life, they claim to solve a problem which is the bane of women and agony aunts throughout the country. This war on fatty deposits fills many magazine column inches and has earned a fortune for the UK's £6 billion cosmetic industry through its self-proclaimed remedies.

The advert for a cream by Estee Lauder, which costs £28 for a 200ml tube, was criticised as misleading by the Advertising Standards Authority. The ASA said the advert implied that Estee Lauder's Body Performance Anti Cellulite Visible Contouring Serum worked directly on the cellulite.

But Estee Lauder said its consumers realised this was a cosmetic treatment which alleviated the appearance of the cellulite by toning and moisturising. And it said 83 per cent of women tested said it worked.

But no quick fix will be found in a bottle, says Dr Susan Mayou, a consultant dermatologist. 'I don't see how a cream can remove the dimples, unless it's Polyfilla.

'Cellulite is beyond people's control. It's a genetic predisposition and I'm sure it doesn't help if you're overweight but I don't think there's any way of improvement, other than rupturing the fibrous bands or removing the fat'.

July 2005

## Competition

All markets are subject to some competition, either directly or indirectly, from what the industry calls **close substitutes**. Consumers can substitute one good or service for another.

For example, there are a number of different ways of travelling from Edinburgh to London. You can travel by train, plane or bus. British Airways and Easyjet are in direct competition for those wishing to fly. However, these consumers can also be lured away by rail operators offering fast, cheap comfortable travel direct to the centre of London, or by bus operators like 'Megabus' with very low travel costs for those not so concerned with the speed of travel.

Some markets have only a few big producers, such as the soft drinks market where the biggest producers are Coca Cola, Pepsi, Cadbury, Schweppes and Barr's. There are many local producers of soft drinks, but they generally have a very limited and local market share. Other markets have many producers, such as the market for electrical goods, where there is a huge choice of different manufacturers.

The number of manufacturers does not always decide how competitive the market is. For example, the market for televisions was very uncompetitive during the 1980s and 1990s, as the manufacturers managed to keep prices high through anti-competitive practices such as only supplying shops which would guarantee not to reduce prices.

In order to sell in competitive markets, the manufacturer's product must have something that makes the customer decide to buy their product rather than that of one of their competitors.

This is called a **unique selling proposition** (**USP**). To do this, the manufacturer must be continually offering new and improved products at prices which the consumer is willing to pay.

Some modern marketing experts believe that a USP is difficult to obtain and maintain with so much competition in the market. No sooner is it achieved than it is lost. They believe that much more important is the **emotional selling proposition** (ESP) – 'Do I like you?' Here, it is believed that consumers will respond emotionally to product and brands, sticking with what they like and trust, and making it difficult to get them to switch brands.

## Info Point

Competition amongst the supermarkets drives most of their marketing. Price competition is always fierce and not very profitable. Sainsbury's and Waitrose have always tried to gain competitive advantage through high quality. Tesco competes through opening hours, banking and insurance services, and non-food sales. The Co-operative competes by having an ethical policy which sees them sell the widest range of 'fair trade' goods. Asda competes through selling low priced goods.

However, any competitive advantage is easily lost by other supermarkets copying good ideas.

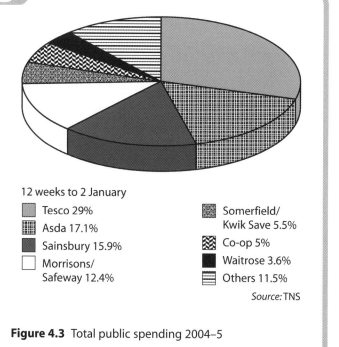

12 weeks to 2 January

- Tesco 29%
- Asda 17.1%
- Sainsbury 15.9%
- Morrisons/ Safeway 12.4%
- Somerfield/ Kwik Save 5.5%
- Co-op 5%
- Waitrose 3.6%
- Others 11.5%

*Source:* TNS

**Figure 4.3** Total public spending 2004–5

## Technology

The continuing development of technology means that in order to keep up with the competition or to gain some competitive advantage, organisations have to use the very latest technology available.

In the home computer market, advances are being made at such a fast rate that new models can be issued within a few months of the previous model being launched on the market. It is now likely that new computers will be sold with a specification far in excess of what will be needed for home use for the foreseeable future. However, manufacturers see this as the only way to keep ahead of the competition.

The introduction of more and more sophisticated production methods allows for higher quality, faster and cheaper production. New technology has allowed far better communications and made more information available to consumers.

The internet and the saturation usage of mobile phones allow businesses new ways to tap into new markets for their products.

## Economic forces

The economy has a major influence on consumer behaviour and on organisational behaviour. During times of economic growth and high confidence, consumers are willing to spend more money and feel more confident about their job security; organisations spend more on developing and marketing new products. During recession, consumers spend less and organisations tend to concentrate on reducing production costs and prices.

When interest rates are high, borrowing becomes more expensive so consumers are less likely to buy the high-value, high-cost products. At the same time, organisations will attempt to reduce their own borrowing and make offers like interest-free credit in order to attract sales.

Exchange rates will affect imports and exports, as when the value of the pound is high, foreign goods and services will become cheaper for consumers. Scottish manufacturers will find their products more difficult to export because the products will now be more expensive for consumers abroad. When the pound's value is low, UK goods become more attractive in terms of price.

## Consumers

### Demographics

Demographics is the study of the structure of the population, in terms of age, gender, household income, buying patterns and lifestyle. It is very important for marketing because it gives the manufacturers a great deal of information about their customers and potential customers.

A vast range of information on demographics is available. Market research companies and the government constantly update their statistics. Some of this is free, but the most up-to-date and detailed information usually has to be paid for.

BUSINESS DECISION AREAS

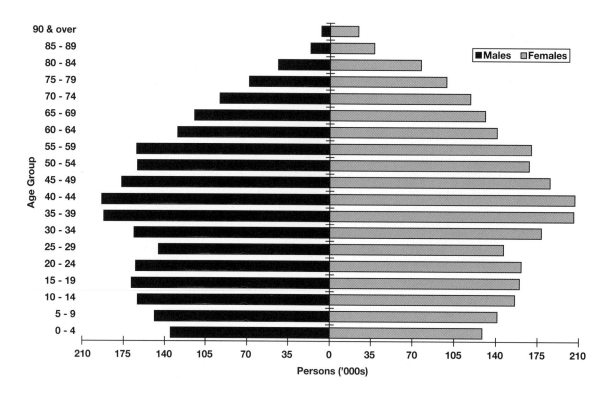

*Source*: www.gro-scotland.gov.uk

**Figure 4.4** Estimated population by age and sex, 30 June 2004

## Household income

The make-up of households has changed dramatically in recent years. Far more people are living on their own, leading to a growth in the market for convenience goods for single-person households. There are many more one-parent families, and combined families where couples who are divorced set up home with the children from previous marriages. Each of these factors leads to different or new demands for goods and services.

At the same time, the disposable income (income left after tax) of families has greatly increased. This has led to a big increase in demand for clothes, holidays, DIY, cars, leisure and furnishings.

There are now more women than men workng in the economy. They obviously have less time to spend on household chores and so this has led to growth in demand for convenience foods, childcare services, labour-saving devices and more flexible shopping hours, such as supermarkets opening 24 hours a day.

It is becoming more common for men to stay at home and become 'house-husbands'. Television companies take this into account when drawing up the schedules for daytime television.

## Location

Consumers living in different parts of the country have different needs and spending patterns. For example, those living in the rural areas of Scotland have to spend much more on travel, and more of their disposable income on food, as supermarkets in rural areas tend to be more expensive. Different parts of Scotland have different weather patterns which will lead to different house types, clothing, diet, etc.

## Social class

Although marketing professionals categorise consumers by their disposable income, they also split the population into six general classifications, as this tends to reflect their spending more accurately. The reason for this is that people tend to have similar interests and tastes within these broad classifications.

One set of classifications used is:

| Classification | General description and examples |
|---|---|
| A | Upper or upper middle class – senior managerial/professional: company director, surgeon, professor |
| B | Middle – intermediate managerial/professional: bank manager, head teacher, accountant, lawyer |
| C1 | Lower middle – supervisory: shop manager, bank clerk, sales representative, nurse |
| C2 | Skilled working – electrician, heating engineer, mechanic |
| D | Working – semi-skilled: machine operator, slater, driver, call-centre worker |
| E | Lowest subsistence level – unskilled, low paid: cleaner, porter |

So although an electrician can earn much more than a bank clerk in some cases, their spending patterns will be more likely to match those within their social classification than those on the same income level.

## Lifestyle, taste and fashion

Consumers' lifestyles affect what products they buy. For example, those who are interested in a healthy lifestyle will be much more conscious of what they eat and drink, and of exercise. They are far more likely to buy organic produce, and eat less fast food, sweets, and high sugar-content drinks. They will be far more likely to buy bikes, sports equipment and clothes.

Those who are concerned with environmental issues will opt for products that suit their beliefs. They will only buy dolphin-friendly tuna; they are far more likely to use bikes and public transport, and use only ozone-friendly aerosols. They will try to use energy-saving products like solar energy or wind turbines.

Those who are concerned with their own self-image will be very interested in fashions. They will look for the most up-to-date clothing, house decoration, mobile phones, etc.

## Personality

Consumers' personalities will dictate what products they will be interested in buying. Extroverts are more concerned about being noticed and will opt for products that make them stand out from the crowd, such as unusual clothing. Introverted consumers are much more concerned with fitting in and will tend to buy well-known brands in an attempt to be more socially acceptable. All consumers have one of these traits to a greater or lesser extent, and so marketing based on personality types can be successful.

## Political

Many consumers have strong political views and this will influence their purchases. Newspapers support different political parties, so consumers will buy a newspaper that most agrees with their own politics.

# Topic The marketing mix

In order to market or sell its product successfully, a business must develop a strategy based on four key elements – **product**, **price**, **place** and **promotion**. Together, these elements are called the four Ps. How these elements are combined in the marketing strategy is called the **marketing mix**.

## *Place*

This refers to how the product is taken from the production line and made available to consumers. There are two parts – firstly the channel of distribution, and secondly the type of retailer or outlet that will sell your product to the consumer.

## The channel of distribution

This is how the product gets to the market. There are a variety of methods that are available to manufacturers. These can involve wholesalers, retailers, agents and importers/exporters; which methods are used depends on the product itself.

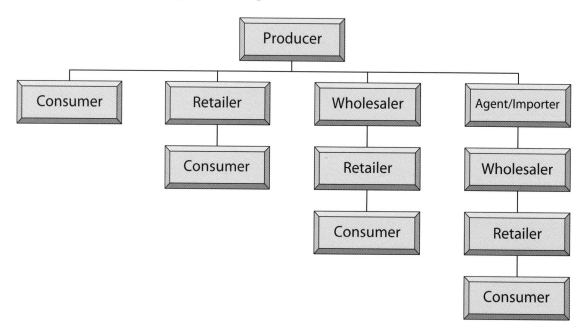

### Direct selling

The manufacturer can sell directly to the public. This is common when the manufacturer is a small local business like a baker, who will have their own shop(s) to sell to the public. It is also widely used where products have to be made individually to a customer's specific requirements, as in double glazing; and where the product is highly technical, such as machines which are made for another manufacturer. Direct selling is common in the industrial markets.

However, the growth of the internet has made it much easier for all businesses to sell direct to the public. For example, Dell sell their computers etc directly to their customers through the internet. They use advertising on television and in the press to direct consumers to their website.

Websites can give potential customers information about the organisation and its products, and are able to attract a much wider audience. Discounts are often available online, and the consumer has the convenience of shopping from home. However, it depends on the consumer being able to find the website; organisations can pay to make sure that they have links to other websites and will appear near the top of any searches.

The organisation may have much higher advertising and administration costs, and the cost of postage and packaging may make it more expensive for the customer too. On the other hand, the business does not have the expense of setting up a chain of outlets, and the consumer may receive credit facilities.

### Retailer

The retailer is the local outlet for the business's products, where the consumer can physically buy the goods or services. They offer a variety of goods and services from a variety of producers. They store the goods on their premises, prepare them for sale and display them for sale.

They provide information for consumers through advertising, displays and trained staff. They also offer related services such as credit facilities, hire purchase, after-sales service, guarantees and delivery for large items.

### Types of retailers

There are a number of different types of retailer, and which one or ones are used depends on the product being sold. The most common type is the independent retailer, usually with just one shop such as your local corner shop. However, they do sometimes join forces in order to buy in bulk and offer some competition to the larger chains, e.g. Mace.

Multiple chain stores have a number of outlets spread across the country. They are usually well known, such as Next or Marks and Spencer. Supermarkets offer a wide range of groceries, clothing and household and electrical goods. Department stores, such as House of Fraser, offer a range of goods in the different departments within the store. They tend to specialise in higher-priced premium brands. Franchises, which were examined in Chapter 1, offer new businesses the opportunity to trade using an established name, such as McDonald's.

### Wholesaler

The wholesaler provides a link between the producer and the retailer, and in doing so can provide a good source of market research, marketing information and services for the retailer in order to improve sales.

The wholesaler buys in bulk from the retailer and breaks the product down into smaller quantities for the retailer, or even direct to the consumer.

For example, it is far cheaper for Cadbury to deliver large quantities of its products to the wholesaler, who will then break up the pallets into smaller boxes for the corner shop to buy. This leaves Cadbury free to concentrate on production rather than distribution to thousands of small outlets across the whole of the Scotland. Also, it can arrange for delivery of finished products straight to the wholesaler and avoid the high cost of storage, and the cost of stock going out of date.

Some wholesalers finish off the product in terms of packaging and pricing, again reducing the cost to the producer. It should be remembered, however, that the wholesaler has to make a profit on their activities, which adds a further cost to the consumer.

The wholesaler has to play their part in the marketing strategy. If they do not promote the product in the way the business wants, they could destroy the business's marketing mix.

### Agent

Agents attract the customer by carrying out promotional activities, and then selling the product to the consumer. For doing this they take a commission (a percentage of the sales price). Examples are estate agents, travel agents, insurance brokers, etc.

Many smaller car manufacturers use agents to sell their cars in foreign countries. This is because the agent will have a good knowledge of the local market, including any local customs or legal requirements that have to be met.

### Importer/exporter

Importers and exporters play an important role in identifying new or potential markets for products around the world. Their role is similar to that of the agent, in that they will have a good knowledge of local markets around the world, and can generate sales through their own promotional activities. In many cases they act as retailer as well.

## Choice of distribution channel

How the product reaches the consumer will be decided by a number of factors:

- the product
- the market
- legal requirements
- buying habits
- the business.

### The product

This is probably the most important factor to consider. If the product is perishable with a limited shelf-life, then a direct channel is best. For example, McDonald's cannot cook and then distribute its products through other outlets; it has to sell them direct from the restaurant.

However, many perishable products like fish, fruit and vegetables are sometimes handled by specialist wholesalers, who buy from a large number of small producers in order to make up the bulk needed for many retailers.

Manufacturers often treat new products differently. They select which wholesalers or retailers to use in order to keep control over the marketing of the product. Highly technical products will usually go direct to the buyer, but convenience goods such as tinned food will be distributed in bulk, either directly to the major supermarkets' warehouses, or to the wholesaler who will break down the bulk for individual retail outlets.

High-quality premium brands will only be sold through very selective outlets in order to protect their brand image.

### The market

Where the market is large and spread throughout the country, the use of wholesalers and retailers is much more efficient. Mars, for example, would find it very expensive and time-consuming to deliver the small quantities of Mars Bars to every shop and outlet in the country.

Where the market is small and local, direct selling is more likely to be appropriate as the producer can sell directly to the consumer. The location of potential customers also influences the choice of channel. For example, products aimed at the tourist market will be sold at the major tourist destinations in Scotland.

### Legal requirements

Some goods and services can only be sold through licensed premises or authorised outlets. For example, chemists are the only shops that are allowed to dispense certain drugs, and the Post Office offers services that are not available at other outlets. And, of course, alcohol can only be sold through licensed premises.

### Buying habits

Consumers often decide how products will be distributed. Remember that one of the main functions of place is to get the products to the consumer and in a place where the consumer would expect to find them. The increase in car ownership has led to the growth in out-of-town shopping centres, so consumers expect to find supermarkets, carpet stores, furniture stores, DIY and gardening outlets in these places.

### The business

Some companies have their own distribution networks with their own warehouses and transport. This was common with the larger businesses, although many have now outsourced these functions.

Other types of outlets available are mail order, where rather than having the expense of a chain of shops, the business (such as Freeman's) issues catalogues to consumers who can choose products in the comfort of their own home and at their own pace. They are successful because of the credit facilities that they offer.

Other companies such as Avon offer a door-to-door selling service with a catalogue. With the growth in the popularity of cable and satellite television the use of television shopping channels has increased, which again allows consumers to buy from the comfort of their own home.

## Pricing strategies

Price is important for a number of reasons. First, consumers will only pay what they can afford, and what they think is a reasonable price for the product. Secondly, consumers use price as a measure of quality. A high price would infer high quality and vice versa, although this is not always the case.

When setting price there are a number of factors which a business should consider. The price of the product has to cover the costs of production and allow the business to make a reasonable profit in the long run. New products can often sell for a higher price due to their novelty value. For example, DVD players were originally very expensive. Today you can buy one for less than £25, which is about a twentieth of the price charged when they were introduced, in real terms.

The business must take into account the market price, or the price charged by competitors, and also how price can be used to increase sales.

Finally, some markets are regulated by the government in terms of price; e.g. the government wants unleaded petrol to be cheaper than leaded.

### Long-term pricing strategies

Businesses can adopt a number of different pricing strategies for different markets and different market conditions.

### Low price

A business may decide to charge a price lower than those of competitors where there is **price elasticity of demand**. This means that consumers respond positively to changes in price, and lower prices will result in much higher sales. It is most appropriate where there is little brand loyalty and competition in the market is high. Supermarkets attract high volume sales of DVDs, CDs and computer games by charging lower than market prices.

### Market price

Setting your price at the market rate means that your prices are broadly in line with those of competitors. This usually happens in markets where price competition does not benefit any of the businesses, such as in the petrol market where there are a few large companies, with very little difference between the competitors' products. Petrol price wars in the past have simply led to one firm cutting the price, just for another to match it, or even better it, the next day. This was good for the consumers but resulted in a loss of profits for the petrol companies and no real change in demand. These businesses tend to compete on things other than price, such as offering air miles.

## Info Point

**Nintendo DS in festive price cut**

The Nintendo DS is getting a price trim in the UK in the run-up to Christmas.

From 7 October, it will on sale for £89.99, a cut of £10. To coincide with the release of the hit Nintendogs, gamers will be able to grab two bundle deals for the original £99 price tag.

The lead up to the festive season is one of the most crucial periods for the games industry as they battle for space in the living room and pockets.

The DS now faces stiff competition from Sony's PlayStation.

*Source*: www.bbc.co.uk, August 2005

### High price

High price is adopted in the long term by businesses offering high-quality premium goods and services where image is important, such as in perfumes. You can often charge higher prices for well-known brands, or where marketing is particularly successful.

In some markets there is a lack of competition, which means a high price can be charged. Or the product may have an established USP or patent which allows for a high price.

In other markets when the supply of goods is restricted, it is also possible to charge a high price.

In the short term a high price can be charged for innovative products when they are first introduced to the market, such as the latest high definition televisions.

## Info Point

### Apple head attacks record firms

'Greedy' record companies are pushing for an increase in the price of music downloads, Apple's chief executive Steve Jobs has said. Mr Jobs vowed to resist such pressure, after revealing that music firms were pushing for higher prices on Apple's iTunes internet music store.

He said companies already made a bigger profit through iTunes than in CD sales. Mr Jobs said that by cutting out manufacturing jobs, selling through iTunes was already proving lucrative for record companies. 'So if they want to raise the prices it just means they're getting a little greedy,' he said. Big music companies are currently trying to alter the terms of their deals with Apple, with many contracts in the US due for renewal.

The iTunes site in the US charges 99 cents (55p) per song, with prices typically higher in Europe and Japan – it is 79p per song in the UK.

'Customers think the price is really good where it is,' said Mr Jobs. 'We're trying to compete with piracy, we're trying to pull people away from piracy and say "you can buy these songs legally for a fair price". But if the price goes up a lot, they'll go back to piracy. Then everybody loses.'

Apple has sold about 22 million iPod digital music players and more than 500 million songs though its iTunes music store.

*Source*: BBC News, September 2005

## Short-term pricing strategies

### Skimming

This involves using a high price initially, usually for a new product where there is little competition. Consumers are willing to pay a high price for the novelty value of the product, but as more competition enters the market, the price will be lowered.

### Penetration pricing

This is usually used in order to introduce a product to an established market, and allows the business to achieve sales and gain market share very quickly. It involves setting a low price, sometimes at a loss, to attract customers to the product in an established market with strong competition. As the product becomes established in the market, the business can increase price.

### Destroyer pricing

Again, this involves setting a price below those of competitors, but this time at an artificially low price in order to destroy competition. The business will probably be running at a loss in terms of its sales, but as soon as the competition is eliminated, the price will return to market price or above. It is often used by established companies to prevent new companies entering the market, although it may be considered anti-competitive by the government and could result in legal action.

### Promotional pricing

This is used to boost sales in the short term by lowering the price of the product. It can also be employed to create interest in a new product. Supermarkets use promotional pricing for some of their sales lines, as loss leaders. They will advertise the low price for these products, attracting customers into the store in the hope that they will buy a whole range of other goods at the same time.

### Demand-orientated pricing

Here, price varies along with the demand for the product. It is usual in crop markets such as the market for coffee. When the harvest has been poor, successful producers can charge a higher price due to the number of manufacturers chasing a limited supply.

---

## Info Point

### Why do petrol prices vary around the UK?

In the wake of Hurricane Katrina, petrol prices have passed the £1 a litre barrier in parts of Britain. But why do prices vary so much around the country? In Northern Ireland petrol stations were charging as much as £1.04 for a litre of unleaded petrol and prices reached £1.03 in parts of Wiltshire and £1.02 in East Sussex.

But the average cost is 94.6p, with the lowest recorded price being 90p, according to industry analysts. So why do prices vary so much?

It all comes down to size, according to experts. The size of the company running the petrol station, the size of its customer base and the size of the competition. Prices are usually higher in rural areas where there is less competition and fewer customers. Petrol stations in those areas are also more likely to be run by smaller, independent retailers, who have to charge more to cover business costs.

The cheapest prices are found in major cities, where petrol stations have to compete for customers. They are also more likely to be run by big companies – like supermarkets – who can offer more competitive rates.

'Supermarkets use motor fuel to promote the rest of their business, so they hide the cost in other goods they sell,' says Ray Holloway, director of the Petrol Retailers Association (PRA). 'Local services are often seen as not being as cheap as supermarkets, but people don't do all the sums. In rural areas fewer people means there will be fewer sales, whereas in urban areas more people mean more sales. It is supply and demand.'

*Source*: BBC News, September 2005

---

## Product/service

The good or service which the business is trying to sell must be one that the customers want, and are willing and able to buy. The product tends to be the most important element of the marketing mix as it determines what the price will be, how it is promoted and where it is sold.

For example, a top fashion designer will not sell their garments for a low price; they will not advertise in a local newspaper, nor will they allow their products to be sold in Poundstretcher. The garments will have a very high price, promotion will be through the major fashion shows, and they will sell the clothes themselves, directly to clients.

Each product has to satisfy a basic need of the consumer if it is to be sold. For example, the basic function of clothing is to keep you warm. Any clothing that satisfies this need is called the **core product.** However, if all we wanted from clothing was something to keep us warm, we would simply buy the cheapest and most effective clothing that serves this basic need.

Very few consumers purchase clothes in this way. What we actually buy meets a whole range of needs – to make us feel good, to be comfortable, to look good, to fit in or to make a statement, and to suit the various social or work activities. This is what we call the **product concept**.

Most product markets tend to be very competitive, so businesses continually try to add new features to the product or its packaging in order to make their product more attractive to the customer. The product with the additional features is called the **augmented product**.

What decides whether or not the consumer thinks the product is desirable, is how well it meets their needs in terms of its basic function, plus the features which make it attractive, which may include reliability, value for money, design, image, status and quality. The value of the product will reflect the quality the consumer expects from it. A Rolex watch has a very different level of quality from a Swatch watch, but both may be successful in meeting their own customers' requirements.

Other features which can influence the consumer to buy your product include credit/finance facilities, after-sales service, manuals and guarantees.

## The product mix

Most businesses produce a range of products which have similar uses and have similar characteristics.

Cadbury produces a huge range of chocolate-based products, most of which are very well known – from the basic product of Dairy Milk Chocolate to all the other sweets that have been developed for different tastes and occasions, e.g. Cadbury's Creme Egg.

The benefits involved in having a product line are:

- It spreads the risks. If the market for one product fails, then the organisation has many other products to fall back on.

- It gives the consumers the impression that the organisation is a specialist producer in that particular line of products.

- It allows new products to be launched, with existing customers at least willing to try them.

There are a number of possible disadvantages to having a product line:

- Bad publicity for one product could affect the sales of other products.

- Operations within the business can become very complicated, with lots of different machinery and processes needed for each of the different products.

Most businesses will see their product lines grow over time. For example, Mackie's ice cream now comes with a wide variety of flavours, and more recently it has added organic ice cream

and responded to trends for health with low fat Dairy Sorbets and Iced Fruit Smoothies. Firms tend to add new lines in order to make more profits, show innovation to retailers and add interesting new tastes for consumers or if their product line is too long, profitability may be increased by dropping products.

To keep their product line fresh, it is important that organisations invest in research and development. New products allow them to gain a competitive edge over their rivals, and improve the quality and safety of their products. If the product is the first on the market it will give the business a monopoly position for some time, allowing them to charge higher prices.

Having a product line is also very important to meet the changing needs of customers; if done properly, it will ensure that the new products do not fail.

## The product range

The product range is the combination of the different types of product that a business manufactures and sells.

As with the product mix, having a wide range of products spreads the risk for the business, but here the company is operating a number of different industries, so is not relying on one industry.

## The product life cycle

It is said that a product has a natural lifespan, through which it passes until it is withdrawn from the market. For some goods or services it is easy to see, e.g. the PS One has now been withdrawn from the market and the PS2 will soon be replaced with the latest model. For others, it does not seem to be true. Barr's 'Irn Bru' is still very popular after more than 50 years on the market.

It may be that some products have a much longer lifespan than others, or that the manufacturer has been very successful in using extension strategies to prolong the life of the product. However, all products do go through a number of distinct phases:

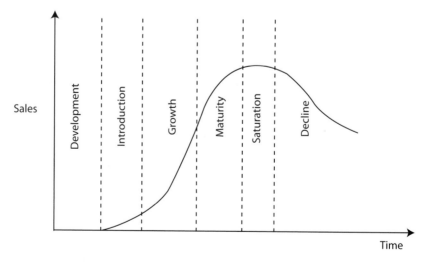

The **development** stage is when the product will start its life. A large number of products will never progress past this stage, perhaps as much as 80 per cent. There are a number of reasons for this. It may be impossible to make the product at a cost which will allow sufficient profit from the price which consumers would be willing to pay, or management may decide that the risk in entering the market is too great.

Development is essential for most businesses in order to bring out new or improved products; however, the costs involved can be very high. The first Ford Mondeo model took six years and $6 billion for research and development, market research, and start-up costs such as setting up plants with new machinery.

If the business decides to go ahead at this stage then, as there have been no sales, the product will initially make a loss for the organisation.

Before launching the product on to the whole market, the business may decide to **test-market** the product. This is part of the organisation's market research. The product is launched to a small segment of the market to see how it reacts. The organisation will quite often use one television area, such as Grampian Television, as the launch can be backed up with appropriate advertising on television and the local press.

Modifications can be made to the product as a result of consumers' reaction to it, prior to the launch on the whole market. Choosing the correct market for testing is very important; e.g. Yorkshire Television area has very similar characteristics in the proportion of age, gender, class, etc to the whole of the UK, so it is often used for test marketing.

At the beginning of the **introduction** stage, the product is launched onto the market. Heavy advertising spending is necessary at this stage as consumers are generally unaware of the product and will be loyal to other products or brands. Sales are slow and the selling price at this stage does not cover the development and start-up costs, so losses are usually made on sales.

How long this stage last varies between products. A new chocolate bar will have a fairly short introduction stage, but a new technical product will take some time before consumers feel confident that the product works and is superior to the others on the market. Such was the case with the Dyson vacuum cleaner. Although it is now the market leader, consumers took some time to decide that such an expensive machine was worth the additional cost.

During the **growth** stage consumers become more aware of the product and sales start to grow rapidly. It is during this stage that the product begins to become profitable.

As the product reaches the **maturity** stage its sales reach their peak. This is the highest level of sales that the product will achieve without the business taking some action. Spending on advertising will be much less as the product is fully established on the market, and any advertising will be aimed at maintaining sales levels rather than making consumers aware of the product.

At this stage all the development costs should have been repaid, and the product will be at its most profitable. These profits can then be used in part to fund development of new products. The business will work to keep the product in this stage for as long as possible. This can be done by using **extension strategies** (see below).

Eventually, all products will reach the **decline** stage. Sales and profits will start to fall, and the business's new replacement products should be in the growth stage. Life cycles are becoming shorter, especially in industries that are based on new technology. For example, new computer models tend to last for no more than six to twelve months, by which time new specifications from competitors have led to a rapid reduction in sales.

### Info Point

**Sony pulls out of PDA marketplace**

Sony is to stop selling personal digital assistants (PDAs) outside Japan, exiting a declining market that has been overtaken by mobile phones.

Just a few years ago a PDA was a must-have for professionals who wanted an electronic diary or contacts book.

Yet despite increasing technologies, such as wireless internet connection, they have been overtaken by the unstoppable rise of mobile phones.

Today's mobiles offer more and more PDA facilities – and the ability to phone.

'We consider mobile (phone) devices a key aspect of our strategy to converge contents like music, movies and games with hardware,' said Sony.

*Source*: BBC news, June 2004

## Extension strategies

These are the methods employed by businesses to prolong the life of their products and stop them going into the decline stage. The most successful extension strategies will actually lead to periods of sales growth.

### Promoting more frequent use of the product

Perhaps the most obvious way of achieving this would be by reducing the price. For mobile phones, this could mean reducing the costs of making phone calls or receiving email and text messages. This would be risky, but the success of low-cost airlines such as Easyjet, Ryan Air, Buzz, etc has been based on the fact that they can offer much lower air fares. Air travel was suffering from slow growth for many years prior to the introduction of these services.

### Developing new markets for existing products

Mobile phones and computers were both originally manufactured for the business market. However, they both managed to achieve huge growth in sales by selling to the home market.

### Finding new uses for existing products

A classic example here is in the market for fire-lighters. As consumers switched to gas and electric heating, demand for the product fell. A new market was found in the growth of the use of barbecues. Manufacturers were able to switch their attention to this new market.

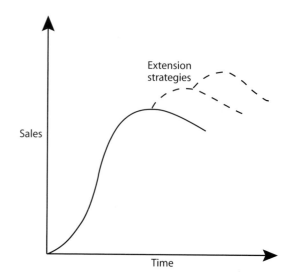

**Figure 4.9** Extension strategy diagram

**Develop a wider range of products**

Introducing new versions of the same product can develop new interest from consumers, and can also generate new interest in the original product.

The makers of the traditional 'Irn Bru' bottle have added a range of can and bottle sizes and fruit chews, and have even entered the alco-pop market with this product.

**Developing styling changes**

By simply introducing a slightly different product, manufacturers can stimulate new sales growth.

Football clubs in Scotland generate much-needed income by introducing new strips each season which they can then sell to their fans.

A successful advertising campaign can stimulate a short-term extension to the product's life. However, it will be much more effective to combine the advertising with one of the above.

## Product portfolio

It does not make sense for a business to wait until its product goes into decline before launching a replacement. Sales and profits would be lost, so businesses plan the introduction of new products to replace existing ones before they become unprofitable. The range of products that a business produces is known as its **product portfolio**.

Each of the products in the portfolio will be at a different stage in its life cycle. This allows the business to spread its investment across a range of products, thereby reducing the level of risk.

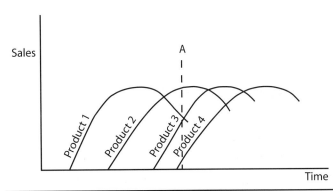

| At point A: | |
|---|---|
| Product 1 – decline phase | • Profit levels remain steady |
| Product 2 – maturity phase | • Risk spread across product range |
| Product 3 – growth phase | • Profitable product support |
| Product 4 – introduction phase | • Launch of new product |

**Figure 4.10** Product portfolio diagram

By having a portfolio of products at different stages in the life cycle, profit levels can be relatively stable. This makes the business easier to manage, and the most profitable products can support the development and launch of new products.

Sony has a huge product range including televisions, DVD players, cassette players, CD players, digi-tape, Mini-disc players, digital cameras, digital cam-corders, etc. Its televisions are constantly being replaced with new and improved models with extra features such as plasma screen and high definition.

The needs of different markets and market segments can be more easily met with a wide product portfolio. Having more products raises the profile of the organisation and allows it the opportunity of achieving greater profit levels.

## Branding

Branding can be a very successful marketing tool, and is widely used by businesses to create USPs and ESPs. The business chooses a word or symbol, or both, then registers them so that they can only be used on its products. It then designs a marketing strategy to distinguish its products from all other similar products by using this brand. Baxter's, Oxo, Cadbury and Heinz are all well-known brand names. Using branding, you can create a form of **product differentiation**.

BUSINESS DECISION AREAS

**Simon Edwards, marketing director at Cobra Beer**

'Here's the bad news. Most markets have been saturated for a very long time and every day, even more companies try to break into these markets.

The principles of branding have been put together to try to help establish a company in a crowded market and to help it compete and grow.

But you don't need huge marketing budgets to start building an enduring brand. In fact you don't need any marketing budget at all.

Building an enduring brand starts long before you spend money on advertising and promotion – it starts with your product and/or service – what can you offer customers that your competitors can't? What can you do operationally that will make your customers want to work with you?

Examine every point at which your company operates and try to find ways of doing it better. Look at all the competing products and make sure yours is outstanding. It is this collective aspect of your company that will establish its identity.

Giving your company a name is not branding. Giving your customers a reason to want to remember your name is.'

*Source*: BBC News, September 2005

### Benefits of branding

A well-known brand allows for instant recognition of the product by the customer. The colours used by Cadbury make their products easy to identify, even from a distance. This makes it easier for the buyer to choose that brand from among a range of very similar products.

Because the consumer knows, trusts and likes that brand, they have brand loyalty which will lead them to buy that product again and again – **repeat purchases**. This leads to a stable level of demand for the product, which is good for the manufacturer and the retailer. For the manufacturer, it allows for better production planning.

Because of the level of trust the consumer has, it is very difficult to persuade them to change brands, or experiment with new brands. We do not like to spend money on things we may not like. Consumers believe that the product will be better than its competitors, and so the manufacturer can charge premium (higher) prices. This also allows the brand-holder to launch new products using the brand name, or even to enter new markets in new countries.

Brands can also convey an image onto the consumer, and if successful can lead to a 'snob value' that makes the consumer who owns the branded product look 'cool'.

A good, well-established brand name actually has a money value which can be added to the balance sheet of the brand holder as an intangible asset.

### Drawbacks of branding

It takes a great deal of time to establish a brand. During this time, promotion costs will be high, and even after it is established it is necessary to keep promoting to maintain brand visibility.

While the business can quickly launch new products successfully under the brand name, a single bad event with bad publicity can affect the whole range of same-brand products.

You have to be able to protect your brand name worldwide, and this can often be difficult with huge markets producing 'fake' products. These imitators are very difficult to stop and legal actions against the imitators can be time-consuming and costly.

Major brand manufacturers who can charge premium prices for their products suffer most at the hands of the forgers. They find it almost impossible to prevent the production of fake items, particularly in the Far East. Trading Standards and organisations such as FACT (Federation Against Copyright Theft) spend a lot of time working to prevent the sale of counterfeit goods in Scotland.

Brands which develop through fashion can suffer badly when fashions change.

## Info Point

Profits at fashion retailer French Connection have fallen nearly 70 per cent after disappointing sales of its key summer clothing range.

The firm saw its profits drop to £5.1m in the six months to 31 July, compared with £16.2m a year ago. The company said challenging trading conditions had contributed to a 9 per cent fall in like-for-like sales over the period. The company's sales fell 8 per cent to £117.9m over the period. Future wholesale orders for its winter collection and next summer's range are currently 15 per cent lower than last year, it said.

French Connection – best known for its FCUK advertising slogan – is the latest in a string of retailers to warn of tough times following a sharp slowdown in consumer spending.

However, the retailer said it was encouraged by the positive response to its winter range from buyers.

*Source*: BBC News, September 2005

### Own brands

Most of the major supermarket chains, and many large retailer chains such as Boots, offer a wide range of products under their own brand names. Asda for example uses the Smart Price label to sell its own brand of groceries.

Any product that sells in high volume would be considered for own-brand labelling. These retailers have a good reputation for value and/or quality, and their own-brand goods, sitting next to premier brands such as Heinz (who may also make the supermarket's own brand), offer an additional choice to their customers.

Asda does not make any of its own-brand goods; it asks various manufacturers to do it. The advantages for the manufacturer are that they have a guaranteed sales contract with Asda,

and they are protected from direct damage should any of the brand products attract bad publicity, as it is Asda's name on the label.

Asda has the goods made to its own specification and at its own price. The own-brand products are often cheaper, and attract more customers and more sales within the store. However, they may be seen by consumers as being of lower quality than established brand names ('you get what you pay for'). Some of these own-brand products look very like the real thing. Own-brand colas tend to look very like Coca-Cola in their packaging.

## Promotion

Marketing is about communicating with consumers, and promotion is the method used to pass information to the consumer. It is an essential way of keeping existing customers and reaching new ones. There are a number of different methods of promotion:

- advertising
- sales promotions
- public relations
- exhibitions and trade fairs
- merchandising
- direct mail
- personal selling.

### Advertising

Advertising is the method that most of us would consider first when talking about promotion. However, it can be very expensive and is not always successful. There are four main types of advertising:

#### Informative advertising

This is used to pass information to the consumer about new or improved products, or to give information about a technical product. The government uses informative advertising in the press, on television and in its own publications.

For example, the Health Education Board for Scotland regularly runs adverts on television about the dangers involved in smoking, taking drugs and alcohol abuse.

#### Persuasive advertising

This is an attempt by the manufacturers to persuade us to buy their product. It is usually used in very competitive consumer markets, where consumers see little difference between one product and another. They use powerful images and language to imply good things about you if you buy this product. They are an attempt to build an emotional reaction in the consumer and use qualitative statements (opinions) rather than fact. An example is: 'Probably the best lager in the world'.

## Corporate advertising

This is more concerned with promoting the whole company rather than individual products. The advertisements will often put forward their image as being responsible and caring. For example, BP adverts do not tend to try to persuade you to buy their petrol, but to convey a 'green', socially responsible image.

There is often a growing pressure for the company name to become a brand in its own right, and businesses will use slogans or catchlines to help this become established: e.g. 'The world's favourite airline' (British Airways).

## Generic advertising

The red meat industry in Scotland has used generic advertising to promote and give reassurance about the quality and safety of the product following recent food scares. Generic advertising is where a number of advertisers or the whole industry come together to promote the industry rather than individual products.

## Choice of advertising media

How and where an organisation carries out its advertising depends very much on how it can best reach its existing and potential customers. Targeted advertising can be much more successful and effective. For example, if you are targeting a younger audience, then using magazines aimed at the youth market, or advertising during television programmes popular with young people such as *Hollyoaks*, will be more effective. However, if you are targeting older people, then advertising in the Sunday newspapers and during daytime television will be best.

Products that are aimed at the whole market are usually advertised best during very popular television programmes such as *Coronation Street*.

There are three main types of advertising media:

1  print media, such as newspapers and magazines

2  broadcast media, such as television, radio and the internet

3  outdoor media, such as billboards, around football grounds and on buses.

Which is used will depend on the following factors:

### Cost

Television advertising can be the most expensive, particularly during the most popular programmes. However, it does reach a huge audience either nationally or in the local television area such as STV or Grampian. It is best used for mass marketing.

### Target audience

National newspapers can also be expensive. However, they can be read again and again, although the adverts here are less entertaining than television adverts. The newspapers tend to be designed for different socio-economic groups, so the advertising is more targeted. If the market is local, a local newspaper would be most appropriate.

### Competitors' advertising

In order to compete effectively it may be necessary to match your competitors' choice of media. Most banks and building societies use newspaper adverts extensively as they allow the reader to spend time going through the sometimes complicated offers. In order for the consumer to make comparisons, the competing products will appear in the same types of media.

### Impact required

If you are launching a new product, it is likely that you would use a wide variety of different media to get as much attention and interest in the product as you can, as quickly as possible.

### The law

There are legal restrictions on what advertising can take place where, and also advertising guidelines which have to be followed. There are restrictions on tobacco and alcohol advertising, and also restrictions on adverts which may be unsuitable for young children.

## Sales promotions

As part of the overall marketing strategy, sales promotions are short-term inducements used to encourage customers to react quickly and make a purchase. Sales promotions can be given to the wholesaler/retailer or to the consumer.

### Promotions into the pipeline

These are designed to encourage the wholesaler or retailer to take more stock than they would otherwise and they include the following:

- Dealer loaders where for example the retailer is given six boxes for the price of five.
- Point-of-sale displays, posters or video cassettes. Video hire shops are given display material to encourage hires of new videos. Some stores run videos of new products for customers to watch.
- Dealer competitions where customers can win prizes that would appeal to them.
- Staff training for the shops' staff in order for them to deal more effectively with customer enquiries.
- Sale or return (offered by most newspapers), where if businesses do not sell all their newspapers, they can simply return them without charge.
- Extended credit – where the shop does not have to pay for the products for some months, allowing it to take stock and receive payment for sales before it actually has to pay for them.

### Promotions out of the pipeline

These are promotions which give a direct benefit to the consumer in order to encourage them to make the purchase. They include:

- Free samples or trial packs which are given away in-store or with other products. Magazines are a common way of distributing free samples.

- Bonus packs where for example 50 per cent is given free. These are common with many convenience goods such as coffee or washing powder.

- Price reductions, which are short-term pricing strategies to encourage sales. For example, a pack may carry '50p off' on its packaging.

- Premium offers where one product is given free when you buy another.

- In-store demonstrations or tastings. Tastings are common in supermarkets where customers are allowed to taste and try new products.

- Merchandising.

The benefits that are gained from sales promotions tend to be short term, and must be combined with the other elements of the marketing mix if they are to be successful in the longer term.

## Public relations

Public relations is the way in which the organisation communicates at a corporate level with the rest of the community. This would include the public, the press, the government and shareholders. These are planned communications by the company in order to enhance the image of the organisation.

The role of the public relations department is an important one and may involve issuing press statements, making charitable donations, sponsoring events and arranging for product endorsement by well-known personalities. In some organisations, the customer care or services department will be involved in public relations.

## Publicity

Publicity arises either within the organisation by the company itself through press releases or public announcements, or outside the organisation through news reports or through consumer programmes or publications. It is not usually paid for by the organisation, but can become advertising for the business if it is good publicity.

## Packaging

Sometimes referred to as the fifth P, packaging is a very important element of the marketing strategy. Good packaging can increase sales of the product, whereas poor packaging can result in a loss of sales.

There are a number of factors to consider:

### Shape and weight

These can affect how easy the product is to distribute and handle, which can lead to higher costs.

### Protection

The packaging must be robust enough to ensure that the product and its packaging are not damaged in transit or storage. The packaging must also protect the product from possible damage from light, heat and dust.

### Convenience

It is important that the packaging is easy for the consumer to handle; awkward shapes and sizes will put the customer off buying.

### Design

The design should be eye-catching to allow it to be distinguished easily from competitors' brands. Colour may be important as for example some foodstuffs and colours do not mix. As with Cadbury, the colour of the packaging may be used to promote the brand image.

### Information

Food products are subject to legal requirements about their ingredients appearing on the packaging, and some technical products, such as light shades, must show the maximum wattage of bulbs that can be used.

### Environmental factors

There has been a great deal of public concern regarding recyclable materials being used on packaging, coupled with a pressure to reduce the amount of unnecessary packaging.

## Merchandising

Merchandising is an attempt to encourage the customer to buy at the point of sale in shops, petrol stations, etc. Display material such as window displays, in-store posters, etc. will attract attention from customers.

The actual layout of products can encourage customers to follow particular routes around stores, with popular items at the back or sides of the store in order that customers have to pass other products. Stores keep related items together, such as all washing detergents in the same lane. The position of a product on the shelves is also important, with those at eye level being in the best position to achieve sales.

The shelves should always be well stocked, otherwise sales will be lost. The creation of the right atmosphere within the store will affect customers' buying, e.g. using bright lighting close to fresh food items to give an image of cleanliness, and bread or coffee smells to make the customer hungrier and more likely to buy food.

# Topic Target markets

Marketing is a major cost for many businesses, so it must be effective in communicating with the consumers who may buy their product.

## *Market segmentation*

### Differentiated marketing

This is when businesses offer different products to different groups within the total market. This is done by altering products to suit the needs of different consumers.

Businesses are able to use differentiated marketing by using market segmentation. This is when the whole market is split into different groups who have similar wants and needs, and so a business can produce goods and services specifically for that group. In doing so it can more closely meet the needs of those customers, and so is more likely to make a sale.

### Methods of segmenting markets

The marketing can be targeted at those who are most likely to want to pay for the product, and so costs can be reduced. Businesses can dominate specialist parts of the market for their product, which should lead to higher sales, and so increase the businesses' profitability.

How a business can identify these segments of the market depends very much on the product it has for sale. It may be based on the tastes or preferences of consumers. For example, Scottish country dancing appeals mostly to females, but of various age ranges. This does not mean that it will appeal to all females, but producers of dancing shoes are more likely to advertise in publications which women read, or more specifically in any publication available for Scottish country dancing, or concerned with Scottish country pursuits.

Using the example of targeted publications, we can look at the other ways in which the market can be segmented, e.g. by age – *Smash Hits*; by gender – *Heat*; by socio-economic group – *The Daily Record*; by education level – *The Scotsman*; by income – *Ski Monthly*. The market can also be split by the structure of the household, by geographical location, or by religion.

### Undifferentiated (mass) marketing

Some products appeal to the majority of consumers and so marketing is directed at all consumers, the whole market. An example could be milk, which appeals to consumers of all ages, gender, income groups, etc. It is seen by many as an essential item, so the Scottish Milk Marketing Board does not need to spend too much on advertising.

Another example is the Mars Bar. Although young people tend to buy more sweets, older people also enjoy them, and with Scotland having a very high consumption rate of sugar and fat-based foods, advertising tends to be based on beating the competition rather than trying to convince people that they will enjoy them.

Undifferentiated marketing is where one product is sold to the entire market. There tends to be very high-volume sales, so the manufacturers involved benefit from economies of scale. There is usually a lot of competition in the market, with Mars competing with Cadbury and Nestlé for the same snack-sized chocolate bar.

## Niche marketing

Niche marketing involves a business aiming a product at a particular, often very small, segment of the market, where the consumers' needs and wants can be clearly identified. It can be a local market or a small national market.

The advantages involved in niche marketing are that you can take advantage of small markets that will have been overlooked or ignored by other firms, and so you are able to avoid competition in the short term. You can focus on the needs of consumers in these segments, which will give you an advantage over businesses which target the wider market. In the case of Mackie's ice cream, it has been producing its quality ice cream in volume since before Haagen Dazs or Ben and Jerry's entered the Scottish market.

The disadvantages of niche marketing are that if the business is successful it may attract competition. Niche markets are often too small to accommodate two or more firms in competition. Large national firms deciding to enter the niche market can often force other businesses out. Secondly, as niche markets contain small numbers of consumers, they tend to be faced by bigger and more frequent swings in consumer spending than larger markets.

## Info Point

Luxury brands like Chanel, Gucci and Louis Vuitton used to be for the select few, but these days everyone seems to be brandishing them. Why? By 'going cheap' fashion houses can win the loyalty of shoppers at a younger age.

The fashion world has had to revaluate its target market and is now taking on the top end of the high street and creating cheaper lines.

Today's celebrity culture, and the public's hunger for a bit of the 'bling' lifestyle lived by their idols, is seen as fuelling the move and 'revolutionising' access to luxury brands.

The ranges – including keyrings, baseball caps and underwear – are being credited with pulling the luxury goods market out of a financial slump. Following three years of falling profits, the market is now worth more than £41bn and is predicted to rise to £59bn by 2008, according to new research.

The likes of David Beckham, pictured in celebrity magazines in the latest Versace outfit, has also led to designers developing a devoted following among young consumers. And the fashion industry is embracing them – and their pocket money – with delight.

**Example of luxury bargains:**

- Louis Vuitton keyring – £54

- Prada robot keyring – £100

- Versace underpants – £20

- Dior Pure Poison perfume – £27.

'The leading luxury goods companies hope that by recruiting customers at an earlier age, they can ensure greater product loyalty and grow sales at the same time.'

The new ranges have also allowed some of the fashion houses the freedom to do something different and keep their upmarket client base.

*continued ➤*

Designers also see their cheaper lines as a way of keeping control of their brands and fighting back against the flow of cheap fakes flooding the High Street. They see counterfeit goods as devaluing their brand, as well as costing them millions of pounds a year.

They now make sure they are represented in the way they want or the brand loses value. The Burberry baseball cap is a good example. Now associated with so-called 'chavs' the company has discontinued it.

*Source*: BBC News, September 2005

## Market share

A market is made up of all the consumers and producers, buying and selling a product. For example, the market for mobile phones includes all the manufacturers such as Nokia and Motorola, all the network operators such as Vodafone and Orange, and all the consumers who buy and use mobile phones.

For the manufacturers, their share of the market will be the percentage of all users with one of their phones; for the networks, their market share will be the percentage of users connected to their network.

The businesses involved in the market are continually trying to keep or increase their market share. For the networks, this means that they will have more customers, and so will make more sales which should make them more profitable.

Changing the marketing mix should allow an organisation to increase their market share at the expense of one of their competitors. However, it will depend on how successful the marketing strategy is, and how effective is the competitor's marketing mix.

Many organisations use market share as a measure of success. An increasing share of the market would indicate that the business is doing well compared to their competitors.

## Market growth

As we have seen, by increasing its market share a business will increase its sales at the expense of those of its competitors. However, firms can also increase their sales if the whole market grows. Market growth takes place when the number of people buying or using the product increases.

Just as products go through a life cycle, so can markets. New products will experience market growth, then market saturation, and finally decline. And just like products, extension strategies can be used to prolong the life of markets and also increase the market size. This can be done by finding new uses for products, finding new sectors of the market, etc.

BUSINESS DECISION AREAS

### Info Point

Emerging markets are the key to future growth in the mobile phone market, according to leading business figures speaking at the 3GSM World Congress in Cannes.

As the mobile phone markets have become saturated in Western Europe and North America, India, China, Russia, Brazil and Africa were highlighted as regions that would drive growth over the next five years.

'China is a multi-billion market for us,' said Ed Zander, chief executive of US handset maker Motorola.

'China was cool for us before anyone else thought it was cool.'

Jay Naidoo, chairman of the Development Bank of Southern Africa, argued that the developing world is where new subscribers are going to come from.

'There are a billion people in Africa but only 51 million using cellphones,' he said.

'By 2006, we could see a quarter of Africa's billion people using them.'

*Source*: BBC News, February 2005

## Topic Market research

If promotion is the communication from the business to the consumer, then market research is the communication from the consumer to the business. It is very important because it is the method that businesses use to identify and anticipate consumers' needs and wants, and so will affect how profitable or successful the business is.

If no market research was carried out, the first sign that something is wrong would probably be that sales start to decline. By then it would be too late to take effective action. The success of new products depends on them meeting consumer demand; without market research, there is a very high chance that the product would fail.

It includes research on:

- what types of consumers buy the product now
- what the consumers think of the product
- what prices consumers are prepared to pay for the product
- what competition exists in the market and what potential competition there is
- what types of packaging and promotion are most appropriate
- how best to distribute the product and where to sell it
- whether any legal restrictions or regulations apply to the product.

Good information in sufficient quantities is essential for good decision-making. Failing to carry out market research will lead to lower sales and revenue.

## *Primary and secondary information*

There are two main types of market research: field/primary and desk/secondary. These have been dealt with extensively in Chapter 2, and you should refer to them at this stage.

## *Desk research techniques*

This is usually much cheaper and easier to obtain than primary information. It can be obtained from a variety of sources such as:

- the internet
- government statistics
- trade magazines
- reports prepared by market research companies
- internal company reports.

It can give a good indication of what is going on in the business's external environment. However, the value and reliability is limited because:

- much of the information is historic
- it was collected for another purpose
- it is available to competitors
- you cannot normally go back to the initial source to check its accuracy or ask follow-up questions.

The most useful tool in terms of marketing advantage is your own sales force's estimates of future demand. However, like all market research, it may not be accurate.

## *Field research techniques*

Field research involves going outside the business to gather the marketing information you need. The main benefits of field research are:

- the information is up to date
- it is collected for the exact purpose required
- it is not available to competitors, giving the organisation a competitive advantage over its rivals.

### Surveys

One of the most common methods of collecting primary information is through a survey. The survey can take a number of forms, and the choice of survey type will depend on the budget and the importance which the organisation places on the information needed.

### Personal interview

This means stopping people in the street or visiting them at home. Street surveys are often more brief, and do not allow for as many follow-up questions as home interviews. They allow

*(sidebar, right margin)* BUSINESS DECISION AREAS

two-way communication, so the researcher can encourage the person to answer. Any mistakes or misunderstandings can be cleared up.

### Postal survey

This involves sending out questionnaires to people to complete and return. Because it is a relatively cheap method, a much larger number of people can be asked to respond, although few will reply. Postal surveys tend to be simple tick-box questionnaires, which allow for ease of collation.

### Telephone survey

This requires phoning customers at home or work to ask their opinion. Again, this is a relatively cheap form of survey, so a large number of people can be entered into the sample. You receive the information straight away, but people do not normally like to be phoned at home.

### Purchase surveys

This involves asking customers to provide information when they make a purchase. This can be done in-store by the sales person, or with a survey form when registering the product for warranty cover. It is successful in that nearly all of those asked to complete the form will do so. However, you are only asking people who have bought your product, so the usefulness of the information will be limited.

## Population

How do you carry out market research? You could survey every possible consumer in the market, but this would be very expensive and time-consuming. The information would probably be out of date by the time you had collected and analysed it.

The 'population' for a survey refers to all the persons or companies to which you would like to direct questions. Rather than survey the entire population, it is more appropriate to take a sample of that population. The sample should be representative of the population as a whole.

## Sampling

There are three decisions to be taken when planning a sample to research. The first is '**Who is to be surveyed?**'. This will be the population that you plan to target in your research. Once this has been established you then develop a **sampling frame** – this is a way to make sure that everyone in the population you are targeting has a chance of being included in the sample.

The second question is '**How many people/companies should be surveyed?**'. The larger the sample, the more accurate your survey will be; however, it will also be more expensive. It has been shown that samples of less than 1 per cent of a population can provide sufficiently reliable information if the sampling frame is correctly developed.

The final questions is '**How do we choose those to be included in the survey?**'. There are two main methods – **random** sampling and **quota** sampling.

### Random sampling

Random sampling involves producing a random list of individuals to survey. Those picked for inclusion in the sample could be generated randomly, using a computer and the telephone directory or the electoral register. Many market research companies hold huge amounts of information on all different types of consumer, and have access to government information from which they can generate random lists.

The main advantage of this method is that there is no chance of bias being introduced when selecting individuals for the sample, and it is simple to do.

The main disadvantages are:

- It may not be focused on any particular market segment.

- It assumes that all members of the group are the same, which is not always the case.

- The random sample must be maintained – if someone is chosen for the sample then they must be interviewed.

### Quota sampling

This type of survey is preferred when carrying out research. Here, those chosen to be surveyed are selected in proportion to the whole population by social status, gender, age, etc. Once they have reached the quota for, say, males aged between 15 and 21, then no more are surveyed.

The advantages of this method are:

- It is cheaper to operate than random sampling.

- Statistics showing the proportions of different groups within the population are readily available.

- Interviewers can substitute someone else if the interviewee is not at home at the time of the visit or phone call.

The main disadvantage is that the results from quota sampling can be less representative than using the random sampling method.

## Questionnaires

Once you have decided how you will sample and who will be included, you then have to decide how you are going to obtain their responses. The two most common methods are interview and questionnaire.

The questionnaire will be filled in by the person who has been chosen to be included in the sample. The purpose of the questionnaire is to gain information from the respondent on a wide variety of different issues, including what they own, what they would like to own, what they plan to buy, and about their values, attitudes and beliefs.

In order to be successful, the questionnaire must be one that the respondent is willing to complete. The purpose of the questionnaire should be clear, with an explanation of why they would benefit if they take the time to fill it in.

The questions should be clear and easy to understand, and not too heavily based on the respondent's memory, as the information given may be guessed at. The opening questions should be easy, keeping the more complicated questions for nearer the end to avoid putting them off. The closing 'filter' questions should categorise the respondent by age, income group, etc. However, you should use banded questions, e.g. age 30–39.

The questions should follow a logical order, with questions on the same topic grouped together. The questions should use terms that mean the same to all or most people; e.g. the term 'often' can mean once a day to one person, and once a month to someone else. You should vary the question types to maintain the respondent's interest.

## Interview

Where the questions have to be more detailed, using a trained interviewer has a number of advantages. First, because of the two-way communication, the interviewer can explain questions, encourage answers, and ask follow-up questions where appropriate. It also allows for more detailed responses than the questionnaire where answers will usually be no more than one- or two-word answers.

These are time-consuming and expensive, and poor interviewers may influence the answers given. However, they can give much more detailed information.

The interview can take place in a number of ways. They can be personal interviews, face-to-face in the street, in an office or at home, and they can be carried out over the phone provided that the respondent is willing to answer the questions.

## Test marketing

This involves selling the new product on one small part of the market before launching it onto the full market. The benefits of this are:

- Consumer reaction to the product can be gained on a large scale.
- Changes can be made to the product in response to the consumers' reactions.
- Potentially unsuccessful products can be withdrawn before full launch.
- The full launch is much more likely to be successful.

## Other methods

There are a number of other ways to gather primary data:

### Consumer panels

Small groups of consumers are brought together to gather their views on a number of different new and existing products. Detailed questions can be asked, and feedback on changes can be obtained.

### Hall tests

A larger number of consumers are asked to comment on a range of products. Most major cinema releases are shown first to a test audience who will then be asked to discuss what they thought of the film. Changes can be made, or scenes re-shot; even changing the ending is common. Once the test audience's changes are made, the film will be put into general release.

## Collection of customer data

Businesses now use a variety of methods to keep up to date research on their customers.

### Loyalty cards

These contain information on the customer, and every time they use it, it records what that customer purchased. This allows the business to track customer spending patterns.

### EPOS/bar codes

These can keep track of what is being purchased in different parts of the country in different stores.

**The Internet**

The Internet has become very important in collecting consumer information. The growth of e-commerce or e-tailing gives organisations access to consumers in their own homes. Customer information can be gained through registration which asks for personal details of the consumer. The customer can also be asked to complete questionnaires online which provides the organisation with very useful market research information.

You can also use the Internet to find out about what your competitors are doing by visiting their websites; or find secondary information from government, market research companies, and newspapers' websites.

These methods are examples of how modern technology is being used in market research.

## Info Point

**Now here's a question: What actually is the point of 3G phones? Finding the answer is a bit more tricky, as the phone companies are discovering.**

All the UK's mobile phone operators have launched 3G services and are now working hard to persuade existing customers to trade up and make efforts to poach new patrons from rivals. But although the operators think that their customers are ready for 3G, it is far from clear that their networks are as well prepared.

At first glance 3G phones seem to be very similar to the 2.5G ones we have now except that everything happens a bit faster or looks and sounds a little better. But the big difference between 3G and existing phones lies in the network. To begin with, the vastly greater carrying capacity of 3G networks means that voice calls get much cheaper. This is a big problem for phone firms which currently get most of their money from people talking to each other.

To compensate, operators running 3G networks have to get people using, and paying for, data services such as video clips, music tracks, games, weather reports etc. And this is where the problems start.

'We really don't know what people are going to do with these networks,' said Stirling Essex, from mobile testing firm Ubinetics.

Third-generation networks are inherently more complicated because of the amount and sorts of data that people will want. Serving up a video clip to one person is straight-forward.

Serving up a video clip of a winning goal during the moments after it happens in a key match of England's 2006 World Cup campaign to millions of people, balancing the load across servers holding the clip, making sure the clip does not stutter, that it is adequately protected, that all the rights holders are acknowledged, that everyone is paid properly and customers are charged correctly, is a much bigger task.

Many operators are realising that they are going to have to upgrade to a faster form of 3G, that goes by the graceful name of High-Speed Downlink Packet Access (HSDPA), which boosts airborne bandwidth to new heights. Until that is widely deployed and handsets that can use it reach consumers, there are likely to be problems, said Mr Essex.

'We would all benefit from operators spending more on infrastructure,' he said.

*continued* ➤

And that leads to another problem with 3G – the sites of the base stations that provide coverage. Third-generation services need many more base stations than earlier generations so simply adding a 3G aerial to an existing site will not do. Physics dictates that the coverage of each 3G base station shrinks as more people use its available bandwidth to make calls, browse the web or listen to music. This means that base stations have to be packed tighter than ever which is tricky at a time when mobile masts are viewed with suspicion.

'The problem is the planning constraints,' said Mr Essex. 'If an operator has a certain number of cell sites, they have to sweat those assets as much as they can.'

Finally, there remains a question over how many people will even bother to use all the new services that 3G makes available. Research by mobile phone firm Mobeon could come as something of a shock for 3G operators. The company surveyed 16–19 year-olds to find out what they want from their future phones and found that most were utterly turned off by the perceived complexity of getting data services. For this young group the most important thing about 3G services was the handset.

'Almost all of them want very simple services,' said Robert Vangstad, Mobeon spokesman. 'It was important for them to identify themselves with their telephone. Everything about their telephone was helping to create their identity.'

The research revealed that there was little loyalty to the operator or affection for any particular service. What might make a difference was avatars – animated characters – that can tell a phone's owner about things that might interest them.

*Source*: BBC, February 2005

# End of chapter revision questions

1   Why is marketing important to organisations?

2   Describe the main objectives of marketing.

3   Explain why it is likely that product-orientated organisations are less successful in modern markets.

4   Describe the difference between goods and services, giving examples of each.

5   Explain what you understand by the terms 'market share' and 'market growth'.

6   Describe the governmental constraints placed on marketing.

7   What do the terms unique selling proposition (USP) and emotional selling proposition (ESP) mean?

8   What are the main factors that affect the buying decisions of consumers?

9   Describe how differentiated marketing can be more effective than undifferentiated marketing.

10   Describe the difference between the core and augmented product.

11   Describe the benefits for a business of having a range of products.

12   Describe the product life cycle referring to costs, sales and profits at each stage.

13  Identify the life cycle extension strategies available to an organisation.

14  What are the advantages to an organisation of creating a successful brand?

15  Describe the various pricing strategies that a business could use.

16  Identify the factors that will affect a business's choice of channel of distribution.

17  Identify the factors that will affect the business's choice of advertising media.

18  Identify the different types of promotions into and out of the pipeline.

19  Describe the differences between public relations and publicity.

20  Explain why packaging is important in marketing.

21  Describe the differences between random and quota sampling.

22  Describe how interviews can be used to gather market research information.

## Chapter Summary

At the end of this chapter you should be able to:

★ describe the role and importance of marketing in organisations

★ identify and describe the role of marketing in relation to different types of organisations in the public and private sectors

★ discuss marketing as a strategic activity, and the marketing of products and services

★ discuss place, including distribution channels; pricing strategies; product/service; promotional strategies; and their relationships in context of a marketing strategy

★ describe market segmentation; methods of segmenting markets; including niche marketing, market share, market growth

★ discuss the costs and benefits of primary and secondary information

★ describe market research techniques including desk research, survey, questionnaire, interview, test marketing, sampling, the assessment of customer requirements and the collection of consumer data.

# CHAPTER 5

# Operations

This part of the course contains the following topics.

| | |
|---|---|
| **Operations** | Role and importance of operations in organisations. |
| **Input, process and output** | Production systems, quality assurance, stock control, quality standards, purchasing, payment systems. |
| **Distribution and delivery** | Warehousing, transport (road, rail, air, sea), scheduling. |
| **Types of operations** | Job, batch, flow. |
| **Quality** | Quality control, benchmarking, quality circles, quality management. |

## Topic Operations

Operations management is concerned with the way in which organisations produce goods and services. It is a transforming process, turning inputs (resources) into outputs (goods and services).

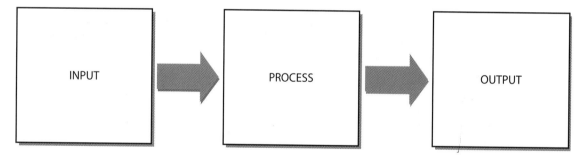

It could be described as the core activity of the organisation, as it actually produces the goods or services for sale. However, marketing could also claim to be the core activity as it achieves the sales that create revenue and profits for the organisation.

### Info Point

In 2000, the then chief executive of the Ford Motor Company announced that they were considering outsourcing the production of their motor cars (this means contracting someone else to make them) as the company's profits were created through sales, not production. That particular chief executive has since been replaced, and Ford continue to make the cars themselves.

# Topic Input, process, output

## *Production systems*

It is much easier to identify the inputs such as information (e.g., sales forecasts), raw materials, labour, machinery, factories, the process of making the goods, and the output of finished goods. However, in the service industries, the operations process can be much more complicated. For example, for an airline such as Easyjet, the inputs would include the passengers who are transported (process) to their destination (output).

Although the diagram for operations management is very simple, operations management itself is a very complicated function. We can split it into a number of key areas:

- planning

- production

- purchasing

- warehousing and storage – including stock control

- distribution/logistics

Each of these interact with the other functional areas of the organisation. For example, the planning of what to produce, how to produce it, and how much to produce, will require input from marketing, finance, human resources, etc. Marketing will provide information on consumers' wants in terms of the product itself (features, quality, colour, etc), how they wish to make their purchases (place), and how much they will buy. Finance will provide input on the costs of various suppliers, machinery and labour costs. Human Resources will provide information on the available workforce and their skills, and any legislative requirements (employment laws, health and safety, etc).

### Activity

Visit the Institute of Operations Management at: www.iomnet.org.uk.

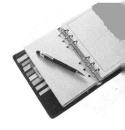

BUSINESS DECISION AREAS

## Production planning

Successful planning is essential to the success of operations management and for the organisation to achieve its objectives. Planning on how to produce involves creating a production system that will most efficiently produce the goods for output.

Ideally, production should be at a constant level for good planning. The exact number of workers required, the materials to be used, and the number and type of machinery will be known in advance. The diagram here shows the ideal for production planning.

It is more likely that production will vary over time, because of changes in consumer demand, staff shortages, machine breakdown and maintenance. So production will vary from day to day or week to week. The production curve will look more like this diagram.

In reality it is rarely possible to have a continuous level of production, so the production system must be flexible.

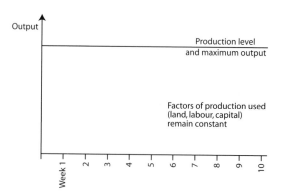

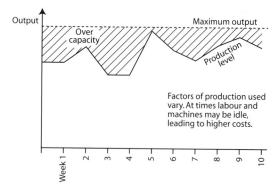

## Manufacturing production systems

This is about how the manufacturer produces the goods for the consumer. The first job in the production system will be deciding the layout of the factory; then where each part of production will be done by which workers/machines, and how many workers/machines will be needed for each part of the production process. The splitting up of production into a number of different jobs is called the **division of labour**. A successful system will need a flow of stocks from one job to another to make sure that there are no delays due to **shortages** or **bottlenecks**.

There are a number of key factors that affect the decision on what type of production system to use:

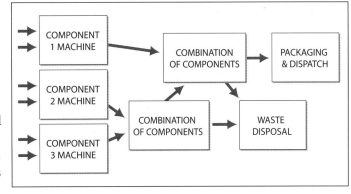

## The nature of the final product

Different products will be produced in different ways; e.g. the products in farming are tied up with the land that they are produced on, whereas producing a new bridge requires very different processes.

## The market size

Where the firm is producing large numbers of standardised products (such as cans of Irn Bru), production can be simplified into a number of stages; whereas if you were producing customised software for individual clients, the processes would be more complicated and need a great deal of customer input.

## The resources available

The production system will be restricted by the finance available, the number and skills of the workers, the size and capacity of the premises, machinery and tools available.

## The stage of development of the business

When firms are first set up they tend to produce small amounts, and their production system will be limited. However, as the firm grows it can increase its capacity and so the production system can grow and produce a greater variety of goods.

## Labour-intensive versus capital-intensive production

Labour-intensive production is where the cost of labour is greater than the cost of capital. There are few industries in the UK that use labour-intensive production because of the high labour costs; machines are much more cost-effective. However, in other parts of the world where labour is very cheap, labour-intensive production becomes more cost-effective.

## Availability of technology – automation

The continuing developments in technologies such as **Computer-Aided Manufacture (CAM)**, **Computer-Aided Design (CAD)** and **automation** (robotics to replace workers) allow firms to design, develop and produce products quickly. It also allows firms to produce a much wider variety of similar products to appeal to different segments of the market.

Using robotics has the advantage of machines which can carry out very complicated tasks very quickly, and with a high degree of accuracy. Machines can perform in seconds jobs that may take even the most skilled workers hours or days to achieve; indeed machines can do jobs which are impossible for human workers. There is far less waste when machines are used, and the quality is usually consistent.

The main problems with machines are they are far more likely to break down than humans, and will only be able to carry out a very narrow range of tasks.

**BUSINESS DECISION AREAS**

## Info Point

Sony have at least 12 different versions of the Sony Walkman on the market at present. Each has the same basic features, all of which are made on the same production lines. However, by using technology in the design and production of the Walkmans, they can add different features to each model to appeal to different consumers, with prices ranging from £12–£60.

This can sometimes be taken a step further, where mass manufacture can take place with production being tailored to the individual customers' needs.

## Activity

For case studies visit the biz/ed catalogue at:
http://catalogue.bized.ac.uk/roads/opman.html

## Materials management

The materials that are included in the input stage have a direct influence on both the process stage and the final product. Poor quality will increase waste during production and lead to some poor quality output. It is essential that the correct suppliers are selected in order that the organisation can achieve what it wants, in terms of the quality and cost of the output.

## The purchasing mix

This refers to the main factors which have to be considered by the purchasing team. The choice of which suppliers to use depends on a number of factors:

### Alternative suppliers

Are the suppliers dependable? Most manufacturers run a series of checks on suppliers, including credit reference checks to make sure that they are able to supply as they have said. Should the business use a local or a national supplier? A local supplier will be able to supply at short notice if needed, but may not have the range of materials and may be more expensive than national suppliers. Will using local suppliers bring any other advantages?

## Info Point

Supermarkets have adopted a policy of using local suppliers for some of the produce they sell. This is part of their corporate responsibility in encouraging local producers, which in turn provides good publicity for the supermarkets.

Are there additional costs? Some suppliers make additional charges for delivery and insurance. Some will have already added this to the quoted price; other will add it on as an extra which will increase the overall price.

## Delivery time

The time taken from placing an order to receiving the materials is called the **lead time**. How important this is depends on the needs of the organisation; e.g. it may operate a **Just In Time** system of stock control, where only enough stock to keep production going is held (see p146 for a fuller explanation of Just in Time). If this is the case, the supplier must be able to deliver the materials directly from their own stores. In other instances, the supplier may not be able to supply straight from stock, so there would be a further delay in delivery. Delays can be acceptable provided they have been planned for, so that an order is placed far enough in advance for the materials to arrive when they are needed.

The suppliers have to be reliable in their promised delivery times. If materials do not arrive when they are needed, this could mean that production has to stop. The organisation will lose sales and customers, and this will affect profitability.

## Price

Ideally the best price would be the lowest price. However, prices are often open to negotiation. Discounts for bulk-buying may be available and this must be balanced against how much stock the organisation can buy and store at a time. There may be other discounts available if there is a guarantee that the organisation will place regular orders. The credit terms on offer are also important. The longer these are, the longer it is before the organisation has to pay for the materials it has received. This has to be balanced against any discounts that may be available for paying quickly.

Many organisations enter into a contract with their suppliers which will set out the terms and conditions of supply and payment. Purchasing and finance departments work together to obtain the best price on the best terms.

> ### Info Point
>
> McDonald's do not have contracts with any of their suppliers, which means they can change suppliers without notice. Although this may seem hard on the suppliers, the size of McDonald's orders make it a very attractive proposition. The suppliers must meet McDonald's very strict quality standards.

## Quality

What quality means is different for different organisations. The quality that the supplier can provide for the organisation should be acceptable for the organisation's needs, in terms of being suitable for the production process and for the customers' requirements. For consistent production the quality of materials used should be consistent. If the quality is variable this will lead to increased wastage and poor quality of output on certain occasions. The supplier must be able to guarantee that the materials will be of a minimum standard.

## Quantity

Although there may be discounts for buying in bulk, this has to be weighed against the cost of storage. It is thought that storage adds a further 15–30 per cent to the cost of purchasing, so ideally the quantity bought should be as low as possible. The stocks may deteriorate over time, leading them to being scrapped. The organisation could also be left with unwanted stock as fashions change. These all mean further cost for the organisation, which should be avoided where possible.

### Storage facilities

When making purchasing decisions, the organisation must consider what facilities it has for storage. The capacity of storage should be more than the supplies held at any one time. The storage has to be suitable for the products to be stored. They should be safe and secure to ensure there is no loss through theft or poor control systems. Some materials need weather-proof storage, whereas others can be left out in the open; some need refrigeration, others need heated storage. The cost of insuring the stock also has to be considered.

## Service production systems

Service production systems exist where the output is not a good, as in a manufacturing production system, but rather a service.

Hospitals are a good example of a service production system in operation. For example, the day surgery unit carries out many small operations for patients on a daily basis. The production system may operate the following processes:

1　Patient arrives at reception area of hospital.

2　Patient is 'checked in' and processing begins.

3　Patient undergoes various checks before undergoing surgical procedure.

4　Patient undergoes surgical procedure.

5　Patient is examined/briefed before being released.

6　Patient is discharged from hospital.

The above system can be applied to many different operations in the same way.

## Stock control

Also known as **inventory management** when considered with purchasing, this is a very important part of operations management because inefficient stock control can lead to a large increase in cost to the business. Ideally the organisation would operate with as little stock as possible, but this is not always possible. There has to be a balance between the cost of holding stock and the cost of lost production and sales. Efficient production needs a continuous supply of stock.

The decision of how much stock to carry at any one time will be decided at the planning stage. However, if the organisation wants to ensure continuous production it must calculate the economic stock level.

### Economic stock level

This is the lowest level of stock that ensures that production is not interrupted by shortages, but at the same time also makes sure that it is not carrying too much stock and keeps cost to a minimum.

The economic stock level will ensure that there is enough stock on hand for production to continue. This will be based on the following:

**Minimum stock level**

This is the level which ensures that there will always be stock for production, allowing for ordering and delivery times (lead time).

### Re-order stock level

When stock falls to this level, new stock must be ordered to make sure that the organisation does not run out. For example, if it takes a week for new stock to arrive, the reorder level will be at the point where there is at least one week's stock left. In real life there will always be problems with delivery from time to time, so the organisation might re-order when there is ten days' supply of stock left, just in case.

### Re-order stock quantity

This is the amount of stock needed to bring the level back to the economic stock level.

## Automation in stock control

Most organisations use a computerised stock control system, where the computer automatically orders more stock when the stock falls to the re-order stock level. There are a number of ways that such a system can be operated, but many use a bar-code system similar to the bar codes used by supermarkets. The principle is the same: as stock leaves the warehouse or stock room, it is scanned by the bar code reader which automatically adjusts the recorded stock level; the same happens as new stock comes in, and it date-records its arrival to make sure that stock is issued in date-order to avoid deterioration. This allows for an accurate check on the running balance of each stock item. Physical checks of the stock must be made from time to time, to make sure that the recorded stock levels are accurate. There may be discrepancies due to theft, natural wastage, or deterioration.

In supermarkets, the bar-code system allows management to make decisions about what products are popular in what areas of the country, and so the stock levels can be easily adjusted to take account of local tastes.

## Info Point

Bar codes have now become the global language of business. They are standardised and regulated so there is no danger that two companies will pick the same bar code for different products. Bar codes celebrated their 25th birthday in the UK in 2002. They are widely used by companies who trade electronically, and make it very easy to describe the raw materials and products that are being bought and sold. In the future, bar codes will be augmented with radio-frequency identity tags that can be scanned more quickly and can also update the information encoded on them.

ISBN 0-340-91369-X

9 780340 913697

'Without bar codes our operations would not work,' said Robin Kidd, supply chain manager at Nestlé UK.

*Source:* BBC News

## Activity

To find out more, visit www.e-commerce.org.uk who look after bar codes used in the UK.

BUSINESS DECISION AREAS

## Just In Time (JIT)

This is a popular method of operations for mass manufacturers as it limits the amount of stock held by the organisation to near zero. It works best where there is a very close relationship between the manufacturer and their suppliers.

In practice it is very simple: the stock is held by the supplier and is only brought to the factory as and when it is needed. The whole production process has to be geared to working with the JIT system. The cost savings can be very high as there are none of the stock-holding costs:

- Capital tied up in stock – money can be used for other purposes or removed entirely from the manufacturer's expenditure.

- Storage costs – space, equipment, warehouse and stores staff, services, etc.

- Stock losses/wastage – theft, accidental damage, stock exceeding its shelf-life, stock obsolescence.

In a JIT system, these costs are paid by the suppliers.

The whole production operation works on the JIT system in that nothing is produced unless there are customers to buy the products. The marketing department give figures on expected demand or actual orders, and only then will production take place. Supplies are ordered 'just in time' to become parts for the final product, these component parts are assembled 'just in time' to become finished products; 'just in time' to be sold to the customers.

### Info Point

Just In Time production was first developed in Japan by Toyota, the car manufacturer. In order to reduce the costs involved in holding stocks of materials and work-in-progress, Toyota devised a card ordering system known as **Kanban**. Toyota devised a policy that no components would be made, or supplies ordered, unless the instruction appeared on a Kanban. For example, if a worker fitted six steering wheels, a Kanban card would be sent to the production team to order another six steering wheels. These would arrive just in time, before the worker ran out of steering wheels.

In order for this to be successful, Toyota had to ensure that their suppliers understood the system and were able to supply on demand. When they opened their UK plant, they trained their suppliers in operations and quality procedures to make sure that they delivered the exact product at the right time. In some cases the suppliers had their factories next door to the Toyota plant to ensure that they could operate with the JIT production system. To secure long-term contracts with Toyota, suppliers had to deliver small quantities of high quality goods at short notice. The suppliers had to be completely reliable and would have to pay the costs of lost production if they could not deliver, or if they delivered faulty materials.

The advantages of using a successful Kanban system are that significant savings are made in the purchase and storage of materials and so production costs are lower; all stock purchased is used in production and so there is no waste; a close relationship is developed with suppliers which ensures that there are no production delays and the materials exactly match the organisation's needs. The main danger is the heavy reliance on suppliers who must be willing to co-operate fully with the organisation.

The JIT system does not suit all organisations, and so many still hold stock. In manufacturing this can often be because the organisation makes some or all of its own component materials. Where organisations decide that they must hold stock, they have to manage the storage of the stock.

The first decision is whether the stock should be held in a centralised storage area, or spread around different departments. Holding it centrally has several advantages:

- The stock is secure, with specialist staff to receive, check and issue stock.

- Standard organisational procedures can be developed for ordering, receiving, and issuing stock.

- Storage costs can be better controlled.

The main costs would be the recruitment, training, and salaries for the specialist staff, and the cost of creating an area for storage. There would be time delays between ordering and receiving the stock.

Having a decentralised stock system allows for better decisions to be made about what stock to buy and how much to order, and makes sure that stock is always available for production.

## Payment systems

Workers must be paid for their work. Most production workers, but not all, receive a basic weekly wage for a basic number of hours worked per week. However, it is common for organisations to offer some additional incentives to encourage them to work harder or better. How the worker is rewarded for their labour varies between organisations.

**Overtime** is paid when the employee works longer than their contractual hours, usually at a higher rate than the basic rate. This allows the employee to increase their earnings. In some jobs guaranteed overtime is available as part of the contract of employment, or it may be essential to ensure the organisation runs efficiently. For example, the police force and ScotRail depend on employees working overtime.

### Info Point

ScotRail depends on drivers working overtime to maintain services. During the recent overtime ban by the drivers, 180 trains had to be cancelled on the first day as drivers were not available to work on their rest days.

A report by the TUC in March 2002 said that the average employee works seven hours longer than contracted every week, worth about £5,000 per employee per year. The number of employees putting in unpaid overtime has risen to over 5.5 million, with women in professional jobs more likely to work longer than their contracted hours. The TUC estimate that unpaid overtime is worth £28 billion each year to employers.

The CBI stated that tighter controls on the number of hours worked by employees was not the answer, and that people want to make their own decisions about working extra hours.

*Source*: www.tuc.org.uk, March 2002

In small-scale manufacturing, **piecework** is commonly used. Here the worker is paid a certain amount (**piece rate**) for each good unit they produce. In some cases they receive no basic wage. This system allows for low levels of supervision, and staff will be motivated to work hard enough to earn a reasonable living. However, workers may not pay attention to the amount of waste they create, and may work hardest when they want the most money (e.g. before their summer holidays), which may not be when demand for the product is highest.

**Performance-related pay (PRP)** is an additional payment or **bonus** to staff who are seen to be working better than average, or who have met targets set by the organisation. On the face of it this seems a good idea to encourage workers to work harder. However, it is now recognised that it only encourages the individual, creating unhealthy rivalry between managers, and the possible destruction of teamwork.

A more modern approach which is becoming increasingly popular is **profit-sharing**. Here staff are given a share of the annual profits of the organisation. This can have a number of benefits. Firstly, the staff can see the success of the organisation in terms of profit-making as being directly good for them, putting them in the same position as the shareholders. Secondly, they will be encouraged to work more efficiently for the organisation without affecting teamwork. In some cases, the share of profits is paid in the form of free shares which gives the employee part-ownership of the organisation.

**Share Save** schemes or **share options** are other ways to create share ownership amongst employees. With share save schemes, employees save a regular amount each month for a set time period (usually five years), after which they can turn their savings into shares to keep or sell at a substantial profit. This ensures the loyalty of key employees, and provides an incentive to keep profits up, which will in turn increase the value of shares. Share options are sometimes available for senior managers, where they are given the option to buy a certain number of shares at a discount at some point in the future. Again, this creates loyalty and motivation.

## Info Point

In August 2001, the former chairman of the food chain Iceland made a £3 million profit from the controversial sale of share options. The former Chief Executive had also sold shares, making over £2.5 million profit despite spending just under five months in the job. Both the former senior members of Iceland sold their shares prior to announcing a profits warning for the group, and just before they resigned.

**Fringe benefits** are types of reward other than wages or salaries which the organisation offers to its employees. There are a wide range of fringe benefits covering many different jobs. For managers this may include expense accounts, company cars, cheap loans, private medical insurance, etc. For other workers this could include free travel, subsidised canteen or crèche facilities, discounts on products, etc.

Many of these are taxed as income by the government and so have become less popular then 15 years ago. However, they are still widely used.

### Activity

To get case studies and up-to-date information on pay levels and other benefits visit www.irseclips.co.uk.

# Topic Distribution and delivery

Distribution and delivery are an important part of business operations. The successful manufacture of goods is only one part of the overall business, and safe and efficient distribution to wholesalers or delivery to the customer are essential.

Companies often make use of warehousing facilities to bulk store their goods. Warehouse space may be owned by the company, leased or rented. The warehouse may be a centralised function of the business or it may be decentralised and located at a distance from the main operations.

The main reason for utilising warehouse space is that most businesses are unable to match exactly their output to the demand for their products. Stocks of finished goods are stored in the warehouse in order to meet demand quickly.

It is important that the warehouse space is of suitable quality and offers security for the protection of stock. It should also offer the correct environment for the storage of stock, e.g. dry, temperature maintained.

The main aspects of warehousing are as follows:

## Design and layout

The design and layout of the warehouse are essential to the smooth operation of the business. Ideally, warehouses should be on ground level only, as storage and retrieval of stock from additional floors above ground level will increase handling times. A system of stock rotation should be in operation to avoid deterioration of stock quality.

## Mechanical handling

Some businesses may decide to utilise specialist stock handling equipment that can be incorporated into the design of a new building. This may be costly but there are substantial benefits to be gained, in terms of the space used and time required to move stock.

Pallets are often used in warehouses, and are a relatively cheap method of organising stock. They can be easily moved using a forklift truck and enable stock to be stored off the floor. They can also be re-used.

## *Transportation*

Businesses have a choice in the transportation that they use: their own, hired or public transport. The decision on which type of transport to use will be based on the needs of the particular business and the costs involved.

The advantages and disadvantages of each are summarised in the table below.

| Type of transport | Advantages | Disadvantages |
|---|---|---|
| Own | Complete control | High initial investment and continuing running costs |
| Hired | No capital investment, ability to change requirements quickly | Less control |
| Public | No capital investment, cheaper | Unreliable, poor value for money, little control |

## *Transport and delivery of goods in Britain*

During the last decade, British businesses have become more and more dependent on the roads network for transport and delivery of goods and services.

The use of the railways has decreased and the road system is under constant pressure. Nowadays, over 80 per cent of goods are delivered by road. The pie chart below shows the most common methods of transport used in Britain today.

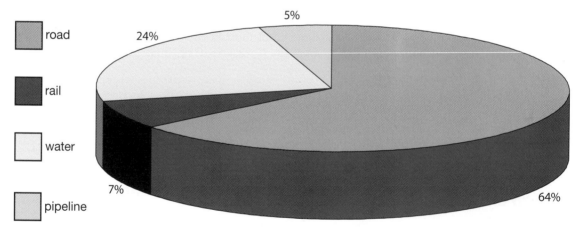

*Source:* www.transtat.dtlr.gov.uk

**Fig 5.8 Methods of transporting goods in Britain**

Over 60 per cent of goods are transported by road in Britain. There has been a steady decline in the use of the rail network as a bulk carrier of freight, with more and more goods being delivered via the road network instead.

The UK Government has consistently opposed the increasing use of the road network by imposing greater taxes on road users (e.g. fuel duty, road tax) and also by freezing expenditure on the upgrading of existing roads and building of new roads.

Ultimately, the choice of transport will be determined by assessment of the costs and benefits of each type of transport that is available, and also taking into account the timescale involved for delivery.

Other forms of transport that may be used include air and sea. Transport by sea is rare within the UK, but large ports such as Portsmouth in the south of England and Leith, near Edinburgh, still serve as busy areas for ships docking from all over the world.

Air transport is the most costly form of transport, but in some cases it may be the only option where a delivery is to be made quickly to the other side of the world. Large freight carriers have their own fleet of cargo planes although most other air carriers offer a freight service on their flights to almost every worldwide destination.

Prestwick International Airport in Ayrshire is the largest cargo airport in Scotland, dealing with freight from all over the world.

## Scheduling

Scheduling is essential to any business operation. This is making sure that all the factors of production are taken into account and are working in harmony with each other. This ensures that from initial production to final delivery to the customer, every operation works smoothly and delivery times are met.

# **Topic** Types of operations

There are three types of production:

- job
- batch
- flow.

## Job production

Job production means that one 'job' is done at a time, through to completion before another 'job' is started. This effectively means that one product is made at a time.

Examples of businesses that use job production are house building, bridge construction and designer clothing.

Job production is typical in smaller businesses which rely on individuality to sell their products.

## Batch production

Batch production involves all stages of the production process being completed at the same time. Products may be similar, although different ingredients may be used for different products.

A number of products (called a **batch**) will be produced at once, and although each product in a batch is the same, the products may vary from one batch to another.

Batch production is most commonly found in the food business, but it is also common in other businesses e.g. construction where the foundations for a row of houses may be dug at the same time, and then the kits to assemble the frame for the houses erected at the same time.

## *Flow production*

Flow production is common in a factory with a production line, where the product being produced flows through various stages with parts being added at each stage. This is common in almost all instances of mass production where a standard product is being produced.

Examples of this type of business include car production and magazine printing.

This type of production results in a continuous output of products which are essentially the same.

As with any type of production method, there are advantages and disadvantages. Some of these are listed in the table below:

### Job production

| Advantages | Disadvantages |
|---|---|
| 1. Easy to organise production<br>2. 'One-off' orders can be easily accommodated<br>3. Workers are involved in the entire production process from start to finish and see the results of their labour | 1. Production costs are likely to be higher for job costing since there are few economies of scale<br>2. Production time may be longer than using other methods since individual requirements of the job have to be met<br>3. Capital investment may be higher since specialist machinery may be required |

### Batch production

| Advantages | Disadvantages |
|---|---|
| 1. Allows flexible production<br>2. Stocks of partly finished goods can be stockpiled and completed later, allowing a quick response to new orders | 1. Production runs of small batches may be expensive to produce<br>2. If production runs are different from each other, there may be extra costs and time delays in setting up different equipment |

### Flow production

| Advantages | Disadvantages |
|---|---|
| 1. Economies of scale<br>2. Automated production lines save time and money<br>3. Quality systems can be built into the production | 1. A standard product is produced which may not suit all customers<br>2. High costs associated with setting up automated production line<br>3. Work can be repetitive and boring for workers<br>4. If production runs are high, there may be too much produced and supply will exceed demand |

# **Topic** Quality

Quality is an important factor to the consumer in today's competitive market. It is difficult to define and means different things to different people. It may mean the quality of fit and finish, or the price paid for the goods. Some consumers will place greater value on the reliability and useful life of the product.

The producer of the goods may have different aspirations relating to quality, e.g. meeting specifications or having very few customer complaints.

Quality assurance aims to make sure that quality standards are:

- set
- agreed
- met

through the **entire** organisation.

## *Quality control*

Quality control and quality assurance are different concepts which are linked to the management of quality within an organisation.

Quality **control** is a historic concept and assumes that there will be a degree of waste, up to 25 per cent, where an organisation has in place a system of quality checking at the end of the manufacturing process.

This type of 'control' can lead to significantly increased costs of production and often the goods that are tested for quality control purposes need to be destroyed.

This can lead to such syndromes as the 'Friday car syndrome' and does not ensure that all goods that leave the production line are of the highest quality.

Quality **assurance** assumes that the wastage caused by quality control can be prevented. This means that quality is checked at every stage of the process instead of just at the end. This reduces waste to levels as low as 5 per cent. Most modern businesses now rely on a system of quality control through the use of quality assurance at each stage of production, to produce a better product and reduce their costs of wastage.

## *Quality standards*

If you were to ask anyone on the street for their views on quality, it is likely that they would at some point indicate a specification of standards that has to be met.

However, although there are quality standards in place, these are not widespread and may be limited to certain industries. There may not even be a requirement for all businesses operating in a particular business sector. Measurements of quality can include appearance, safety, availability, value for money, consumer support and the overall reputation of the product and the company. A good example of perceptions of quality is to be found in the car industry. Some car producers have developed a reputation for quality based on the fit and finish and general feel of their products. German car manufacturers such as Volkswagen, Mercedes and BMW have developed a reputation for quality cars, whereas manufacturers from the Far East such as Kia, Perodua and Skoda have developed a reputation at the budget end of the market.

There is also the effect of legislation in the UK linked to the quality of products. Consumers have a right to expect that goods are of 'satisfactory quality' and that they are 'fit for the purpose for which they are intended'. Indeed, the UK courts have been quite liberal in their interpretation of legislation, falling more often than not firmly on the side of the consumer.

In a recent case in which the writer was involved, the failings of quality control were highlighted and the need to rely on current legislation was necessary. The facts were that the writer purchased a brand new 'quality' German motor car. After 250 miles, there was a catastrophic failure of the turbo unit in the engine; a fault that had not been discovered at any point in the production process or in the subsequent inspections prior to the customer taking delivery. The writer had to invoke his statutory right of rejection as the car was not of 'satisfactory quality' taking into consideration the price paid and the age of the car. Subsequent delivery of the replacement car revealed poor quality in the panel fit of the bonnet, and again the writer had to rely on his legal rights to have the problem rectified.

The UK Government has over recent years promoted the benefits of the British Standards Institution (BSI). The aim is to promote quality at all stages of the production. As previously mentioned, this is a move away from the more traditional approach of testing for quality at the end of the production process, and merely trying to rectify faults at that stage.

The British Standards Institution is able to certify companies with the British version of this international standard of recognition, BS EN ISO 9001. Many companies will only deal with other companies that are certified to this quality standard.

Organisations which aim to achieve this standard have to go through a process of producing quality manuals to set out their policies and procedures for quality assurance, and take part in inspections to ensure that these policies and procedures are being implemented. Once a certificate has been issued, it will be subject to further regular inspections to ensure that standards are maintained.

BS EN ISO 9001 is the benchmark for quality in the UK. The international equivalent is ISO 9000 and is recognised in over 90 countries worldwide.

There are other organisations which offer quality assurance marks:

- Association of British Travel Agents (ABTA)
- Investors in People (IIP).

## Info Point

### Baxters Today

In 2000, Baxters ventured into something slightly different and new for the company when they opened a retail outlet at Aberdeen Airport. Today the retail side of the business continues to grow. Baxters Food Group now has five retail outlets at its Highland Village in Fochabers. It also has a large store at Ocean Terminal in Edinburgh, and has recently opened a new flagship store at a unique new visitor attraction and shopping experience, at Tullibardine, Perthshire.

A new state-of-the-art factory opened at Grimsby in early 2001 which now produces the popular range of Baxters fresh soups.

Also in 2001, Baxters made its first aquisition – Garner's Foods Ltd, owner of Garner's pickles, chutneys and salad dressings. The businesses continues to be run from its premises in Pershore, Worcestershire where the Baxters' experience, knowledge, resources and passion is now ensuring that Garner's continues to achieve its fullest potential.

A second acquisition took place in 2003 when Baxters acquired CCL Foods Plc based in Earls Colne, near Colchester in Essex. Through this, Baxters has expanded its range of premium brands and private label businesses in the UK to include condiments and pickles under some of the UK's best-known brands, such as PizzaExpress, Peppadew, Simply Delicious, Olivaise and Mary Berry.

In September 2004 Baxters made its third and biggest acquisition to date with the purchase of Canada's leading private label soup manufacturer, Soup Experts Inc, providing them with the opportunity to grow the Baxters brand in the region. Based in St Hyacinthe in the Provence of Quebec, SoupExperts will operate as a wholly owned subsidiary of Baxters Canada Inc and, in addition to retaining the well-established private label business, will produce Baxters branded soups for the North American market.

In many respects, Audrey and her management team run a company of which their great-grandparents could never even have dreamed. The sheer scale of the operation, the science and technology that underlies it, the sophisticated sales, marketing and distribution – these things are light years away from the business that was conducted in the little grocery shop in Fochabers.

From having a sole salesman in the early days, Baxters now have distributors throughout the world and products are exported to USA, Canada, South Africa, Australia, Hong Kong and Europe.

*Source*: www.baxters.co.uk

BUSINESS DECISION AREAS

## *Quality management*

The aim of quality management is to produce a perfect product every time.

This system was first seen in the UK over 20 years ago when it was adopted by the Ministry of Defence.

Quality management uses the principles of quality assurance, but the view of quality is such that the exact needs and requirements of the customer must be regarded above everything else. This means that there is a change in the focus of the quality culture from the manufacturer to the client. The client tells the manufacturer what they want and it is up to the manufacturer to use this as his benchmark for quality.

To achieve quality management, it is essential that quality is evident at every stage of the production process. When properly implemented, wastage can be reduced to less than 3 per cent.

Quality management therefore requires:

- a whole company focus on quality
- a commitment from each individual in the company
- consultation with every employee at every level of the organisation in setting standards
- a focus on teamwork and the creation of a feeling of worth among the workforce
- viewing quality management as a long-term concept
- the creation of a plan for quality
- training for employees
- constant checking and review of performance
- constant checking for improvement.

The introduction of a system for quality assurance or quality management requires four key elements to be managed:

### The definition of quality at each and every stage of production

This depends on the requirements of the customer and their ability to provide detailed specification. This may take into account such factors as intended use, safety standards, efficiency, materials to be used and cost.

### The commitment of all the workforce

This requires several important points to be taken into account:

- a commitment from the organisation to quality; this should be included in their mission statement
- the production of a quality manual
- a clear definition of staff responsibilities within the organisation
- established standard operating procedures
- quality audits
- use of benchmarking
- use of quality circles.

### The operation of a system in which the established quality can be assured

This includes:

- systems to help in the definition and specification of products/services
- systems for checking and monitoring quality at all stages
- keeping records
- establishing a system of review, monitoring and feedback
- appraising staff
- setting targets.

### The ability to meet quality requirements

This can be measured both quantitatively and qualitatively.

## Benchmarking

Benchmarking is a process of quality assurance which uses the best performers in a particular industry to set standards for others to meet.

This means that organisations from the same business sector can compare their performance to the market leaders in the same field.

The setting of benchmarked standards is somewhat subjective, as it may be identified from sources such as customers, journalists and business analysts.

## Quality circles

Quality circles are groups of people that meet regularly within the organisation to identify, discuss and resolve problems in the production process.

Members of the quality circle should include a wide range of people from the workforce from shop floor workers up to senior management.

They were first established in the Japanese car industry several decades ago and are well-suited to production where there are a lot of individual processes.

# End of chapter revision questions

1. What factors influence the type of production system that a manufacturer chooses?

2. What are the main factors that affect purchasing decisions?

3. What are the four main decisions to be made in minimising stock holding costs?

4. Describe three different methods of transport, giving advantages and disadvantages of each.

5. Why are barcodes important in modern business?

6. Explain why JIT systems can reduce costs to business.

7. Describe the main types of payment to ordinary workers and those available to senior managers.

8  Explain why quality is important to a business.

9  Give a definition of benchmarking.

10  Explain the term 'quality circle'.

11  How does quality management affect the organisation as whole?

12  How might a lack of quality control affect a business?

## Chapter Summary

At the end of this chapter you should be able to:

★  describe the operations process of input, process and output and apply it to different types of production system

★  identify and describe the main elements in the operations function including purchasing, systems design, automation labour requirements and system operations such as stock control

★  describe the distribution and delivery systems including warehousing, transportation and scheduling

★  describe the different types of production (job, batch, flow) and identify the situations in which they should be used

★  describe the factors that affect quality in operations including quality control, benchmarking, quality circles and quality management

★  identify and describe quality assurance, stock control, quality standards, purchasing function and payment systems.

# CHAPTER 6

## ● ● ● Finance

This part of the course contains the following topics.

| | |
|---|---|
| **Finance** | Role and importance of the finance function in organisations. |
| | Payment of wages and salaries, payment of accounts, maintenance of financial records. |
| **Financial information** | Purpose of profit and loss account, balance sheet, cashflow management, purpose of ratios. |
| | Description of components of and interpretation of profit and loss account and balance sheet. |
| **Cashflow management** | Liquidity, decision-making, projection. |
| **Budgetary control** | Uses of budgets, e.g. to monitor and control activity. |
| **Ratio analysis** | Purpose and interpretation of gross profit/sales, gross profit/cost of goods sold, net profit/sales, return on capital, acid test, current ratio. Use of ratios in decision-making. |
| **Uses of financial information** | Controlling costs and expenditure, monitoring performance, inform decision-making. |
| **Users of financial information** | Management, owners, creditors, employees, citizens. |

## Topic The role and importance of the finance function

The finance function of any modern business plays a vital role in the overall success or failure of the business. It exists to carry out such functions as the maintenance of financial records, the payment of bills and expenses, the collection of accounts due, monitoring of business funds, payment of wages and salaries, and reporting to management. The main role of the finance function is to provide information to managers and decision-makers within the business.

### *Payment of wages and salaries*

The staff, or human resource, of any business are its life-blood. Without staff to carry out the daily duties of the business, it will not survive. Therefore, one of the most important tasks performed by the finance function is the payment of wages and salaries to the organisation's staff.

The finance function works in close proximity with the human resource department when calculating and paying staff wages and salaries. The human resource function holds personal information for all the staff employed by the business. Certain personal information is required by the finance function in order to calculate and pay staff wages and salaries. For example, names, addresses, wage or salary amounts, bank account details and any sickness days all have to be reported before payment of wages and salaries can take place.

Depending on the nature and type of business that an organisation carries out, staff may be paid either a wage or a salary. Typically, the difference is that a wage is paid weekly (i.e. once every week) and a salary is paid monthly (i.e. once every month or sometimes once every four weeks).

Wages and salaries are not normally paid in cash to staff, although some businesses do still operate on this basis. Developments in electronic banking over many years ago mean that most businesses use a system called Bank Automated Credit System (BACS) to transfer electronically wages and salaries directly to employees' bank accounts. There are several advantages in using this service:

- no need for large sums of money to be kept on the business premises
- no need for large sums of money to be transported to the business premises
- cheaper for the business.

## Payment of accounts

Depending on the size and nature of the business, there may or may not be a distinct section or department dealing with the business accounts that must be paid.

Accounts that are payable by the business fall into two different categories:

- cash
- credit.

Accounts which are payable in cash are normally to companies or individuals that the business does not usually deal with in the course of regular business. These bills would normally be settled using the **petty cash** system in operation within the business. The petty cash system is normally administered by an employee and audited by a more senior member of staff in order to maintain its security. Petty cash works by setting aside a sum of money called the **imprest**. This amount is decided by the business and may be several hundred pounds or more. The purpose of petty cash is to meet the daily cash expenses of the business. At the end of each week (or month), depending on the frequency of use, the petty cash is audited and the imprest amount restored to the original amount, with money taken from the business bank account. Each amount of money that is paid out from petty cash must be authorised, and a receipt offered in exchange to be entered in the petty cash record of account.

For larger amounts of expenditure, it is normal for a business to have a line of credit with other business organisations. This means that the business is able to receive the benefit of goods and services from another business and make payment for them at a later date; usually one month later. The amount of credit and the timescale for payment will be decided by the organisation providing the credit. It will be dependent on the 'credit history' of the business and its reputation, as well as any reference taken up from other providers of credit to the business, e.g. a bank.

Credit must be managed carefully, and it is normal for most businesses to employ someone who is responsible for the control and payment of credit invoices. Too much credit can overcommit the business and lead to financial difficulties. It is the responsibility of the employee in charge of credit control to provide information to management on the control and payment of credit within the business. It is normal for most credit agreements to require payment within one month of the business taking delivery of goods or using services that have been provided on credit.

Some companies offer a discount for early settlement of accounts to encourage fast payment.

All businesses must be careful not to abuse the provision of credit facilities, because it is a valuable source of free credit for them which aids the smooth running of their businesses. Companies which are regularly late in paying their invoices will quickly build a reputation as slow payers, and may eventually have the provision of free credit removed so that they have to pay in cash immediately for all goods and services that they require. Conversely, businesses should not make payment too soon, as by doing so they fail to utilise fully the provision of free credit.

## *Maintenance of financial records*

All companies must maintain financial records. Financial records are an essential part of every business as they are a history of all the business's activities. They provide the basis for internal control, internal reporting and external reporting to agencies such as the Inland Revenue.

The Inland Revenue requires that businesses retain financial records and related documents for a period of six years for the purpose of possible investigation. It is an offence if this is not done.

Furthermore, limited companies fall under the scope of the Companies Acts of 1985 and 1989 where it states that it is an offence not to maintain proper financial records.

Financial records form the basis of many business decisions. Without proper financial records, the business would not be able to operate effectively or efficiently.

Financial records can take several forms:

- daily record-keeping

- manual record-keeping

- electronic record-keeping

- information presented for internal decision-making

- information presented for internal reporting

- information presented for external reporting

- information presented as a requirement of statute (law).

In the next section of this chapter we will consider some the financial documents that are of most importance to the business.

### *Activity*

If you have access to the Internet, find out about some of the software that is available for financial record-keeping. You could start by visiting www.sage.com.

# **Topic** Financial information

Financial information may be presented by a business in different formats. For example, the business will have different formats for information that is used internally and information that is presented externally.

There are three main financial statements that all businesses use:

- profit and loss account
- balance sheet
- cashflow statement.

In addition to these statements (which are usually produced for both internal and external use), most businesses also find it useful to calculate accounting ratios based on their financial records. The three main financial statements are normally used as the basis for the calculation of the accounting ratios.

## *The Profit and Loss Account*

The profit and loss account is used by businesses as a statement for both internal and external reporting. The form that it takes differs according to its use, but nonetheless it will still provide the same basic information. For example, the profit and loss account used for internal reporting may be produced on a monthly basis and go into great detail, whereas the profit and loss account that is produced as a statutory requirement at the end of the financial year will take a much reduced form and will contain much less detail.

What does the profit and loss account show? The profit and loss account details the business income and expenditure over the course of the financial year. The business expenditure is matched to the business income, and where the business income is greater than the expenditure, a profit is recorded. Conversely, where the business expenditure is greater than the income, a loss is recorded.

It is an important feature of the profit and loss account, and a requirement of accounting conventions, that the business properly matches its income and expenditure for the period for which the profit and loss account is drawn up. This ensures that the profit (or loss) calculated is not overstated and that a true reflection of the business's trading activities is shown.

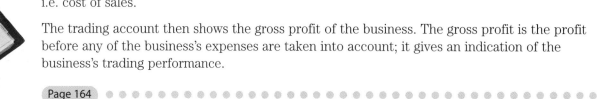

The profit and loss account is a continuation of the business's trading account. The trading account records the difference between how much money the business generates from selling and how much the goods it is selling actually cost, i.e. cost of sales.

The trading account then shows the gross profit of the business. The gross profit is the profit before any of the business's expenses are taken into account; it gives an indication of the business's trading performance.

A simple trading account might look something like this:

General Traders

Trading Account for the year ending 31 March 2006

|  | £ | £ |
|---|---|---|
| Turnover |  | 150,000 |
| Cost of Sales |  |  |
| Opening stock of goods | 20,000 |  |
| Purchases | 75,000 |  |
|  | 95,000 |  |
| Less Closing stock of goods | (25,000) | 70,000 |
| GROSS PROFIT |  | 80,000 |

The profit and loss account follows on from the trading account and a simple version would look something like this:

General Traders

Profit and Loss Account for the year ending 31 March 2006

|  | £ | £ |
|---|---|---|
| Gross Profit |  | 80,000 |
| Other Operating Income |  |  |
| Rent received | 9,000 |  |
| Interest received | 1,000 | 10,000 |
|  |  | 90,000 |
| Expenses |  |  |
| Rent and rates | 25,000 |  |
| Heating and lighting | 8,000 |  |
| Telephone | 900 |  |
| Advertising | 250 |  |
| Postage | 400 |  |
| Wages and salaries | 45,000 |  |
| Insurance | 2,000 | 81,550 |
| NET PROFIT |  | 8,450 |

A more complicated format of the profit and loss account is used for limited companies. Limited companies fall under the jurisdiction of the Companies Act 1985 and they must produce their year-end accounts in accordance with the formats prescribed by the law. All other types of business produce a similar type of profit and loss account, but it will usually be less detailed than that required by the limited company.

BUSINESS DECISION AREAS

An example of a profit and loss account for a limited company is shown below:

*Johnston Computer Systems Ltd*

*Trading, Profit and Loss Account for the year ending 30 June 2006*

| | £ | £ |
|---|---|---|
| TURNOVER | | 5,200,000 |
| Cost of Goods Sold | | 2,100,000 |
| GROSS PROFIT | | 3,100,000 |
| Operating Expenses | 120,000 | |
| Other Operating Income | 100,000 | |
| Net Operating Expenses | | 20,000 |
| OPERATING PROFIT | | 3,080,000 |
| Investment Income | | 320,000 |
| NET PROFIT BEFORE INTEREST PAYABLE | | 3,400,000 |
| Interest Payable | | 260,000 |
| PROFIT ON ORDINARY ACTIVITES BEFORE TAX | 3,140,000 | |
| Corporation Tax | | 740,000 |
| PROFIT ON ORDINARY ACTIVITIES AFTER TAX | 2,400,000 | |
| Preference Dividend | | 350,000 |
| PROFIT ATTRIBUTABLE TO ORDINARY SHAREHOLDERS | | 2,050,000 |
| Ordinary Dividend | 150,000 | |
| Transfer to reserves | 700,000 | 850,000 |
| UNAPPROPRIATED PROFIT FOR THIS YEAR | | 1,200,000 |
| Balance brought forward | | 2,700,000 |
| **Balance carried forward** | | **3,900,000** |

If you have access to the internet, you can look at a huge variety of company reports online at the following site – Company Annual Reports On Line: www.carol.co.uk. Once you have registered, you can choose which accounts you would like to access. This is a free service.

An example of a company profit and loss account is shown below:

### Summary of consolidated profit and loss account

Year ended 31 December

| 2004 US $m | Summary of consolidated profit and loss account | 2004 €m | 2003 €m | 2002 €m | 2001 €m | 2000 €m |
|---|---|---|---|---|---|---|
| 2,773 | Net interest income before exceptional items | 2,036 | 1,934 | 2,351 | 2,258 | 2,022 |
| – | Deposit interest retention tax | – | – | – | – | (113) |
| 2,773 | Net interest income after exceptional items | 2,036 | 1,934 | 2,351 | 2,258 | 1,909 |
| 25 | Other finance income | 18 | 12 | 62 | 67 | 71 |
| 1,648 | Other income before exceptional item | 1,210 | 1,230 | 1,514 | 1,426 | 1,304 |
| – | Exceptional foreign exchange dealing losses | – | – | – | (789) | – |

*continued* ➤

| 2004 US $m | Summary of consolidated profit and loss account | 2004 € m | 2003 € m | 2002 € m | 2001 € m | 2000 € m |
|---|---|---|---|---|---|---|
| 4,446 | Total operating income after exceptional items | 3,264 | 3,176 | 3,927 | 2,962 | 3,284 |
| 2,569 | Total operating expenses | 1,886 | 1,960 | 2,318 | 2,284 | 1,997 |
| 1,877 | Group operating profit before provisions | 1,378 | 1,216 | 1,609 | 678 | 1,287 |
| 184 | Provisions | 135 | 177 | 251 | 204 | 134 |
| 1,693 | Group operating profit | 1,243 | 1,039 | 1,358 | 474 | 1,153 |
| 274 | Share of operating profits of associated undertakings | 201 | 143 | 9 | 4 | 3 |
| – | Share of restructuring & integration costs in associated undertakings | – | (20) | – | – | – |
| (71) | Amortisation of goodwill on acquisition of associated undertakings | (52) | (42) | – | – | – |
| 12 | Profit on disposal of property | 9 | 32 | 5 | 6 | 5 |
| 23 | Profit/(loss) on disposal of business | 17 | (141) | – | 93 | – |
| 1,931 | Group profit before taxation | 1,418 | 1,011 | 1,372 | 577 | 1,161 |
| 458 | Taxation on ordinary activities | 336 | 318 | 306 | 55 | 319 |
| 41 | Equity and non-equity minority interests | 30 | 11 | 24 | 23 | 38 |
| 7 | Dividends on non-equity shares | 5 | 5 | 8 | 15 | 20 |
| 1,425 | Group profit attributable to the ordinary shareholders of Allied Irish Banks, p.l.c | 1,047 | 677 | 1,034 | 484 | 784 |
| 696 | Dividends on equity shares | 511 | 452 | 429 | 380 | 335 |
| 2.0 | Dividend cover – times | 2.0 | 1.5 | 2.4 | 1.3 | 2.3 |
| 167.4c | Earnings per € 0.32 share – basic | 122.9c | 78.8c | 119.1c | 56.2c | 91.6c |
| 181.3c | Earnings per € 0.32 share – adjusted | 133.1c | 109.5c | 122.7c | 108.6c | 106.7c |
| 166.7c | Earnings per € 0.32 share – diluted | 124.4c | 78.4c | 117.9c | 55.9c | 91.0c |

**Fig 6.5** Allied Irish Bank

The type of profit and loss account that is produced will depend on the type of business, e.g. sole trader, partnership, private limited company or public limited company.

Partnerships and limited companies produce an extra and final section in their profit and loss accounts called the **appropriation account**. This simply shows how the business's profit or loss is to be shared. Profits may be distributed in a number of different ways:

- payment of corporation tax
- payment of a dividend to shareholders
- appropriated among the business partners
- retained in the business.

BUSINESS DECISION AREAS

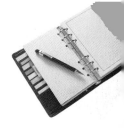

BUSINESS DECISION AREAS

| Profit and Loss Account terminology | |
| --- | --- |
| Trading account | Provides a summary of the business's trading activity during the financial year |
| Sales | Monies that the business has received from selling goods and/or services |
| Turnover/net sales | The value of the business's sales less the value of any returns |
| Cost of sales | The cost of the sales to the business, i.e. before a sales or profit margin is added |
| Opening stock | The value of the stock of goods at the start of the financial period |
| Purchases | The cost of goods that the business has bought for resale to its customers |
| Carriage inwards | The cost of transporting or delivering goods purchased by the business for resale |
| Purchase returns | The value of goods purchased but returned to the supplier, e.g. wrong colour, faulty |
| Closing stock | The value of unsold stock at the end of the financial period |
| Gross profit/loss | The profit (or loss) recorded as the difference between the business's sales and purchases |
| Expenses | Any expenses incurred by the business in the course of its normal operation |
| Net profit/loss | The profit (or loss) recorded after all business expenses have been deducted |
| Corporation tax | A tax on business profits payable to the Government |
| Dividend | Proportion of the business profit paid to shareholders and dependent on the number of shares that they own |
| Unappropriated profit | Profit retained in the business, i.e. not distributed to owners or shareholders |

## The balance sheet

The profit and loss account records a history of the business activity throughout the financial year, but the balance sheet shows a snapshot at a particular date in time; usually the last day of the financial year.

Whereas the profit and loss account details trading activity, the balance sheet records the financial worth and the financial position of the business at a particular point in time. For this reason alone, the balance sheet of any company is out of date by the time it is published. It forms part of the **historic accounting** records of the business.

Historic accounting is so called because it uses information from the past to compile statements and reports that are useful to other businesses and individuals.

The balance sheet shows three different things:

● assets

● liabilities

● capital.

We can combine each of these three categories of items in the accounting equation:

CAPITAL = ASSETS – LIABILITIES

| Balance Sheet terminology | |
|---|---|
| Fixed asset | Something the business owns and depends on to operate on a daily basis. Usually has a degree of permanence |
| Current asset | Assets that are likely to be changed into cash in the short term. They frequently change in value |
| Current liability | Something that the business owes money for in the short term, i.e. a debt. They must usually be paid within a period of 12 months or one year |
| Long term liability | Debts of the business that are not due to be repaid for more than 12 months |
| Capital | A special kind of liability. The money invested by the owner(s) of the business to set it up. This money is owed back to the owner(s) by the business |
| Net current assets | This is the difference in value between the total current assets and the total current liabilities. The total of the current assets should normally be more than the total of the current liabilities |
| Reserves | Money and profits that are retained in the business, perhaps to buy new assets or to safeguard against future losses |
| Net assets/net worth | The financial value or worth of the business |

The balance sheet is presented in two parts. The top half of the balance sheet displays the assets and liabilities of the business, and the bottom half displays the capital. **Assets** are things that the business owns, and these are categorised as either fixed or current. **Liabilities** are the opposite of assets and are things that the business owes money for. They can be either current or long term.

**Fixed assets** are the productive assets of the business. Without these assets, the business would not be able to function on a day-to-day basis. These are things like buildings, machinery and other equipment. They are normally listed in descending order of permanence, i.e. the one that is expected to last the longest will be listed first.

**Current assets** are assets that change on a daily basis and can be turned easily into cash. They are listed in descending order of liquidity, i.e. how easily they can be turned into cash. The most illiquid (or most difficult to turn into cash) is usually listed first. Examples of current assets are money in the bank, stocks of goods and debtors.

**Current liabilities** (sometimes called creditors falling due within one year) are also listed on the top half of the balance sheet and are shown as a deduction from current assets. This is because the business will (eventually) turn all of its current assets into cash and subsequently use this cash to pay its current liabilities. These liabilities are known as current because they will normally have to be repaid within a period of 12 months. The most common example of a current liability is a creditor; i.e. people or other businesses to whom the business owes money for goods or services supplied on credit.

BUSINESS DECISION AREAS

The difference between the total current assets and the total current liabilities is highlighted on the balance sheet. This is known as **net current assets**. This figure is extremely important because it highlights the business's ability to meet its short-term debts. This figure should normally be positive, i.e. the total of current assets should always be more than the total of current liabilities. Where the total current liabilities is greater than the total current assets of the business, this shows that the company is in potential financial difficulty as it may be unable to meet its most immediately payable debts. In extreme cases, where the company does not have sufficient current assets to pay its short term debts, it may have to resort to selling off some of its fixed assets to survive. This is, however, a dangerous practice as without its fixed (productive) assets, the company will not be able to function properly and may ultimately fail.

**Long-term liabilities** (sometimes called creditors falling due after more than one year) are listed on the top half of the balance sheet after net current assets. These represent liabilities that the business must repay after more than one year. Examples include debentures and other longer-term loans which may or may not be secured on assets belonging to the business.

The total of fixed assets plus the net current assets minus long-term liabilities is known as the business's Net Worth. This means the value of the business in monetary terms on the particular date specified on the balance sheet. The relative usefulness of the balance sheet is however limited, as it only provides a snapshot of the business, and like other accounting records, is based on transactions from the business history.

The bottom half of the balance sheet represents the 'capital' side of the accounting equation. Depending on the type of business, this half of the balance sheet may comprise owner's funds or share capital contributed by the shareholders of the company.

As the balance sheet is comprised of two halves that represent the accounting equation, the total of the top half of the balance sheet must equal the total of the bottom half of the balance sheet; i.e. the accounting equation must be satisfied.

An example of a balance sheet is given on p169.

Example of a published balance sheet for a limited company:

| | | | | Year ended 31 December | | |
| 2004 US $m | Summary of consolidated balance sheet | 2004 € m | 2003 € m | 2002 € m | 2001 € m | 2000 € m |
| --- | --- | --- | --- | --- | --- | --- |
| 139,261 | Total assets | 102,240 | 80,960 | 85,821 | 89,061 | 80,318 |
| 91,473 | Total loans | 67,156 | 53,326 | 58,483 | 57,445 | 50,239 |
| 113,913 | Total deposits | 83,630 | 66,195 | 72,190 | 72,813 | 65,210 |
| | | | | | | |
| 2,619 | Dated capital notes | 1,923 | 1,276 | 1,287 | 1,594 | 1,836 |
| 470 | Undated capital notes | 345 | 357 | 389 | 426 | 413 |
| 677 | Reserve capital instruments | 497 | 497 | 496 | 496 | – |
| 1,651 | Equity and non-equity minority interests in subsidiaries | 1,212 | 158 | 274 | 312 | 272 |
| 248 | Shareholders' funds: non-equity interests | 182 | 196 | 235 | 179 | 264 |
| 7,354 | Shareholders' funds: equity interests | 5,399 | 4,942 | 4,180 | 4,554 | 4,719 |
| 13,019 | Total capital resources | 9,558 | 7,426 | 6,861 | 7,661 | 7,504 |

**Fig 6.7** Allied Irish Bank, summary of consolidated balance sheet

*Patrick Media Productions Ltd*

*Balance Sheet as at 30 April 2006*

| | £000 | £000 | £000 |
|---|---|---|---|
| **Fixed Assets** | | | |
| Premises | | 1,500 | |
| Computer equipment | | 800 | |
| Motor vehicles | | 200 | |
| | | | 2,500 |
| **Current assets** | | | |
| Stocks | 600 | | |
| Debtors | 400 | | |
| Cash at bank | 200 | 1,200 | |
| **Creditors due in < 1 year** | | | |
| Trade creditors | 500 | | |
| Taxation | 150 | | |
| Dividends | 100 | 750 | |
| **Net current assets** | | | 450 |
| **Total assets less current liabilities** | | | 2,950 |
| **Creditors due in > 1 year** | | | |
| Bank loan | | 200 | |
| Debenture loan | | 1,000 | 1,200 |
| **Net assets** | | | 1,750 |
| **Capital and reserves** | | | |
| Ordinary share capital | | 1,000 | |
| Retained profits | | 750 | |
| **Net worth** | | | 1,750 |

# Topic Cashflow management

Cash and cash management are the most important aspects of business. Without cash, the business will fail. In a recent online survey of the top 65 reasons for business failures, poor cash management was the second most popular reason.

The role of cash in any business at any time (whether business is good or bad) cannot be underestimated. The cashflow cycle demonstrates the role of cash in business. Take a minute to study the following diagram.

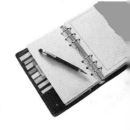

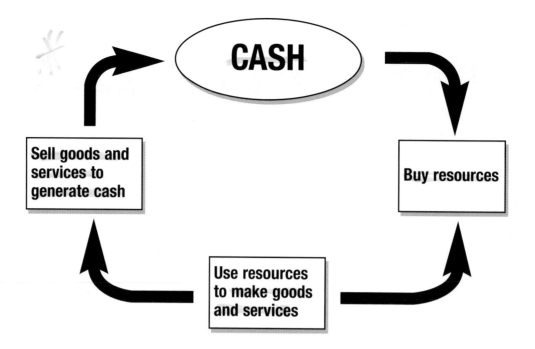

As the diagram suggests, the movement of cash (or cashflow) in and out of the business is central to the success and efficient operation of the business. We have already looked at the component parts of the balance sheet and identified the need for the business to maintain sufficient liquid assets to meet its ongoing debts. The concept of cashflow is centred around liquidity, which is the provision of or the ability to have access to cash or near cash assets to meet the everyday commitments of the business.

The terminology of cashflow is concerned with the movement of money in and out of the business. In this context, the following terms are used:

- Cash inflow – a movement of cash into the business, e.g. cash sales

- Cash outflow – a movement of cash out of the business, e.g. cash purchases.

A cashflow statement is produced as part of the year-end accounts of a limited company and also as a useful financial statement by many other businesses. It shows the movements of cash in and out of the business over the course of the financial year. The term 'cash' has a special meaning in the context of a cashflow statement and can mean cash, money in the bank and other cash equivalent assets (assets that can be converted to cash quickly).

The cashflow statement itself is constructed from the information contained in the profit and loss account and the balance sheet. When a cashflow statement is produced at times other than the financial year end, the business will have to collate information from its accounting records in order to produce it.

The Accounting Standards Board governs the accounting profession, and encourages all businesses, no matter how large or small, to produce cashflow statements on a regular basis. As we have already mentioned, most businesses fail because they run out of cash and not because they lack success or profits. A cashflow statement provides an easy means by which to track the movements of cash.

Here are some common examples of inflows and outflows of cash:

| INFLOW<br>Cash coming into the business | OUTFLOW<br>Cash going out of the business |
| --- | --- |
| Decrease in debtors | Decrease in creditors |
| Increase in creditors | Dividend payment |
| Loan received | Drawings |
| New capital investment | Increase in debtors |
| Profits | Loan repaid |
| Sale of a fixed asset | Losses |
| Sale of stock | Purchase of a fixed asset<br>Purchase of stock |

## Activity

Think about each of the following situations and whether or not a cashflow statement would help to identify problems.

- The local newsagent (a sole trader) makes £45,000 profit this year but has £55,000 in drawings.

- Karen and Kevin buy some business premises and plan to open a new gym. The building is very run down and needs a lot of work before they will be able to open for business. The building works will cost in the region of £60,000. This money is needed before they can open for business and offer memberships to the public.

- A new supermarket has opened less than 100 metres from Jim's local convenience store. He is finding that much of his business has been lost to the supermarket and his takings are down. He decides to offer all his customers credit on all purchases over £25. Business soon picks up again but he finds that many of his customers take more than a month to settle their accounts, while he has to settle the business credit accounts in just 14 days. He is worried that if he withdraws his credit facility he will lose customers again but, at the same time, he is finding it increasingly difficult to meet all of the business expenses and bill on time.

Example of a cashflow statement:

**FORD MOTOR COMPANY AND SUBSIDIARIES CONDENSED CONSOLIDATED STATEMENT OF CASHFLOWS**

| For the periods ended June 30, 2005 and 2004 (in millions) | First Half 2005 | 2004 (unaudited) |
|---|---|---|
| **Cash and cash equivalents at January 1** | 23,510 | 23,208 |
| Cash flows from operating activities before securities trading | 18,275 | 13,235 |
| Net sales/(purchases) of trading securities | (3,679) | (723) |
| Net cash flows from operating activities | 14,596 | 12,512 |
| **Cash flows from investing activities** | | |
| Capital expenditures | (3,572) | (2,780) |
| Acquisitions of retail and other finance receivables and operating leases | (28,951) | (31,727) |
| Collections of retail and other finance receivables and operating leases | 25,150 | 23,795 |
| Net acquisitions of daily rental vehicles | (2,997) | (2,902) |
| Purchases of securities | (2,451) | (6,026) |
| Sales and maturities of securities | 2,395 | 5,703 |
| Proceeds from sales of retail and other finance receivables and operating leases | 12,506 | 3,760 |
| Proceeds from sale of businesses | 2,070 | 125 |
| Cash paid for acquisitions | (1,296) | (30) |
| Other | 71 | (48) |
| Net cash (used in)/provided by investing activities | 2,925 | (10,130) |
| **Cash flows from financing activities** | | |
| Cash dividends | (367) | (366) |
| Net sales/(purchases) of Common Stock | 184 | (101) |
| Changes in short-term debt | 821 | 8,412 |
| Proceeds from issuance of other debt | 14,765 | 7,831 |
| Principal payments on other debt | (25,769) | (24,401) |
| Other | (6) | (35) |
| Net cash (used in)/provided by financing activities | (10,372) | (8,660) |
| Effect of exchange rate changes on cash | (526) | (145) |
| **Net increase/(decrease) in cash and cash equivalents** | 6,623 | (6,423) |
| **Cash and cash equivalents at March 31** | 30,133 | 16,785 |

*Source:* www.carol.co.uk

# Topic Budgets

A budget is simply a statement of anticipated future expenditure. It usually covers a specific time period, e.g. a month or a year. Budgets are usually financial in nature although they can be expressed in other units.

The main uses of budgets are:

- Monitoring and control – setting a budget and then comparing it to actual performance means that comparisons can be made on a regular basis and changes adopted quickly to remedy problems.

- To gain information – budgets allow managers to see how well the business is performing.

- To set targets – this gives managers and employees limits to reach.

- To delegate authority – the use of budgets means that managers can give responsibility to employees.

**Cash budgets** are a common type of budget that are used by most businesses to monitor, control, obtain and present information.

They can be used to monitor the cash position of a particular department, section or project, or the business as a whole. They can also be used as a management decision-making tool to assess the validity of a particular project or scenario. A cash projection may be used as part of a submission to a lender to secure finance.

Budgets are often produced using accounting software or a generic spreadsheet package. This means that changes can be made to the budget very easily, and the effects of these changes will be automatically updated in the rest of the budget.

An example of a cash budget is shown below:

**Airwave Ltd**

| Budgets for the 6 month period – April 2006 to Sept 2006 | | | | | | | |
|---|---|---|---|---|---|---|---|
| **Cash Receipts Budget:** | Apr (£) | May (£) | Jun (£) | Jul (£) | Aug (£) | Sep (£) | Total (£) |
| Receipts from debtors | 5,000 | 5,000 | 6,000 | 7,000 | 4,000 | 6,000 | **33,000** |
| *Total Cash Inflows* | 5,000 | 5,000 | 6,000 | 7,000 | 4,000 | 6,000 | **33,000** |
| **Cash Payments Budget:** | Apr (£) | May (£) | Jun (£) | Jul (£) | Aug (£) | Sep (£) | Total (£) |
| Payments to creditors (raw materials) | 2,000 | 3,000 | 4,000 | 4,000 | 3,000 | 2,000 | **18,000** |
| Direct labour | 2,000 | 2,000 | 2,500 | 2,500 | 1,100 | 1,100 | **11,200** |
| Variable overheads | 300 | 400 | 300 | 200 | 400 | 500 | **2,100** |
| Maintenance contracts | 100 | 200 | 300 | 400 | 400 | 400 | **1,800** |
| *Total Cash Outflows* | 4,400 | 5,600 | 7,100 | 7,100 | 4,900 | 4,000 | **33,100** |
| **Cash Budget:** | Apr (£) | May (£) | Jun (£) | Jul (£) | Aug (£) | Sep (£) | Total (£) |
| Opening Cash/Bank Balance | 1,000 | 1,600 | 1,000 | (100) | (200) | (1,100) | **1,000** |
| Cash Inflows | 5,000 | 5,000 | 6,000 | 7,000 | 4,000 | 6,000 | **33,000** |
| Cash Outflows | 4,400 | 5,600 | 7,100 | 7,100 | 4,900 | 4,000 | **33,100** |
| *Closing Cash/Bank Balance* | 1,600 | 1,000 | (100) | (200) | (1,100) | 900 | **900** |

**Fig 6.11** A cash budget

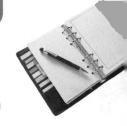

Sidebar: BUSINESS DECISION AREAS

The cash budget is just one example of the use of a budget. It is normal for other budgets to 'feed into' the cash budget. These other budgets are usually referred to as **functional budgets**.

An example of a functional budget is shown below:

**The Central Company Ltd**

**Budgets for the 3 month period – April 2006 to June 2006**

| Raw materials usage budget (units): | | | | | |
| --- | --- | --- | --- | --- | --- |
| | kg Per Unit | Apr (kg) | May (kg) | Jun (kg) | Total (kg) |
| Opening stock | | 15,000 | 21,290 | 25,085 | **15,000** |
| Purchases | | 5,000 | 2,500 | 3,000 | **10,500** |
| Materials available for production | | 20,000 | 23,790 | 28,085 | **71,875** |
| Used for budgeted production | 5.00 | (1,290) | (1,295) | (1,290) | **(3,875)** |
| Closing stock | | 21,290 | 25,085 | 29,375 | **29,375** |

**Fig 6.12** A functional budget

The main benefits to management of using cash budgets can be summarised as:

- **Planning** – look ahead to set aims and strategies. This allows problem-solving to be planned, rather than having to react to situations as they happen.

- **Organisation** – allows the right resources to be in the right place at the right time.

- **Command** – when management are able to make informed decisions, this enables them to instruct their subordinates. The management will have access to all the budgets for each department which will be fed into the master budget, e.g. the cash budget.

- **Co-ordinate** – management can give instructions to those in charge of departmental budgets and keep a clear overview of the business as a whole.

- **Control** – evaluation and review of budgets allows management to exert control over the organisation.

- **Delegation** – management should make subordinates responsible for a suitable range of tasks and give them the authority to carry them out.

- **Motivation** – management have a responsibility to motivate their staff. This can be done through setting realistic targets in the budgets and introducing concepts and practices such as teamwork, empowerment and incentives for meeting targets or operating within budget.

## Activity

Prepare a simple cash budget of your own, detailing your income and expenditure over the course of a four-week period. Do you have enough money to operate?

# Topic Ratio analysis

## Interpretation of profit and loss account, balance sheet and cashflow statement

The final accounts of a business are made up of:

- Profit and loss account – to calculate the profit earned by the business over the last year

- Balance sheet – to show the assets and liabilities of the business

- Cashflow statement – to show all the money that has flowed into and out of the business over the course of the last year.

These financial statements are of limited use if we just look at the figures as they are presented. Careful interpretation of the final accounts can give much more information. One tool which can be used is ratio analysis which is considered below. Another useful source of information is statements issued by the company themselves. Consider the statement that follows.

### Info Point

**TESCO PLC**

**INTERIM RESULTS 2005/6**

**24 Weeks ended 13 August 2005**

**TESCO makes good first half progress – oil price a concern**

Terry Leahy, Chief Executive, comments:

'By improving the shopping experience for customers in our businesses around the world, we have been able to deliver another good performance in a more challenging year. Looking forward, the accumulating effects of rising oil-related costs, both on consumer confidence and on our business, are a cause for concern, but we remain confident that we will make further progress in the second half.'

**Group highlights**

- Sales up 14.1 per cent to £18.8bn, up 12.4 per cent at constant exchange rates

- Pre-tax profit up 18.7 per cent to £908m

- Profit growth of 14.4 per cent to £940m using pre-IFRS underlying profit definition (last year £822m)

- Diluted earnings per share up 15.7 per cent to 8.10p

- Interim dividend per share up 10.5 per cent to 2.53p

- On track to create a further 7,500 new jobs in the UK and 9,500 worldwide in the second half

**UK**

- Sales up 11.1 per cent to £14.6bn

*continued* ➤

BUSINESS DECISION AREAS

- Operating profit up 19.2 per cent to £801m

- Like-for-like sales up 8.2 per cent, up 6.7 per cent excluding petrol

- Deflation of 2 per cent (excluding petrol) as we cut prices again for customers

- One million more customers join Clubcard in its 10th anniversary year

- Second quarter like-for-like sales up 7.6 per cent, up 6.6 per cent excluding petrol

**International**

- International now 54 per cent of group selling space, making a significant contribution to group growth

- Sales up 25.6 per cent to £4.2 bn, up 17.3 per cent at constant exchange rates

- Operating profit up 23.5 per cent to £163m, up 16.0 per cent at constant rates

- Positive customer response to strategic investment in Central Europe

**Non-food**

- UK non-food sales up 13 per cent to £2.8 bn, including growth of 17 per cent in home entertainment, 15 per cent in clothing and 33 per cent in seasonal

- Extended Extra stores at Bar Hill and Slough feature wider non-food ranges

**Retailing services**

- Tesco Personal Finance (TPF) customer accounts grow to over 5m. TPF delivers £50m profit – Tesco share is £25m.

- Tesco.com sales up 31 per cent to £401m and profit up 37 per cent to £21m

- Tesco Mobile customer numbers up to 750,000

*Source*: www.tesco.com

Interpretation of the profit and loss account may include answering questions such as:

- How did this year's trading compare with last year's?

- How did this year's trading compare with our rivals?

- Has the net profit improved when compared to last year?

- Are we making efficient use of our stock?

Interpretation of a balance sheet may include answering questions such as:

- Do we have sufficient liquid assets to meet our short-term debts?

- Are we making enough use of free credit facilities available to us?

- Is our level of debt comparable to that of our competitors?

Interpretation of a cashflow statement may include answering questions such as:

- Has the net debt position of the business changed dramatically over the last year? If so, why?

- Have we kept proper control of cashflow throughout the year?

- How does our liquidity compare to our rivals?

## *Accounting ratios*

Accounting ratios are used as a tool in the decision-making process and as an aid to financial interpretation and planning. They may be used by managers within the business, as well as outsiders who are interested in the performance of the business.

Ratios can be categorised according to the function that they perform:

- Profitability

- Liquidity

- Efficiency.

Several different ratios can be calculated under each of the headings. Comparisons can be made between different years for the same business, with other businesses in the same sector, or with averages for a particular business sector. This process is often referred to as **ratio analysis**.

Ratio analysis may also be used for more sinister purposes, e.g. by another business or individual planning a takeover. It may also prove to be a useful tool in the forecasting or budgeting process.

It is worth noting, however, that accounting ratios have their limitations:

- The accounting information used to calculate the ratios is historic, i.e. it is based on information that is out of date.

- When comparisons are made with other businesses, the comparison is only valid where the business is of the same type and size.

- Comparisons with other businesses can be difficult as many businesses publish only very limited financial information.

- Comparisons must be made using the same ratio calculations – many businesses 'tweak' the ratio formulas to suit their own needs.

- When comparisons are made over a series of years, either for the same business or in the same business sector, the external effects of the general economy are not reflected in the ratio calculations, and this must be taken into account.

- Comparisons of ratios with different businesses in the same sector may be meaningless if the ratios are not calculated on the same basis, i.e. using the same formulae.

- Ratios are of little use on their own. They must be used as an aid to interpretation and in the context of the business sector to which they apply. It is, therefore, essential that the user is also able to understand both how the particular business operates and how it reports its financial results.

- Other sources of information should also be utilised when interpreting the accounts, such as the directors' report, auditors' report, notes to the accounts, accounting policies of the business.

BUSINESS DECISION AREAS

- The users of financial ratios must beware of 'window dressing'. This is where a company temporarily improves its working capital (net current assets) in order to improve its ratios. This effect can be achieved through increasing stock levels or taking out a short-term loan.

The users of financial information can include stakeholders in the business, investors, creditors, customers and employees. They will want to know the answers to questions such as:

- Is the business profitable?
- Can the business pay its debts on time?
- How is the business financed?
- What percentage of the full business worth is financed?
- How does this year's performance compare with last year's?
- How does the performance of the business compare to other businesses in the same sector?

Ratio analysis can provide easy answers to all of these questions without the need to pore over pages and pages of accounts. If you have had the opportunity to access company accounts online at www.carol.co.uk or been able to look at a set of published company accounts, you will appreciate that it can be difficult to interpret the huge amount of information provided.

The most common ratios that are calculated are:

- Profitability
  a) gross profit as a percentage of sales
  b) gross profit as a percentage of cost of goods sold
  c) net profit as a percentage of sales

- Liquidity
  a) current ratio
  b) acid test ratio

- Efficiency
  a) return on capital employed.

For each of the ratios that we will analyse, we will make use of the summarised financial statements of Lena's Laundry Services Ltd which follow:

| Profit and Loss Accounts for the years ending 30 June | Year 1 £000s | Year 2 £000s |
|---|---|---|
| Turnover | 850 | 900 |
| Gross profit | 90 | 110 |
| Interest payable | (15) | (15) |
| Taxation | (50) | (60) |
| Net profit | 25 | 35 |
| Dividends | (15) | (20) |
| Retained profits | 10 | 15 |
| Note to the accounts: | | |
| Cost of goods sold | 600 | 700 |

*continued* ➤

| Balance Sheets as at 30 June | Year1 £000s | Year 2 £000s |
|---|---|---|
| Fixed assets | 600 | 700 |
| Current assets | | |
| Stock | 300 | 350 |
| Debtors | 200 | 100 |
| Cash | 50 | 250 |
| | 550 | 700 |
| Less current liabilities | (250) | (350) |
| Net current assets | 300 | 350 |
| **Net assets** | **900** | **1050** |
| Financed by: | | |
| Shareholders' funds | | |
| Ordinary shares | 700 | 800 |
| Share premium | 60 | 135 |
| Retained profits | 10 | 15 |
| | **780** | **950** |
| 15% debentures | 120 | 100 |
| **Capital employed** | **900** | **1050** |

## Profitability ratios

### Gross profit as a percentage of sales

This ratio is used to calculate the gross profit as a percentage of sales turnover. Where the percentage is high, it may indicate that the business has a prudent buying policy. Changes in the ratio can be caused by an increase or a decrease in the selling price (usually a deliberate company policy) or an increase or a decrease in the cost of goods sold (usually outside the company's control).

The formula used is:

(**Gross profit ÷ Sales**) × 100%

### Gross profit as a percentage of cost of goods sold

This ratio is used to calculate the gross profit as a percentage of cost of goods sold. Where the percentage is high, it may indicate that the business has a prudent buying policy. Changes in the ratio can be caused by an increase or a decrease in the cost of goods sold (usually outside the company's control).

The formula used is:

(**Gross profit ÷ cost of goods sold**) × 100%

### Net profit as a percentage of sales

This ratio is used to calculate the return on sales when compared to the total costs of the business. Where a low figure is calculated, this shows that the company's expenses may be high and should be further investigated. This ratio is often used to highlight efficiency and control of costs.

The formula used is:

(**Net profit ÷ sales**) × 100%

## Liquidity ratios

### Current ratio

The current ratio is used to indicate the business's ability to meet its short-term debts without having to borrow money. There is no ideal figure for this ratio although it should normally fall within the region of 1:1 and 3:1. Where the ratio is very low, this indicates that the business may have problems in meeting its short-term debts. Conversely, where the ratio is high, although this indicates that there is more than enough money to cover short-term business debts, it can also indicate that there is too much cash in the business not being utilised to best advantage. Spare cash can be invested even in the short term, and earn additional income for the business.

The formula used is:

**Current assets : Current liabilities**

### Acid test ratio

The acid test ratio is similar to the current ratio, although it takes into account the fact that stocks of raw materials and goods for resale may take some time to be turned into cash. The business's ability to pay its short-term debts is therefore assessed without the inclusion of the value of stocks. The average figure of 1:1 should be used as a guideline, although anything less than this would indicate that the business would not be able to meet its short-term debts without selling stock or borrowing money. It is worth noting that some businesses can operate with an acid test ratio of less than 1:1, and the typical ratio will depend on the type of business.

The formula used is:

**Current assets – stock : Current liabilities**

## Efficiency ratios

### Return on capital employed (ROCE)

This ratio measures how well or how badly a business has utilised the capital that has been invested in it. This gives a more useful interpretation of performance than merely looking at the profit figure.

For example, imagine that Company X reports a profit of £1m and Company Y reports a profit of £500,000. Company X would appear to be the more successful company based on the information provided, but a quick calculation taking into account the capital invested in these companies shows that Company X earned £1m profit from capital invested of £10m, while Company Y earned profit of £500,000 from just £4m capital invested. Company Y has made better use of its capital, as Company X used more than twice the amount of capital to produce just double the profit of Company Y.

The formula used to calculate return on capital employed:

**(Net Profit ÷ capital employed) × 100%**

The table below shows the ratios for Lena's Laundry Services Ltd.

| Lena's Laundry Services Ltd – Financial Ratios | Year 1 | Year 2 |
|---|---|---|
| Gross profit as a percentage of sales | 10.6% | 12.2% |
| Gross profit as a percentage of cost of goods sold | 15% | 15.7% |
| Net profit as a percentage of sales | 2.9% | 3.9% |
| Current ratio | 2.2:1 | 2.0:1 |
| Acid test ratio | 1:1 | 1:1 |
| Return on capital employed | 2.8% | 3.3% |

### Activity

If you have access to the internet, find the accounts for the year ended March 2005 for Tesco. These can be accessed through the website www.tesco.com – follow the links via Corporate Information to Inside Tesco | Investor Centre | Presentations and Results | Annual Reports | Annual Report and Financial Statements (PDF).

The following ratios have been calculated from the figures in Tesco's annual report.

| Tesco – Financial ratios | February 2005 |
|---|---|
| Gross profit as a percentage of sales | 5.3% |
| Gross profit as a percentage of cost of goods sold | 6.1% |
| Net profit as a percentage of sales | 3.7% |
| Current ratio | 0.57:1 |
| Acid test ratio | 0.35:1 |
| Return on capital employed | 8.6% |

By comparison, the accounting ratios for the period to the end of February 2004 are:

| Tesco – Financial ratios | March 2004 |
|---|---|
| Gross profit as a percentage of sales | 5.2% |
| Gross profit as a percentage of cost of goods sold | 6.0% |
| Net profit as a percentage of sales | 1.7% |
| Current ratio | 0.57:1 |
| Acid test ratio | 0.35:1 |
| Return on capital employed | 7.3% |

Let us consider each of these ratios in turn.

### Gross profit as a percentage of sales

Tesco has a ratio of 5.3 per cent in 2005 and 5.2 per cent in 2004. This means that for every £100 of sales, Tesco made £5.30 in profit before expenses in 2005, and £5.20 in profit before expenses in 2004. Before expenses are taken into account, Tesco was marginally more profitable in 2005 compared to 2004.

### Gross profit as a percentage of cost of goods sold

Tesco has a ratio of 6.1 per cent in 2005 and 6.0 per cent in 2004. This means that for every £100 spent on the cost of sales, Tesco made a profit before expenses of £6.10 in 2005 compared to £6.00 in 2004.

### Net profit as a percentage of sales

Tesco has a net profit percentage of 3.7 per cent in 2005 and 1.7 per cent in 2004. This demonstrates that Tesco may have exerted better control over its business expenses in 2005 compared to 2004. The net profit percentage achieved in 2004 is very low, and it is encouraging to see that it has risen in 2005 despite little change in the gross profit percentage.

### Current ratio and acid test ratio

Both years have yielded very low current and acid test ratios. In fact, they are so low that neither of them would be able to meet their short-term debts if they became immediately payable. However, close inspection of the accounts reveals that neither the current assets nor the current liabilities are particularly substantial. Two conclusions can be drawn from this: any spare cash in the business is invested for maximum gain in the short term, and it is symptomatic of this business sector that these ratios are low (e.g. due to the nature of the goods sold).

### Return on capital employed

The return on capital employed for Tesco was 8.6 per cent in 2005 which represented an increase over the 7.3 per cent achieved in 2004. This means that for every £100 invested in the business, it produced a return of £7.30 in 2004 but rose to £8.30 in 2005. Tesco will be working hard to improve on this figure for 2006 and maximise the return for its investors.

### Conclusion

Care must be taken when using and interpreting accounting ratios. It must be remembered that they are of limited use in isolation, and their usefulness is only marginally increased when used in conjunction with other sources of information. They do, however, remain a popular and useful tool for quickly displaying financial statistics about a company's performance.

## Activity

The following companies (X and Y) operate as supermarkets, providing food and other goods and services to the public. Consider their accounting ratios which have been calculated for you.

| Financial ratios | Company X | Company Y |
|---|---|---|
| Gross profit as a percentage of sales | 8.6% | 5.1% |
| Gross profit as a percentage of cost of goods sold | 7.5% | 4.2% |
| Net profit as a percentage of sales | 6.3% | 2.8% |
| Current ratio | 2.2:1 | 0.76:1 |
| Acid test ratio | 1.9:1 | 0.45:1 |
| Return on capital employed | 10.5% | 3.6% |

Each of these businesses operates in the same sector and in direct competition with each other. Are their accounting ratios similar? Can you explain why there are similarities or differences?

# Topic Uses of financial information

Financial information can be gathered about a business from its financial statements. The main areas that they are likely to cover are profitability, liquidity, efficiency and capital structure.

Managers and other people who have an interest in the operation of the business will use this information to:

- review past performance and compare it with the most recent performance
- assist with planning for the future of the business.

Comparisons should also be made:

- with the same company over a different time period
- with competitors in the same line of business over the same periods of time.

Comparisons are important so that a true picture of the business performance can be drawn up. This also means that management can make informed decisions about the future of the business.

Analysis of financial data may also lead the business to focus on a particular area. For example, spiralling costs may lead to particular focus on one area of expenditure and investigation as to the reasons behind the increase.

Useful financial information should:

- be relevant to the group intending to use it
- be reliable and traceable to its source
- be free from bias and personal opinion
- be clear and understandable

- allow comparisons to be made easily
- be realistic and give a true and fair view
- be consistent
- be presented in a reasonable timescale
- not include irrelevant information
- be disclosed to give a rounded view, even where some of the information is 'not good'.

# Topic Users of financial information

The users of financial information are varied and the range of people who have an interest in the activities of business organisations continues to grow. The following list is not intended to be either prescriptive or exhaustive:

- shareholders
- potential shareholders
- short-term creditors
- long-term creditors
- government and local authorities
- competitors
- employees
- analysts
- management
- customers
- general public.

**Shareholders** have an interest in the financial information provided by a company as they can assess the performance of the board and so make further decisions about investment or disinvestment.

**Potential shareholders** use financial information to assess whether or not the company will be a worthwhile investment, or whether the risk attached is too great to bear.

**Short-term creditors** have an interest as they must decide whether or not credit should be granted in the first instance, and then to assess whether or not future debts will be paid.

**Long-term creditors** must decide whether or not to lend money. They will also be keen to assess whether they consider that interest payments can be made and if the amount of the loan will be able to be repaid when it falls due.

The **government** and **local authorities** will look beyond the financial statements and to the future plans of the business, which are often laid out in the directors' report. They may be interested to see if the company has future plans that will affect the local area. The government (Inland Revenue) will use the accounts to assess the amount of tax that is payable.

**Competitors** will look to see how the company has performed and if it has increased its market share. They will also be interested in any future plans that the company discloses, to see whether or not it conflicts with their own plans.

**Employees** are increasingly taking an interest in the activities of the companies that employ them. Their interest is often linked to the company's ability to pay for wage claims, although they may also be interested in the future viability of the business.

**Analysts** such as **economists** use the financial information as a basis for research, and to compile statistical records.

**Management** require financial information to evaluate their past performance. The results of this evaluation may be plans and predictions for future performance. Linked to this is the attempt to control the future performance of the business through past experiences.

**Customers** and the **general public** may look to the financial statements of a business to assess whether or not it is likely to continue to operate in the foreseeable future. There is also a general interest in business activities, e.g. what effect is Company X having on the environment?

## Activity

Using a copy of published accounts (paper copy or online), make a list of information that would be of interest to each of the groups listed above.

# End of chapter revision questions

1   What four main areas does financial information cover?

2   List some of the factors which may be taken into account when one business is deciding whether or not to provide a line of credit.

3   For what purpose might a manager use financial information?

4   List at least four characteristics of useful financial information.

5   List at least five users of financial information.

6   Using the users of financial information that you have just listed, suggest a reason for each of them to be using the information.

7   Why might an organisation be interested in calculating accounting ratios?

8   Name and describe the purpose of four accounting ratios.

**BUSINESS DECISION AREAS**

## Chapter Summary

At the end of this chapter you should make sure that you are aware of the following:

★ the role of the finance function in an organisation including:
   a) payment of wages
   b) payment of accounts
   c) maintenance of financial records

★ the purpose and use of:
   a) profit and loss account
   b) balance sheet
   c) cashflow statement

★ the main uses of financial information

★ the main users of financial information and the reasons for use

★ ratio analysis

★ budgets are statements showing future expenditure; a management tool; useful for monitoring and controlling business operations

★ they are also useful for gaining information, setting targets and delegating authority

★ a cash budget is a good example of a budget

★ budgets are most easily used when created using a piece of appropriate computer software

★ accounting ratios can be calculated for any business that produces financial reports

★ ratios are normally calculated to highlight the areas of profitability, liquidity and efficiency

★ the use of accounting ratios has limitations

★ the main profitability ratios are:
   a) gross profit as a percentage of sales
   b) gross profit as a percentage of cost of goods sold
   c) net profit as a percentage of sales

★ the main liquidity ratios are:
   a) current ratio
   b) acid test ratio

★ the main efficiency ratio is:
   a) return on capital employed

★ calculation of ratios is not enough; analysis must also take place

★ analysis of ratios may include comparisons over a number of years or comparisons with other businesses in the same sector

★ useful financial information should cover the areas of profitability, liquidity, efficiency and capital structure

★ financial information becomes more useful when it is used as a comparator

★ useful financial information has certain characteristics

★ the users of financial information are a varied group

★ users of financial information have many reasons for showing an interest in a company's financial statements.

**CHAPTER 7**

# Human resource management

This part of the course contains the following topics.

| | |
|---|---|
| **Changing pattern of employment within organisations** | Current trends, e.g. use of part-time and casual staff, core labour force within organisations. |
| **Recruitment and selection** | Techniques: job analysis, job description, person specification, internal and external sources, selection methods, e.g. role of interview, application forms, aptitude tests, psychometric tests. |
| **Training and development** | Reasons for and types of training and development, e.g. flexibility, upgrading skills, costs and benefits to the organisation, induction, on-the-job, off-the-job, staff development, appraisal. |
| **Employee relations** | Main institutions: ACAS, employers' associations, employee organisations. Processes: negotiation, consultation, arbitration. Management of employee relations, e.g. works councils. |
| **Legislative requirements** | An awareness of legislation relating to equal opportunities, employment, health and safety. |

## Topic The role and importance of Human Resource Management (HRM)

The people that work for an organisation represent a big investment in terms of time and money for their employers. Every employee makes a contribution towards the organisation achieving its objectives, through the jobs that they do.

Employees are resources of the organisation, and so human resource management aims to make the most efficient use of these resources; the better they are at their job and the harder they work, the more successful the organisation will be.

### Objectives of HRM

These will vary between organisations, but the main ones are:

- to promote a policy of continuous learning and staff development
- to recruit, develop and retain people with the appropriate skills and attitudes required for present and future jobs
- to manage employee relations, both on a one-to-one and collective basis, and maintain the commitment of the workforce

BUSINESS DESIGN AREAS

- to design, implement and manage remuneration, reward and appraisal schemes, which motivate people towards achieving the organisation's objectives

- to maintain and improve the physical and mental wellbeing of the workforce by providing appropriate working conditions and health and safety conditions

- to take account of all government legislation relevant to human resource management.

Human resource management is still sometimes called personnel management but is becoming increasingly known as 'People'. It is one of the main functional areas of an organisation.

The size of the HRM department depends on the number of people the organisation employs. However, even a small organisation with just one employee has to manage that employee in terms of getting the best out of him/her. In addition, there are a whole range of legal responsibilities that an employer has, and so even a 'one-employee business' has to perform the HRM function.

The department is responsible for drawing up policies and strategies for the management of staff, making sure they are implemented, and for ensuring that the organisation meets all its legal requirements as far as the employees are concerned.

## The motivation of people

It is important for the HRM department to understand what motivates their workforce so that they can use that motivation to increase their productivity. In 1954 an American researcher called Abraham Maslow put forward a theory on workers' needs based on his research. He suggests that people's needs are complex, but can be classified into five main types. Workers will be motivated by trying to satisfy these needs.

The first is their **physiological** needs for things such as food, clothing, shelter and warmth. These needs are satisfied if wages and various financial bonuses bring in enough money to meet weekly bills.

The second are their **safety** needs which can be satisfied through job security, their contract of employment, membership of a trade union, and protection of the various employment laws.

Pyramid diagram showing, from top to bottom: Self realisation of self fulfilment needs; Status or self-esteem needs; Social or interactive needs; Security or safety needs; Basic psychological needs.

The third is their **emotional** needs for love and belonging. These can be satisfied through teamworking, job rotation and social clubs.

**Esteem** needs are the need for self-respect and the esteem of others. This can be done by recognition, promotion, merit awards, job title, even the size of office or desk that you are given.

Finally, **self-actualisation** needs are filled through self-fulfilment. They can be satisfied by promotion, more responsibility, ownership of company shares, or self-employment.

There are two main management schools on what motivates people. They can be described as Theory X and Theory Y.

**Theory X** managers believe that workers are only motivated by money, and that they are lazy and dislike work. They are selfish, ignore the needs of the organisation, avoid responsibility and lack ambition. In order to get the best out of them they need to be controlled and directed by management.

**Theory Y** managers believe that workers have many different needs which motivate them, and that they can enjoy their work. If motivated, the workers can organise themselves and take responsibility. They believe that managers should create a situation where workers can show creativity and apply their job knowledge.

### HRM function within the organisation

The HRM team are involved in all aspects of human resource work and planning, but a major aspect of the job is to provide advice and training to line managers so that they can be fully responsible for their staff.

Line managers may be involved in drawing up job descriptions, selecting new staff, staff training, appraisals, looking at future staffing requirements, initially handling grievances, and of course implementing HRM policy in their departments.

HRM is a support function of the organisation and has a staff relationship with the other departments in the business. Within this function they will support the organisation through a number of roles:

- **Facilitator** – this involves providing guidance and training to other managers within the organisation for all HRM policies and procedures, and on practical aspects of their job such as interviewing for new staff and carrying out appraisals.

- **Audit** – this is the monitoring and reporting on all the HRM policies within the organisation, ensuring that all staff follow procedures.

- **Consultancy** – they provide managers with guidance and advice on specialist assistance to manage potentially difficult situations effectively, such as making staff redundant.

- **Executive** – HRM are the resident experts in all matters relating to HRM management.

- **Service** – providing useful up-to-date information, e.g. on new employment legislation.

## Topic The changing pattern of employment within organisations

The human resource department has responsibility for making the best use of the staff that it employs. The cost of employing staff is a major expense for the business, so part of the HR role is to keep those costs to a minimum. Among the most popular methods that businesses have employed is to change the structure of their workforce.

In previous years, businesses would recruit staff on a full-time basis to perform set tasks, as and when they were needed. This has a number of drawbacks:

- This often led to a large inflexible workforce.

- Staff could become a burden to the organisation when demand for their goods or services fell.

- Redundancy payments can be expensive.

- The workforce can become less co-operative.

BUSINESS DESIGN AREAS

The costs involved in employment not only include the wage or salary, but also other employment costs such as accommodation, national insurance, paid holidays, sick pay, training and development, etc. Having someone else carry these costs often makes it cheaper to employ contractors outside the business.

We have already seen that in order to be successful, organisations must be able to adapt quickly to changes in their markets. As a major part of the organisation, the workforce must be flexible too. This flexibility can be achieved by employing more part-time and casual staff, and the greater use of outside contractors to provide 'non-core' support services such as cleaning, accountancy services, ICT support, etc.

## Core labour force

This means that the people you actually employ are only concerned with the **core activities** of the organisation and are called the **core labour force**. The core activities are those that directly achieve the organisation's objectives.

The core workers will be regarded as essential to the organisation's success and will be employed on a permanent basis. They may be full-time or part-time workers but will receive the full support of the HRM department. The fewer there are of them, the less expensive it will be for the organisation. However, they will in turn be more committed to the organisation's goals, and relying too heavily on contractual or temporary staff will reduce the possibility of success for the organisation.

## Part-time workers

Until recently, part-time workers did not have the same employment rights as full-time workers, and so the cost of hiring, employing, and releasing was much less. The Prevention of Less Favourable Treatment Regulations introduced in 1999–2000 meant that part-time employees had to receive the same benefits as their full-time colleagues.

## Activity

Find out more about part-time workers rights at www.tuc.org.uk.

Employing part-time workers is still attractive because you can often pay them less. In addition, they tend to be more flexible in their working hours. Some workers, particularly women, can only work part-time because of other commitments such as looking after young children.

Part-time workers have been found to have increased productivity levels, mainly due to a lower rate of absenteeism. Research also indicates that part-time managers are more committed and motivated.

## Activity

Find out more at www.dti.gov.uk/work-lifebalance.

## Casual staff

Casual workers tend to be hired and released as and when they are needed. They do not have the same employment rights as full- or part-time workers at present.

## Contractual staff

Another common alternative to employing full-time permanent members of staff is to employ staff on a fixed-term contract of one or two years, or using agency staff.
At the end of the contract the employee will either be released or will be offered a new contract. This brings benefits to the organisation as the contracted worker will not have the same employment rights or protection, and there is no need for the organisation to offer such benefits as

membership of a pension scheme. In effect the employee is self-employed. Agency staff are not employed directly by the organisation, and so can be hired or released as needed.

## Info Point

The EU Fixed-Term Contracts Directive 1999 (which the Government implemented in July 2003) gives many temporary workers similar rights to permanent staff. The TUC fear that they are still not entitled to the same terms of pay and pensions, and wants new laws to cover the increasing number of agency workers.

*continued* ➤

**BUSINESS DESIGN AREAS**

### Info Point

'There are 1.7 million people in the UK on temporary contracts, casual or agency workers, 7 per cent of the total workforce. Sixteen per cent of temporary workers are now agency workers, compared with just 7 per cent eight years ago.

50 per cent pay temporary workers on different pay rates compared with permanent workers (47 per cent get less and just 3 per cent get more).

70 per cent do not offer the same access to occupational pension schemes.

25 per cent do not give access to contractual sick leave to temporary workers.

14 per cent do not give holiday pay to temporary workers.'

*Source:* www.tuc.org.uk

## Women at work

There is a continuing rise in the number of women who are working. Although the highest growth rates in recent years are in full-time employment, there has been an increasing number of women in part-time employment. Across the UK there are an estimated 12.5 million women in work, 843,000 more than ten years ago. This raises a number of issues which the HRM department has to address.

The main problem for HRM departments still lies with equality at work for women. Employers have a legal responsibility to ensure that men and women are treated the same in terms of pay and conditions for doing similar jobs. Failure to do so could result in fines and bad publicity for the organisation.

### Info Point

The Women and Work Commission set up by the government in September 2004 recently reported that many women face 'multiple' barriers to success, according to interim findings of the Women and Work Commission.

The report said that discrimination and fewer opportunities for women are deeply ingrained in our society, and while some women are succeeding in well-respected and well-paid careers, and are managing to combine work and family life although it may be difficult at times, others find it difficult to enter work, perhaps because of their caring responsibilities or through multiple discrimination.

**Women at work: Key facts**

- Between 1971 and 2004: female employment rate rose from 42 per cent to 70 per cent.

- Women make up only 32 per cent of managers and senior officials.

- Sixty-four per cent of public sector workers are women, against 41 per cent in the private sector.

*continued >*

## Info Point

- Having two children reduces earnings by an average of 10 per cent while three or more children cuts earnings by 15 per cent.

- The full-time gender pay gap is 18.4 per cent.

- The part-time gender pay gap is 40.3 per cent.

*Source:* Women and Work Commission, January 2005

## Other changes in the workplace

There have been a number of other methods employed by organisations to reduce the costs of employment and make the workforce more productive.

### Flexi-time

This has operated for a number of years, and involves workers only having to be at their workplace at certain core times of the day. They make up the rest of their daily or weekly hours at times that suit them best. This has the advantages of allowing staff to miss the rush hour and so reduce their time spent travelling, fitting in appointments, picking up children from school, etc. For the employer it means less time off work and a happier and more motivated workforce.

## Info Point

**Employment Act 2002**

From 6 April 2003, for the first time mothers and fathers of young children under six, or disabled children under 18, were given the right to request a flexible working arrangement.

Employers now have a statutory duty to consider such requests seriously and according to a set procedure. They are only able to refuse requests where they have a clear business reason.

Employers should benefit, as new parents with their valuable skills and knowledge are encouraged to stay in work rather than leave to care full-time for their new families.

*Source:* DTI

### Hot-desks

These are areas of the workplace set aside for staff who do not need office space all the time, e.g. salespeople. They have all the equipment they need at the hot-desk, and so the organisation does not need to create office space for them individually.

**BUSINESS DESIGN AREAS**

### Working from home/tele-working

With modern communications equipment, many jobs can now be carried out at home. Why spend hours a week travelling to work at a computer, when you could have the computer at home? This saves on accommodation costs for the organisation, and again can increase the productivity of the workers. The main drawback here is the feeling of isolation by the employee.

## *Drawbacks of the flexible workforce*

Having fewer core staff leads to a number of problems for the organisation. Firstly, the HRM department will spend much more time recruiting staff and ensuring that there is enough staff available. The amount of training required will increase, much of which will be lost as the staff leave when they are no longer required. When dealing with customers, continuity of staff is important to encourage repeat business. And finally, non-core staff are far less likely to be motivated towards achieving the organisation's goals and objectives.

The increased use of automation has changed what workers are expected to achieve in the workplace. Workers are now much more qualified and so there is a reduction in the number of posts which involve manual repetitive work.

Many workers in the UK are unwilling to accept these low-paid unglamorous jobs, and so there has been an increase in the employment of immigrant workers from poorer EU countries.

## **Topic** Recruitment and selection

One of the major roles of the HRM department is to obtain the best possible staff to work for the organisation. The better the workforce, the more able the organisation is to meet its objectives. Even if the cost of employment was not a factor, it would still be difficult to make sure you have the best staff. However, cost is a major factor and always has to be considered in recruitment.

## *Human resource planning*

At the heart of good HRM is **planning**. This involves a range of factors that have to be considered.

### Current labour market trends

There are fewer people being born, which means we have an ageing working population. There will be fewer young people to recruit and train, so other areas of the labour market will have to be investigated.

## Info Point

The Age Partnership Group is a body of representatives from employer organisations, local authorities, trade unions, training organisations, HR and personnel managers, pensions organisations and government departments. The Be Ready campaign urges employers to seize the business benefits of a mixed-age workforce that includes older workers. Businesses of all shapes and sizes are already changing the way they work and gaining the benefits of a mixed-age work force.

Legislation will outlaw age discrimination in employment and vocational training in 2006. It will cover private and public sectors. It will include every member of your workforce, young and old. This means employers will no longer be able to recruit, train, promote or retire people early on the basis of age, unless it can be objectively justified. All employers, large and small, need to review their business now to ensure they are prepared.

*Source:* Age Partnership Group, www.agepositive.gov.uk (2005)

### Forecasting any possible future staffing needs of the organisation

This would include likely staff turnover, promotion of existing staff, retirements, and releasing surplus staff. This will be a continuing process as staff needs change with the organisation's environment (for political, economic, socio-cultural, technological and competitive reasons). The HR department will then compare changing needs with the number of appropriately skilled workers who will be available.

### Support for staff development in training and motivation

This will include the establishment of a corporate culture.

### Any possible increase in workload

This could be caused by increased demand for the organisation's products, the development of new products, or the introduction of new technologies that will require new skills not available in the current workforce.

## Job analysis

This is the first step in the recruitment process. It initially involves establishing whether a vacancy actually exists. If a worker leaves, he or she may not need to be replaced if the work is shared among existing staff. To do this you would have to identify the job's main features.

- What are the main physical and mental elements of the job?

- What specific skills are required?

- What and who would the job-holder be responsible for?

### Hodder Education

A MEMBER OF THE HODDER HEADLINE GROUP

**SCIENCE COMMISSIONING EDITOR**

HODDER MURRAY, one of the UK's leading educational publishers, has an exciting opportunity for a Commissioning Editor to work within its award-winning secondary school team on the **Science** list.

You'll need to have a track record of commissioning books and electronic resources within the secondary school market and ambitions to build and manage a successful list. The ideal candidate will also have an excellent understanding of the author/publisher relationship as well as good project and people management skills and experience of all stages of the production process.

If you have a background in Science, are self-motivating and commercially astute and think that this could be the career opportunity for you, we'd like to hear from you.

*Please send your CV and current salary details to: Tereza*

- Who would they be responsible to?
- Where will they work and what are the main health and safety considerations?

## Job description

Once the job analysis has been completed and a vacancy identified, the next step is to draw up a description of the job that needs to be done. This will also be the basis for any advertisement of the vacancy. It is important because the organisation needs to think through what tasks they want the post-holder to perform. It will include:

- the job title
- the overall purpose of the job
- the main tasks and responsibilities
- what decision-making powers they have
- who they are responsible for and to, and who they will work with
- the skills, qualifications, and experienced required to do the job
- where the job will be based
- the resources required to do the job
- it can also include conditions of service such as details of pay and conditions available to the post-holder, hours of work, and holiday entitlement.

## Person specification

The main purpose of the person specification is to identify the individual that you want to do the job. In addition to the details on skills, qualifications and experience, this will contain the qualities which the ideal candidate will have. Common examples could be, 'Must be a good teamworker', 'Must be able to work on own initiative', 'Must be highly numerate', etc.

The HRM department should identify the:

- physical attributes which the successful candidate should have
- skills, educational qualifications, training and experience required by the candidate
- level of intelligence needed
- kind of personality which is preferred
- special skills required.

This will be used to match against job applicants so it is easier to identify who you want to interview.

Once these stages have been completed, the organisation must decide how they are going to recruit the member of staff. The first decision is whether to recruit internally or externally.

## Internal recruitment

A suitable candidate may already work for the organisation, so you could simply promote someone within the organisation. There are a number of advantages in recruiting internally:

- The costs involved in promoting internally are lower than recruiting externally.

- Advertising the post in newspapers etc, selecting from a wide range of applicants, and the cost of induction training can be avoided.

- The person is already known to the organisation and so the risk of appointing the wrong person is reduced.

- The existing employee will have benefited from the organisation's own investment in training and so this will not be lost if the employee has to leave in order to achieve promotion.

- The prospect of internal promotion can be a strong motivator for employees, and helps in external recruitment where promotion possibilities are available.

Large organisations use internal recruitment as they have a large pool of workers that they can pick from.

### Disadvantages in internal recruitment

There are a number of disadvantages in only using internal recruitment.

- It restricts the number of applicants for the post as the best person for the job, in the long term, may not yet work for the organisation.

- New workers can bring new skills and ideas to the organisation.

- Promotion will probably create another vacancy which will then have to be filled.

## *External recruitment*

There are a wide variety of different methods of recruiting staff from outside the organisation. What methods are used depend on the nature of the post involved.

For example, if you wish to recruit **unskilled** or **semi-skilled** labour, you could use the local Job Centre, or advertise in a local newspaper.

If the post is a **temporary** one you could use a local employment agency. For example, local Health Trusts use nursing agencies to fill short-term shortages in ward staff.

For **management** posts you could use national newspapers who will have set days each week for recruitment. This has the benefit of attracting the widest range of interested applicants with the right qualifications for the post.

For **specialist** staff, such as software designers, there are trade magazines which are read by most of these specialists; or you could use a specialist head-hunting agency who will have lists of specialists for a range of areas.

The government has a range of '**New Deal**' incentives for employers to get people back into work.

There are now a range of businesses specialising in **internet** recruitment. They attract a range of applicants for either specific jobs or for jobs the applicants would like which will be available in the future. They match their database of applicants with jobs. Some sites, such as www.gojobsite.co.uk cover a wide range of occupations. Others, such as www.gaapweb.com specialise in certain occupations for accounting and finance jobs. There is even a site for students to get part-time jobs at www.thestudentclub.net.

Whether the organisation decides to recruit internally or externally, a successful process will achieve a suitable number of applicants from which the business can select a suitable candidate. This takes us to the next step – selection.

## Selection methods

When selecting the most suitable candidate there are a number of steps that should be involved. The first is to find out if the advertising process has been successful. Have you attracted the sort of candidates you were looking for? If not, re-advertisement may be necessary.

## Application forms

The most common form of notification of interest in the position is the **application form**. However, some organisations still prefer to have applicants submit a **Curriculum Vitae (CV)**, while for some vacancies a simple telephone call may be all that is required.

Application forms are popular because they give applicants the same questions and opportunities to describe themselves. This makes it much easier to compare information from a large number of candidates.

The application forms will be compared to the person specification to see which appear to match. The HRM department will then look at all the applications and decide which applicants to reject at this stage. All rejected applicants should be sent a letter advising them that they have been unsuccessful. However, the department may be able to identify candidates for whom there may be a position in the future and retain their details on file.

From the applications that appear to be suitable, a decision must be made as to how many should be invited for interview. The number to interview depends on the organisation, although interviews represent a cost to the business and this should be kept as low as possible.

On the other hand, the business needs to balance this with having a good selection of candidates to choose from. The organisation may select a long-list of ten or more candidates

---

**John Nicholls Department Store**

**Application Form**

Application for appointment of:
Job reference Number:

**PERSONAL DETAILS**

| Surname | Tel: (home) |
| Other name(s) | Tel: (business) |

Title (e.g. Mr Mrs Miss Ms)

Address

Do you hold a full current driving licence?

Town
Postcode

| Previous surname (if any) | Do you own a car? |

**CAREER HISTORY**

| Present Appointment position | Employer and address |
| Date of appointment | |
| Renumeration and Grade (if applicable) | Employees supervised: |

Description of Duties (add further sheets if necessary)

Reason for leaving

---

**PREVIOUS APPOINTMENTS AND EMPLOYERS**

| Employer's name and nature of business | Appointment held | Dates From | To | Grade/Salary on leaving | Reason for leaving |
|---|---|---|---|---|---|

**EDUCATION**

| Secondary School / College / University | Dates From | To | Qualifications gained | Grades | Date |
|---|---|---|---|---|---|

**OUTSIDE INTEREST (hobbies etc.)**

What are your main interests and leisure activities outside work?

**MEMBERSHIP OF PROFESSIONAL BODIES (state whether by examination)**

| Body | Membership Status | Since |
|---|---|---|

**NON-QUALICATION COURSES ATTENDED (Course, Organising Body and Dates)**

An application form

for a first interview, which will then be reduced to around five for a second interview, when a final decision will be made. Applicants under consideration should be invited for interview, and references sought from existing or previous employers or schools.

## The interview

Interviews are the most common form of making a final decision on which applicant will be the successful candidate. This will be based on who is the best match to the person specification.

However, research shows that interviews are not a very successful way of predicting how well a person will perform in a job.

In many instances it is not the HRM department who carry out the interviews; instead, the line manager and possibly other senior managers will be involved. They are not suitably trained or experienced in the process of conducting an interview, and their decision will be very subjective – they will go with how they feel about the candidate. They are too easily persuaded by the appearance, personality and interview techniques of the applicant.

It should also be remembered that the interview is a two-way process. It is an opportunity for the applicant to find out more about the job and the organisation. It may be that at the end of the interview process, the applicant decides that the job is not for them.

Successful interviews happen when the interviewer(s) have prepared fully for the interview, with set questions and full information on what is required. It may be helpful to prepare a checklist in advance. They also require training in interview techniques which allow the interviewer to compare candidates more equally. For example, some candidates find the interview situation less intimidating than others, but this does not make them the better person for the job.

Good interviewers bring the best out of each candidate by being open-minded and unbiased towards candidates, making them welcome and relaxed, controlling the interview, and ensuring that all relevant information is gained and given.

Interviews do help in the selection process in identifying the personality and characteristics of the applicant, and also give some indication of how they react in stressful situations. The problem is that some applicants may be highly experienced in interviews.

Because of the problems of interviews, other selection techniques have been devised to assist in the process.

## Aptitude tests

These tests measure how good the applicant is at a particular skill such as mathematical skills, typing or shorthand speeds, driving ability, etc. They are objective, in that each applicant's performance can be measured and compared.

You must remember that people perform differently under test conditions from how they would in their normal working day. The business would be advised to give the candidate a number of opportunities to perform at their best.

## Psychometric tests

These tests are designed to measure the personality, attitudes and character of the applicant. They are timed tests (usually multiple choice) taken under exam conditions and are designed to measure the intellectual capability of the applicant for thinking and reasoning, particularly logical/analytical reasoning abilities.

They are designed to be challenging but should not depend on having prior knowledge or experience of the post.

Psychometric testing is most commonly used in management and graduate recruitment. However, doubts have been expressed as to their accuracy and validity. If the questions are not prepared properly they will give an unfair advantage to certain types of applicant, and should be checked for social, gender or racial bias.

## Personality tests

These can give an indication as to whether they are a teamplayer or not, and what roles they perform best. For example, Belbin's self-perception inventory is commonly used by organisations to establish how the applicant will fit into an existing team.

### Info Point

'Psychometric' literally means measuring the brain, which sounds more scary than it need be. In this context it applies to tests that have been scientifically devised to measure certain characteristics or abilities. Such tests go through rigorous trials to ensure they do what they claim and can only be bought by people trained to use them, which means that anything you can get hold of to practise on is probably not the real thing. However a close copy can be good to work on so you can familiarise yourself with what's expected.

Lots of employers use psychometric tests because they believe such tests make selecting the right people easier. There are a whole range and any you're asked to do should be relevant to the job you're going for. Tests for applicants to the police force will be different from those used to select engineering apprentices or accountants.

There are two main types, those that measure personality and those that measure aptitude – things like your verbal, spatial or numerical ability. With personality tests there are no right or wrong answers. Employers who use these are looking for people who will fit into their company culture and contribute to their teams. As they're looking for different personalities in different roles the best advice is to be completely honest. These tests have lie detector questions built in that can be hard to spot. Your responses need to be consistent; if you try to answer in a way you hope will please them it's easy to come unstuck. Pretending to be something you're not to get a job is not a good idea – if you end up in work you're not suited to, it will make you miserable. There's little you can do to prepare, personality quizzes are rarely like the tests employers use so can be misleading.

*Source:* www.bbc.co.uk/one life, January 2005

**Activity**

Try some psychometric tests on yourself at www.allthetests.com

### References

These are used to confirm that the person who is applying for the job is who they say they are. They are normally written statements from previous employers or other reliable person who can give information about the applicant to the potential employer, stating whether they are suitable for the post, how reliable they are, etc.

References should be open and unbiased.

# **Topic** Training and development

Training has always been important in business, but the concept of continuous training is seen as increasingly important. The Scottish Parliament has a Minister in charge of what it calls 'Life-Long Learning'. The concept is that modern society requires people to continue to learn after school, further, and higher education in order to be part of the country's economic activity.

## *Staff training*

This is the process of teaching an employee how to do their job, how to do it better, or how to do a new job in which they have no or little experience. It should improve the efficiency of the employee, making them more productive so they are more able to contribute to the organisation's objectives. Developing good skills can also motivate the employee.

This can lead to other benefits such as lower staff turnover and lower absenteeism.

### Flexibility

One target for the organisation of staff development is to achieve a multi-skilled workforce. Where each member of the workforce can do a variety of jobs or task, the organisation can be much more flexible in responding to the changing needs of its customers. Training and development produce a more flexible workforce and allow changes to be introduced successfully.

### Upgrading skills

Successful training helps to update the skills of the workforce and so improve employee satisfaction. Employees represent one of the most important resources of the organisation, so the introduction of a staff training and development programme will assist the organisation to get the best possible return from its investment in the workforce. The other important fact to remember is that it will improve the image of the organisation. Organisations which offer good training find it easier to attract new staff, are more likely to attract business, and may qualify for quality awards. Because of this, training should be a continuous process for successful organisations.

BUSINESS DESIGN AREAS

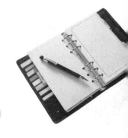

There are four major objectives in the introduction of staff training and development:

1   to allow all workers to achieve the level of performance of the most experienced workers. For new workers this would be included in their induction training.

2   to make a wide pool of skills available to the organisation, both for the present and the future.

3   to develop a knowledgeable and committed workforce, which will be highly motivated.

4   to ensure that the organisation can deliver high quality goods or services.

## The costs and benefits to the organisation in training and development

Sending people on courses involves a number of costs including travel and subsistence, but it also means that they will be away from their jobs, leaving the organisation with a choice of accepting lower output, or bringing in other staff to cover. While training, the quality and quantity of their output could reduce. If the organisation has its own training department, then staff here will add additional employment costs to the business.

Once qualified, staff may leave for better paid jobs; on the other hand, some staff may not want the training.

Research has shown that organisations in the UK fail to provide appropriate staff training and development. Training tends to happen only when problems occur, e.g. when new technology forces it upon the organisation.

### Info Point

In order to try to encourage organisations to be more pro-active in their approach to staff training and development, the government launched the '**Investors In People**' campaign. Organisations can achieve IIP accredited status by developing a more strategic approach in terms of analysing its training and development needs, planning and implementing a programme for training and development, and finally carrying out an evaluation of the effectiveness of its programme.

*Source:* www.iip.co.uk

The benefits from training are harder to identify, and this is why many organisations fail to carry out proper staff training and development programmes. However, the costs of not training are:

● additional recruitment costs when new skills are required

● untrained staff are less productive or motivated and accidents are more frequent

● workers are far less likely to be aware of, or work towards, the organisation's objectives.

Established employees will also benefit from training from time to time.

## *Types of training*

### Induction training

All new employees should go through a process of induction training. This will make them more aware of what is expected of them in terms of the tasks they are expected to perform, and also allow them to develop an awareness of the organisation's policy and practices quickly, and become familiar with their surroundings. This includes simple things like where the toilets are, and much more complicated issues such as health and safety policy. It will depend on the type of organisation but it could include the correct use of equipment, the need for protective clothing, hygiene, etc.

Depending on the job and the organisation, the induction training may take a day or a matter of weeks to complete.

### On-the-job training

This takes place while the employee is actually doing the job. It can be a more experienced employee showing another worker how to do a job ('sitting next to Nellie'); or the more experienced employee may watch and offer advice and instruction while the other worker completes the task (coaching); or the employee may work in different departments or areas of the organisation, learning what each does. This is common for trainee managers so that they can 'learn the business'.

### Off-the-job training

This can take several different forms. The organisation may have its own training department where it organises its own courses, or it may invite specialists to train staff. The employee may be sent to training courses organised by trade associations or employers associations, or to obtain qualifications from college or university.

## *Staff development*

Staff development is the process for helping employees to reach their full potential. It will certainly include training of some sort, but to achieve full development, some of the training will not be specific to the employee's existing job; it will allow them to train in other areas and develop new skills.

## *Staff appraisal*

One of the main methods used for establishing an employee's training and development needs is through appraisal. Appraisals may be used for other reasons, e.g. they may be linked to pay. They are meetings which take place on a one-to-one basis with the employee's line manager or a member of HRM department, to establish how the employee performed in their job, usually over the past year. The process usually involves some preparation by both parties, and an end agreement on a set of goals for the employee. These goals then form the basis of next year's appraisal, and so should be reviewed throughout the year to ensure they are being attained.

The main objectives for the organisation are:

- to identify future training needs
- to consider development needs for the individual's career
- to improve the performance of the employee

- to provide positive feedback and constructive criticism for the employee about their performance

- to identify individuals who have potential for future promotion within the organisation, or who have additional skills which could be useful now or in the future.

It is important that both sides take the appraisal process seriously with proper processes followed, including setting a date well in advance, with an agenda and forms issued with good time for preparation. The employee should be encouraged to contribute effectively and so should not find the process threatening. The outcomes of the appraisal should be clear and any training needs identified with a course of action that includes appropriate training.

# Topic Employee relations

Employee relations is another major area of the HRM department's role within the organisation. It covers how employers deal and interact with their employees, as individuals or a group.

Good employee relations will help ensure that the organisation meets its objectives, as workers are usually much happier in this environment, and more motivated and committed to the goals of the business. They will be more accepting of change, more flexible in their response to requests, and will recognise the need for the organisation to achieve its objectives.

Poor employee relations will lead to less co-operation of the workforce, more industrial action, and a poor image of the organisation for its customers.

The HRM department has responsibility for drawing up and implementing the organisation's employee relations policies. What they cover will vary with the organisation but should include:

- the terms and conditions of employment for staff

- procedures for dealing with staff complaints (grievance), the disciplining of staff, and redundancy including any agreed payments

- the involvement of staff in decision-making

- trade union recognition (some businesses do not recognise trade unions)

- collective bargaining – discussions with trade unions on pay and conditions or changes to working practices for all employees.

## ACAS

Because of the importance of achieving good employee relations, a number of institutions have been created to help ensure that disputes between employers and employees are kept to a minimum.

Perhaps the best known of these is the Advisory, Conciliation and Arbitration Service (ACAS). They describe themselves as employee relations experts, helping people to work together effectively. This ranges from setting up the right structures and systems for employee relations, to finding a way to settle disputes. Nowadays they spend most time advising on how to avoid disputes through good practice and dealing with individual cases.

There are four main ways that ACAS provides helps:

1 Providing impartial information and help to anyone with a work problem, dealing with over 760,000 calls a year.

2 Preventing and resolving problems between employers and their workforces, and helping settle disputes. Their advisory service works with hundreds of companies every year to develop a joint approach to problem-solving.

3 Settling complaints about employees' rights. Over 100,000 people a year complain to an industrial tribunal. Before going to the hearing, most cases are referred to ACAS to see if there is a less damaging and expensive way of sorting the problem out. For unfair dismissal cases, a new scheme has started giving people the choice of confidential arbitration instead of an industrial tribunal.

4 Encouraging people to work together effectively by running workshops and seminars on things like basic employment issues and the latest developments in legislation. Most events are targeted at small businesses with no HRM specialists.

### Activity

Visit ACAS at www.acas.org.uk or try their quiz at www.acas.org.uk/quiz/stage.swf.

## Employers' associations

Businesses in one sector of industry often form an association to look after the interests of all businesses in that particular industry. For example, businesses in the engineering sector may belong to the Engineering Employers Association. They benefit from this association by having a single strong voice to lobby politicians, in their dealings with the engineering unions, and in dealing with the press and other media.

They can pressure and may influence government in areas such as providing support for research and development, taxation, consumer and employment laws. Market research can be gathered for the benefit of the members, many of whom may be small businesses who would otherwise not be able to afford research. The National Farmers Union represented the farmers during the foot and mouth epidemic in 2001, putting forward their views and helping to re-establish export and home markets.

## Confederation of British Industry (CBI)

This body tries to represent the employers from all the UK's industries. They are a much stronger voice in dealing with all of the above, but may voice their opinions on political matters that affect businesses (such as joining the single European currency (Euro), although they are divided on what would be the best course of action).

### Activity

Find out more about the CBI at www.cbi.org.uk.

**BUSINESS DESIGN AREAS**

## Trade Union Congress (TUC)

The TUC represents all trade unions in much the same way as the CBI represents the employers. As with the CBI, they provide information and advice to their members. Trade union membership has risen in recent years after decades of decline. They are now more involved in research into employment and employment rights.

## Trade unions

Trade unions were set up to protect employees from unscrupulous employers, and to provide a political voice for the working people of the country. The Labour Party was established by trade unions. However, following the success of their work in ensuring employment law changes their role has also changed.

They still represent workers in their dealings with employers, and still work to protect their rights and to improve their pay and conditions; they also continue with their campaigns to introduce new laws that will protect and benefit working people. Individually workers have little power in their dealings with employers and government, but by joining a trade union, the worker has a much stronger voice and many more resources to make their point.

Trade unions are much more interested in working with employers and government for the benefit of their members, rather than confrontation and industrial action which could damage their members' jobs. However, to make their influence more effective, unions have merged to form 'super-unions', representing large numbers of employees.

There are still a number of different unions in the UK representing different groups of workers. Some represent a wide variety of different occupations in a number of different industries, such as the Transport and General Workers Union; others represent workers in a specific job or industry, such as the Education institute of Scotland who represent primary and most secondary teachers, and some college and university lecturers.

Trade unions are organised through local and national organisations. They offer their members a wide variety of benefits, which could include discounts on purchases, insurance services, and of course free advice and support on all employment matters.

## Employee relations process

### Negotiation

The purpose of negotiation is to come to an agreement. Here employers and employees meet to discuss issues that affect both parties to agree, plan and implement some changes in the workplace. What is negotiated depends very much on the relation between the two parties, and what existing agreements are in place. Negotiation is often seen as the best method of achieving change in the workplace, as the co-operation and support of employees is essential

to the successful implementation of change in order to meet the organisation's objectives. The success of the organisation should benefit the employee as much as the employers.

## Consultation

Consultation is enforced on employers under employment law for some changes within the organisation. However, what consultation actually means varies from organisation to organisation. The definition of consultation in the dictionary is 'to tell', and many organisations will simply tell employees or their trade unions what changes are planned and why, and then listen to their views. No agreement is necessary and the employer is under no obligation to take account of the views of the employees.

## Arbitration

Where no agreement can be reached between the employer and employees, and a dispute resulting in some form of industrial action is possible, an independent arbitrator such as ACAS may be called in to try to resolve the problem. The arbitrator is unbiased and neutral to the dispute, will listen to both sides, gather other evidence as appropriate and offer a solution.

Binding arbitration is where both parties agree in advance to abide by the decision of the independent arbitrator. Where no agreement exists, both parties will then try to negotiate around the arbitrator's decision to come to some agreement.

## Collective bargaining

It is unusual today for workers to try to negotiate new pay and conditions of employment with their employers. It is much more common for trade unions, staff associations or professional associations to do this for them. Collective bargaining is the process where the trade union or other body negotiates with the employer on behalf of the employees, usually on pay or changes that are proposed in the workplace.

The process starts when either the employees' representatives or the employers propose some change to their existing agreement. For example, the employers could offer a pay rise of two per cent to their employees. The employees' representatives then ask their members whether or not this is acceptable; it usually is not and so they make a counterclaim for a different pay rise, e.g. five per cent. It is generally understood that the employers will probably be willing to pay more than two per cent and that the employees will accept less than five per cent. Negotiations then take place to try to come to an agreement. With both sides keen to avoid any form of dispute, a compromise may be reached. It is common for a larger pay rise to be offered, say three and a half per cent, if the workers agree to some efficiency changes in the existing agreement on working practices. For example, overtime rates may be reduced, or more flexible working hours may be proposed.

Once both parties have an agreement, the employees' representatives take the offer back to their members, recommending they accept. If all goes well then the new pay and conditions agreement will be implemented at an agreed date. To ensure a more settled workforce and better planning, it is now more likely that the agreement will be for a number of years, rather than just one. Within the agreement there will be percentage pay rises for the next few years.

## Industrial action

**Strike** action is just one of the types of industrial action available to workers. In a strike, all or most of the workers stop working (withdraw their labour). This is usually only done as a last resort, as stopping production of goods and services means a loss of sales and customers, which in turn threatens the security of the workforce's employment. There is a legally binding set of

procedures that a union must go through before it can call a strike. This includes balloting all its members in a secret ballot.

In extreme cases the employer may decide to sack the striking workers. However, this is only possible where there is a good supply of other workers who can be quickly trained to do the jobs required. Some big organisations may decide to close the factory or move production elsewhere. This may lead to a **sit-in**, where workers occupy their workplace in an attempt to stop the employer closing the unit.

A **work-to-rule** is where employees work strictly to their terms and conditions of employment. The withdrawal of flexibility leads to a reduction in efficiency and output. An **overtime** ban also has the same effect, which is where workers refuse to do overtime. This would be extremely effective in a police dispute because overtime is essential to the efficient running of a police force. They could simply leave a crime scene when their shift is over.

**Boycotts** can be used when employers introduce new machinery or duties that the employees disagree with. They simply refuse to carry out the new duties or use the new machines.

## Management of employee relations

It is the responsibility of the HRM department to try to avoid disputes and industrial action. There are a number of ways of achieving this, but whatever method is chosen, communication and inclusion of the workforce is essential. If the workers understand what it is that the employer is trying to achieve through the changes and why the changes are necessary, there is less likelihood of a dispute arising. This communication would have to be at each stage of the process. Even more successful is having representatives of the workforce involved in the initial decision-making process. The level of trust that can be built up when workers are included reduces the possibility of dispute to a minimum.

### Works Councils

This is a group of representatives from the workforce who have the legal right to access information from management and have joint decision-making powers on most matters relating to employees. The European Works Councils legislation (2000) states that organisations with at least 1,000 employees across the EU have to set up a Special Negotiating Body (SNB) to represent the workforce. The penalty in the UK for not doing so within three years is a fine of up to £75,000. If the organisation fails to do so, they will have a SNB imposed upon them.

There are some exceptions to the types of information that the SNB can gain access to, but generally this will allow the employees to understand what is happening within the organisation, and involve them with the decision-making process.

**Activity**

Find out more about European Works Councils at
www.dti.gov.uk/er/europe/workscouncil.htm or
www.tssa.org.uk/advice/leg/legewc.htm.

## Motivational techniques

**Quality circles** are groups of between four and ten workers who work for the same supervisor. They meet regularly to identify, analyse and attempt to solve work-related problems. They increase the motivation of the workers by involving them in the decision-making around their own jobs, thus increasing efficiency and raising profitability.

**Job enlargement** increases the number of tasks a worker will perform, making their jobs less repetitive and boring. It works best where the employees are organised into groups, and the workers are trained in all jobs the group carries out. They use **job rotation** to allow workers to change the tasks they perform on a regular basis. It also allows for **multi-skilling**.

**Job enrichment** involves giving workers some opportunities to choose how to complete a particular task, again usually working as a team.

## Grievance procedures

A grievance is a complaint by an employee against their employer. It may be because of the way they have been treated by another member of staff such as their manager. The employee must follow the agreed procedure, which could include several stages involving the HRM department, local trade union representatives and management. If the employee is not satisfied by the response of the organisation, he or she can then approach ACAS; if that fails they can take their employer to an Industrial Tribunal who have some legal powers to enforce their decisions.

## Discipline procedures

Organisations should have written disciplinary procedures in place so that employees know what will happen if they break the organisational rules. The procedure will state the number of warnings that have to be given before dismissal is considered to be fair, and ensures that all employees are treated in the same way.

These are often agreed with trade unions or employee representatives, but they must comply with employment legislation which sets a minimum standard that all businesses must follow. These regulations are in place to ensure that all employees are treated equally.

Disciplinary procedures are undertaken against the employee by the employer when the employee is thought to have done something wrong. This could range from persistent lateness to theft. If the action is very serious then the employee can be sacked on the spot (**summary dismissal**). However, it is more likely that they will be given a number of verbal and written warnings, and be given some support to try to overcome the problem first.

Problems could arise for a number of reasons such as low morale or personality clashes, and these should be investigated. Unless the offence is particularly serious, many employers would try to support their staff through difficult times. They may offer counselling or move the member of staff to another department.

BUSINESS DESIGN AREAS

### Redundancy

This is when the employer finds that they no longer require a number of their employees. Where this is the case, the employer has to make redundancy payments to the employees and give them a certain amount of notice of the redundancy. The business cannot then employ other workers to do the job previously done by the workers made redundant, as they would then have a claim for **unfair dismissal**.

# Topic  Legislative requirements

This section covers the legal responsibilities of the organisation. The laws that an employer has to take account of are varied and complex. They are continually being updated, and this requires specialist knowledge on the part of the organisation. It is normally one of the main functions of the HRM department to ensure that the organisation is fully aware of any legislation and to make sure it is implemented.

The basis for implementation are the HRM policies of the organisation. The department must make sure that all the organisation's policies and procedures are in line with the current laws that affect two main areas: employment, and health and safety.

All managers within the organisation must be made aware of these laws and of any changes, and HRM should monitor how the organisation is performing to make sure that they remain within the law.

### Equal Opportunities

#### Equal Pay Act 1970

This Act was introduced to make sure that men and women would receive the same pay and conditions for doing 'broadly similar' work. Up until that time, employers could pay women less than men. The Act is monitored by the Equal Opportunities Commission, who have found that employers still tend to pay women less money.

---

### Info Point

**Close the Gap campaign**

'Equal pay was meant to have been sorted out 30 years ago yet remains a problem for women in Scotland, businesses in Scotland and the Scottish economy. It is ironic that the Equal Pay Act was introduced in 1970 but not implemented until 1975 so that employers would have five years to sort their pay systems out – 30 years later the gender pay gap lingers on.

*continued* ➤

'We are sending this reminder to employers in Scotland to get the message across that equal pay is not just unfair, it's also illegal and can lead to costly employment tribunal claims. We know that many employers are unsure about how to go about ensuring that they are equal payers. Our message to them is that we can help. We are asking employers to carry out a pay review and then take action on its findings. Too many employers have a misplaced confidence that their pay systems are fine – we know that all too often this isn't the case. Employers can contact Close the Gap and find out how to take action now to protect their company's reputation and make sure that the pay gap will not exist in another 30 years.'

The campaign is supported by Scotland's Enterprise agencies, Scottish Enterprise and Highlands & Islands Enterprise. Both agencies are partners of the Close the Gap Project.

*Source:* www.eoc.org.uk, January 2005

### Sex Discrimination Act 1975 (and the Employment Equality (Sexual Orientation) Regulations 2003)

This Act was introduced to ensure that men and women are treated equally and fairly at work. Although most cases tend to be about discrimination against females, it applies equally to males. It covers a wide range of issue. Discrimination can be one of two types:

1  **Direct** discrimination is where an individual is discriminated against because of their sex.

2  **Indirect** discrimination is where the actions of an employer adversely affects a considerably larger portion of males or females. This covers recruitment, treatment at work and dismissal.

### Race Relations Act 1976 (and the Employment Equality (Religion or Belief) Regulations 2003)

This Act deals with discrimination against employees because of their colour, race, nationality or ethnic origin. It is similar to the Sex Discrimination Act and covers the same areas of direct and indirect discrimination.

## Info Point

The government's plans for a single equalities watchdog are to be published soon in a parliamentary bill.

The Commission for Equality and Human Rights (CEHR) will eventually take responsibility for tackling gender, race and disability discrimination.

It will also promote equality regarding age, religion and sexual orientation.

The proposals have appeased other groups which previously opposed the plan for a single equalities body, such as the 1990 Trust, which describes itself as a black-led human rights organisation.

*continued* ➤

BUSINESS DESIGN AREAS

'The Equality Bill is a massive improvement on the white paper proposals,' said Karen Chouchan, the 1990 Trust's chief executive. 'We are pleased the government has listened to our criticisms and those of the black community.'

The Equal Opportunities Commission and the Disability Rights Commission are expected to be merged into the CEHR when it is formed in 2007.

However, it is believed the CRE will continue in its current form until 2009.

There is a government-backed equalities review due to start work soon, leading a panel of experts to investigate the causes of discrimination and disadvantage.

It will work alongside one by the Department of Trade and Industry, which is responsible for the Equality Bill, aimed at modernising the UK's equality laws.

Amongst other issues, the DTI review will look at outlawing anti-gay discrimination, a key demand by campaigners for many years.

*Source:* www.eoc.org.uk, March 2005

## Disability Discrimination Act 1995

This Act deals with discrimination against an employee or potential employee because of their disability. Again discrimination can be either direct or indirect.

All of these Acts cover a wide range of possible areas of discrimination, but for each there are exemptions. Discrimination is allowed in certain cases, such as advertising for a male attendant for men's toilet; only employing Asian waiters at an Indian restaurant; or excluding a blind person from applying for a bus driver's job. However, employers must be very careful when preparing job adverts, introducing working practices and even in their company advertising to ensure that they do not breach the current legislation. It is also possible that the employer could be sued under the Human Rights Act 1998.

### Info Point

There are two Acts of Parliament which prevent discrimination against disabled people:

- The Disability Discrimination Act 1995: applicable to companies with over 15 employees, it gives disabled people the same rights as everybody else.

- The Disability Rights Commission (DRC) Act 1999 promotes equal opportunities and the elimination of discrimination.

The Acts cover everything from the initial job selection process to doing the work, getting a promotion, career development and redundancy or dismissal.

*continued* ➤

The Access To Work programme has lots of options for disabled people. They can help provide:

- a communicator for people with hearing difficulties
- a reader for someone with visual difficulties
- a support worker for someone who needs help getting to and from work
- alterations to a vehicle or help towards taxi fares or other transport costs for someone having difficulty getting around.

Alterations to equipment:

- alterations to premises or the working environment, such as installing alarm systems or adapting a lift
- the employer only has to pay the first £100 and the programme will foot the rest of the bill.

The employer should help by:

- changing work hours
- arranging extra training
- transferring certain duties to other employees
- making adjustments to help with career development, like making a training venue accessible to wheelchair users.

The disabled person has to show that the change is necessary for them to work effectively and productively.

*Source:* DTI

## Info Point

The Government is consulting on draft regulations prohibiting, subject to substantial exemptions, age discrimination in employment and vocational training. The Age Equality Regulations will implement the age discrimination aspects of the EU Framework Directive on Equal Treatment in Employment and Occupation, 'the Framework Directive'. The deadline for responses to the consultation was 17 October 2005.

**BUSINESS DESIGN AREAS**

## *Employment protection*

There is a wide range of range of legislation covering employment law. In most cases the law protects workers from undesirable practices by employers. Although employers would like to see a reduction in the amount of legislation, they do agree that most laws help to provide better working conditions for employees, and help with employee relations and output. Many employers already exceed the minimum requirements of the legislation, and the laws are continually updated by the government and the EU.

### Employment Rights Act 1996

This states the duties and rights of the employer and employee, and includes the employee's rights to maternity and paternity leave, termination of employment, the right to a written contract of employment within 60 days of starting work, Sunday working, and the right to a written payslip.

### Working Time Regulations Act 1998

This covers the maximum amount of time an employee can be expected to work, their entitlement to breaks and rest periods, the pattern of work, the length of time for doing night work, and their entitlement to leave.

The working time regulations places a limit of 48 hours a week on average which workers are required to work, although they can work more if they want to; a limit of an average of eight hours' work in 24 which nightworkers can be required to work; a right for night workers to receive free health assessments; a right to 11 hours' rest a day; a right to a day off each week; a right to an in-work rest break if the working day is longer than six hours; and the right to four weeks' paid leave per year.

### National Minimum Wage Act 1998

This states the minimum wage that must be paid to employees. The youth rate for 18–21 year olds under the minimum wage legislation is £4.25, and the adult rate is £5.05 from October 2005. It is set on the recommendations of the Low Pay Commission, an expert panel made up of business figures, trade union leaders and academics. Employers now accept the minimum wage, but they are against further rises, while the TUC are looking for a higher minimum wage. The adult rate will increase to £5.35 and the youth rate to £4.45 in October 2006, subject to confirmation by the Commission in February 2006, to check that the economic conditions continue to make it appropriate.

### *Info Point*

**TUC calls for increase to National Minimum Wage**

In its annual submission to the Low Pay Commission (LPC), the TUC will today recommend an increase in the adult national minimum wage to £5.35 for October 2005, rising towards £6 by October 2006. These increases would lift the national minimum wage by more than the projected growth in earnings and give a boost to the pay packets of up to two million workers.

*continued* ➤

In its oral evidence to the LPC today the TUC will point out that previous increases in the minimum wage have benefited fewer than the LPC's target of up to two million workers. A minimum wage set at £5 or less – as the business lobby is suggesting – would mean that the value of the wage would fall against average earnings, which are expected to rise by nine per cent over the next two years.

The TUC is also recommending that the adult minimum wage be paid from the age of 18 rather than at 22. The submission proposes an increase that would sustain the level of the £3 minimum wage for 16- and 17-year-olds in 2005 in relation to earnings, and says that for 2006 it would like to see an interim review to set a rate that benefits larger numbers of young workers.

*Source:* www.tuc.org.uk

## Employment Act 2002

This Act gives additional rights such as paternity leave, and an extension of some existing rights. Mothers and fathers of young children under six, or disabled children under 18, have a right to request a flexible working arrangement. It requires employers to have minimum internal disciplinary and grievance procedures, to avoid the need for so many cases to go to industrial tribunals.

## Employment Relations Act 2004

This Act deals mainly with employee relations and the operation of the statutory recognition procedure for trade unions; the law on industrial action ballots and ballot notices; when arbitration should take place; unfair dismissal, and grievance and disciplinary hearings.

### Info Point

**Employment Relations Act 2004**

Staff will have to be given information and be consulted over major changes to the business, as they currently are in Britain's best companies. Trade unions will be free to recruit members and will find it easier to exclude and expel far-right activists in breach of union rules.

*Source:* www.tuc.org.uk

The main problem which HRM departments face is keeping up to date with the changes in legislation.

## *Industrial Tribunals*

When all other avenues between employers and their employees have not settled a dispute, and for cases of unfair dismissal, the employee has the right to take their employer or former employer to an industrial tribunal. The tribunal is less formal than a court and aims to ensure that employers act legally in respect of the employment legislation.

## *Health and Safety*

The main act here is the **Health and Safety at Work Act 1974** which includes the **Office, Shops and Railway Premises Act 1963**, although many of the other pieces of legislation affect health and safety in the workplace. The aim of the Health and Safety at Work Act is to raise the standard of health and safety for all individuals at work, and to protect the public whose safety may be put at risk by the activities of people at work. What the Act covers and the duties of the employer, are constantly being updated. For example, when research shows that some practices pose a danger to health, then there is a duty on the employer to ensure the safety of their staff. Repetitive Strain Injury (RSI) – when an employee continually uses the same actions in the job (such as working at a keyboard) – is an example of how research overtook existing legislation.

### Employers' duties

The employer must make sure that they take every reasonable step to ensure that all machinery is properly maintained; all hazardous substances are dealt with properly; all staff are trained and informed of potential dangers, and that the environment is safe and non-hazardous to the health of the employees. This will involve a **risk assessment** of the building, operation of machinery, and of each task the employees are expected to carry out.

They have to appoint safety officers and committees to carry out regular inspections of the workplace and assess the dangers involved in each job.

### Employees' duties

The employees are expected to behave in a reasonable manner at work and must take some responsibility for their own actions. They must co-operate with their employers in ensuring that all health and safety requirements are met, and to follow all instructions and accept training where appropriate.

The Act still includes many of the provisions of the earlier Office, Shops and Railway premises Act 1963 which covered minimum working temperatures, toilet facilities, first aid, physical space and levels of cleanliness.

# End of chapter revision questions

1 What are the main objectives of HRM?

2 Describe Maslow's classification of needs and how they are satisfied through employment.

3 Describe three strategies that could be employed to increase employee motivation.

4 Describe how the structure of the workforce has changed in recent years.

5 Describe the growing importance of women at work, and identify the issues that HRM are having to face.

6 What problems have been presented to firms who have reduced their core workforce?

7 Describe the importance of good human resource planning.

8 Describe the five main roles that the HRM department plays within the organisation.

9 Identify the first three stages in the recruitment process.

10 Describe the advantages and disadvantages for both internal and external recruitment.

11 Explain what procedures are involved in the selection process.

12 Identify and describe the different methods of training available to the organisation.

13 Describe the benefits of a staff development policy.

14 Identify the main institutions involved in employee relations.

15 Describe the stages in the employee relations process.

16 Identify the main methods of industrial action.

17 Identify two methods for the successful management of employee relations.

18 Identify and describe the major pieces of legislation that concern HRM departments.

## Chapter Summary

At the end of this chapter you should know the following:

★ The main elements of HRM are:
  **a)** recruitment and selection using internal and external sources
  **b)** staff training and development
  **c)** maintenance of personnel information and records
  **d)** terms and conditions of employment
  **e)** monitoring of HRM procedures throughout the organisation including grievances and discipline
  **f)** the legal requirements of health and safety, employment and equal opportunities legislation.

★ Employee relations refers to the inter-relationship between employees and employers. These relationships are managed through local and national agreements, trade unions and works councils.

★ There has been a change in the way employers use and employ staff, with greater use of part-time and casual staff and the establishment of a core workforce.

★ For successful recruitment and selection the following should be used:
  **a)** job analysis
  **b)** job description
  **c)** person specification
  **d)** interviews
  **e)** application forms
  **f)** aptitude tests
  **g)** psychometric tests.

★ The importance of and reasons for staff training and development, including the flexibility of the workforce and upgrading of skills.

*continued ➤*

BUSINESS DESIGN AREAS

★ The different methods of training available such as induction, on-the-job training, off-the-job training and staff development.

★ The costs and benefits to the organisation of training and development.

★ The main institutions involved in employee relations including ACAS, the various employer's associations and trade unions.

★ The process involved in employee relations of negotiation, consultation and arbitration.

★ The management of employee relations through instruments such as works councils.

# CHAPTER 8

## ●●● Internal Organisation

This part of the course contains the following topics.

| | |
|---|---|
| **Grouping of activities** | Function, product/service, customers, place/territory, technology, line/staff. |
| **Functional activities of organisations** | Marketing, human resource management, finance, operations, research and development. |
| **Forms of organisational structure** | Hierarchical, flat, matrix, entrepreneurial, centralised and decentralised. |
| **Aspects of organisational structure** | Organisation charts, span of control, formal and informal structures, awareness of organisation culture, changes in structure e.g. de-layering, downsizing; the role and responsibilities of management. |

## What is an organisation?

In Chapter 1 we considered the different types of business organisation. There were profit-making and non-profit-making, public and private, each made up of a group or groups of people working towards a set of goals or objectives. What defines an individual organisation is the unique ownership or control from where the organisation gets its leadership and decision-making power.

Businesses are set up by entrepreneurs who organise the resources (human, man-made and natural). The relationships between the people in the organisation form the **structure** of the organisation. Each organisation has a name to give them a corporate identity which their customers can recognise.

So when looking at the internal organisation of these businesses, what we are looking at is how these resources are organised to achieve the business's objectives.

### *Why is structure important?*

- The structure defines how the organisation operates.

- It defines the role(s) of individuals within the organisation, and what authority they have.

- It defines the relationships between groups and between individuals.

- It channels the activities within the organisation towards the goals of the organisation.

- It helps to make best use of scarce resources.

It is relatively easy for one person to make all the decisions in a small business, but impossible in large businesses. We have already seen the importance of making good decisions, so it would make sense to put people in charge of areas of the business who are experts in that area. For example, the business could employ an accountant to look after all the organisation's finance.

BUSINESS DECISION AREAS

●●●●●●●●●●●●●●●●●●●●●●●●●●●●●●●●●●●

Questions which will need to be asked are: 'Who can make decisions, and what can they make decisions about?' and 'Who is responsible for what?'

# Topic Grouping of activities

Organisations have to decide how they should be organised – there is not one single way which suits all businesses. In fact, as every business is different, so is the way they are organised. However, there are some basic ways in which they group their activities. Most businesses will use one or more of these groupings. This mix is called a **hybrid structure**.

## *Functional grouping*

This is a very traditional way of organising the business. It was the main structure used in the UK up until the 1970s when it was seen that British businesses were falling behind other countries in the production of goods and services.

The organisation is split into departments which represent the main functions of the business. These would typically be:

- human resources (personnel)
- marketing
- finance (accounts)
- operations (production, purchasing and distribution)
- research and development
- administration.

Businesses may have different departments from those above, depending on the type of business.

How big the departments are depends on how important they are for the organisation. For example, if the business had only one or two big customers, the marketing department may not be very big; if the business does not employ a large workforce, the human resources department would not be very big. However, it would not be uncommon for departments in a big business to have a large number of staff.

When the business is organised into departments based on these functional activities, it means that all the people within the department have similar skills or expertise in that area, and will use similar resources. This can have many advantages for the organisation.

### Advantages of functional departments

#### The resources of the organisation of the business will be better used

If all human resources work is carried out in one department, there is no need to keep duplicate records relating to the staff. The staff within the human resources department can talk face to face, without having to travel or use costly ICT.

#### Staff become experts in their own field

Staff working in human resources can share their knowledge and experiences and so learn from each other.

### Career paths are created within the departments

Because there are likely to be one or more levels of management within the department, there will be opportunities for staff to move up the 'promotion ladder'.

For example, a human resources department may have a manager, an assistant manager, supervisors for training, staff welfare and recruitment. A new employee can see a possible career progression to supervisor, then assistant manager and manager as jobs for the future.

### Good communication and co-operation within the department

Because the staff in the human resources department see each other every day, they will get to know each other well and become comfortable working with each other. They will be able to talk freely and discuss problems.

### Teamworking improves

Working together means that employees have a feeling of 'all being in it together', and they are motivated to work harder for each other and for the department. This also improves their abilities to solve problems.

### Decision-making is better

The human resources manager makes the decisions for the department, and is the expert that senior managers from other departments can ask for advice in that area. Because each department has its own manager, decisions for the business can be made centrally, with these few departmental managers being able to speak for all their workers under their control. This centralises decision-making, allowing decisions to be made quickly for the whole organisation by just a few senior managers.

## Disadvantages of functional departments

With all these advantages, why change? There are some disadvantages that can arise from organising into departments, and management should be aware of these.

### Staff loyalty to the department rather than the organisation

Forming part of a team of workers can leave staff feeling that their first loyalty is to the department rather than the business. They can see other departments as being competitors, either for business or for the resources of the organisation. Money spent on one department may leave other departments feeling resentful, and less co-operative towards other departments.

---

### *Info Point*

This is not uncommon in schools where the functional departments are created around the different subjects. For example, most Business Education departments need a network of PCs which cost tens of thousands of pounds. Other departments may think that they could use that money better in their own departments.

---

### Communication barriers between departments

Although there is excellent communication within the department, it is often only the managers of the departments who have formal contact with each other.

*BUSINESS DECISION AREAS*

This means that communication between departments can be slow, and can lead to decision-making for the whole organisation becoming less effective and more time-consuming than it should be.

### Slow response to changes in the business environment

This was probably the biggest driving force for moving away from the functional structure. The modern business world changes much faster than it did in the past. If the business cannot move quickly to meet the new challenges then the business will fail, as indeed many have done.

Many of the major manufacturing industries in the UK have disappeared because foreign competitors could react much more quickly to changes in what the consumers wanted; they could produce cheaper goods as they were able to take advantage of changes.

### Some decisions take a long time to make

There will be some decisions that the senior mangers cannot make without consulting their departments. Because of the structure of departments, with several employees at many levels in each, consultation will take a long time.

### Some problems cannot be solved by one department

Many day-to-day problems need the attention of more than one department. Again delays will happen. It may be difficult to identify who has overall responsibility.

We have seen that all businesses need certain core functions such as marketing, finance, operations, etc. Within other groupings these functions still exist, but they may not be individual departments operating within the organisation, e.g. there may be no human resources department. Rather, these departments/functions will be split among other groupings, around which the business is organised and operates.

## Product/service grouping

Here the organisation's activities are grouped around the different products or services that are provided by the organisation. Each product or service requires specialist knowledge and expertise, so it makes sense to gather all staff with this knowledge and skill in one grouping.

### Info Point

#### Royal Bank of Scotland group structure

The RBS Group is made up of eight divisions which in turn incorporate over 41 brands:

| Division | Businesses |
|---|---|
| Retail Banking | Personal Banking<br>Small Business<br>Private Banking |
| • The Royal Bank of Scotland<br>• NatWest | Royal Scottish Assurance<br>NatWest Life |

*continued* ➤

| Division | Businesses |
|---|---|
| Wealth Management | Royal Bank of Scotland International<br>NatWest Offshore<br>NatWest Stockbrokers<br>Coutts Group<br>Adam & Company |
| Retail Direct | The One account<br>Tesco Personal Finance<br>E-Commerce and Internet<br>Cards Business<br>Own Brand Businesses<br>Comfort Card<br>Kroger Personal Finance |
| Corporate Banking & Financial Markets | Corporate<br>RBS Financial Markets<br>Lombard<br>Specialist Businesses |
| RBS Insurance | Direct Line<br>Churchill<br>Privilege<br>Green Flag<br>UKI Partnerships<br>NIG<br>Devitt<br>Finsure<br>Inter Group<br>Linea Directa<br>TRACKER Network UK |
| Ulster Bank Group | Ulster Bank<br>First Active |
| Citizens (USA) | Personal<br>Business<br>Corporate |

*Source:* www.rbs.com

**BUSINESS DECISION AREAS**

## Advantages of product/service grouping:

- Each division is a self-contained unit.

- Each member of staff in that division will have knowledge about that specific product.

- It is easier to see which part(s) of the organisation are doing well and which are having problems.

- This grouping allows for a quicker response to external changes, such as changes in customer requirements.

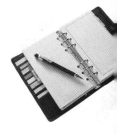

BUSINESS DECISION AREAS

### Disadvantages of product/service grouping:

- Because each division requires its own support staff (administration, finance, human resources department, etc), there is bound to be duplication of resources, tasks and personnel.

- It is difficult to share research and development or equipment.

The divisions are able to make most of their own decisions, as the organisation is decentralised. They all have their own functional staff, and these may be formed into smaller departments.

## Customer grouping

Some businesses have seen the need to put the customer first. Where the individual needs of different customers are important, then businesses will set themselves up in such a way that they have close contact with their customer. A car manufacturer can make a limited range of cars that will suit most consumers, rather than make individual cars to individual customers needs. However, many service industries such as insurance and other financial services find that each customer has their own set of needs.

### Info Point

The Clydesdale Bank employs personal bankers who keep in contact with their customers and provide a service for each individual customer's needs. They carry out a yearly appraisal to see if customers are getting the best products to suit their needs.

Suppliers such as those to the oil companies in the North Sea have a few big customers. It makes sense for them to create teams which work for these oil companies. Often the suppliers will be based in the oil company's office and on their platforms. Each team or group works closely with one customer on a daily basis and can respond quickly to changes in the customer's needs. With such close contact, they can anticipate what the customer will want in the future.

### Advantages of customer groupings:

- Because the customer's needs are identified as a priority, customer loyalty can be built up.

- The customer has the feeling of receiving a personal service even when dealing with large firms.

- The organisation can respond much quicker to the customer's needs.

### Disadvantages of customer groupings:

- Administration of such a grouping can be time-consuming as meeting individual customer needs may take time and effort.

- If the staff changes, the feeling of personal service can be lost.

- Again, there will be duplication of personnel and resources.

## *Place/territory grouping*

Businesses whose customers are spread over a wide area of a country or many countries, often find it better to organise themselves around the place where their products are delivered.

### Info Point

Within Unilever's product/service or divisional structure for ice cream and frozen foods, they have separate companies operating in most countries in Europe.

Bird's Eye Walls make frozen foods and ice cream in the UK. In other countries around Europe, different companies make and sell Unilever's frozen foods and ice cream. This allows them to adapt their products and marketing for local tastes and cultures. Even naming products can be difficult, as a well-known product name in one country can have very different meanings in other countries.

The other main reason for organising this way would be because of where their raw materials are located. The oil extraction industry exists where oil exists, so the oil companies and their suppliers organise themselves in these areas such as the North Sea, Brazil, the Middle East, etc.

In the UK, many national companies organise themselves around the different parts of the country, with regional offices for Scotland, the South-East, etc. This allows them to appoint regional managers who can then better control the activities in their area, and take account of different market conditions in different areas in the country.

For example, the housing market is often very different in areas of the country. At the time of writing, Edinburgh is going through a housing boom, with a shortage of houses on the market and prices being paid above the asking price or valuation. This will allow builders to maximise their profits from sales without having to offer any incentives to buyers, such as free legal fees or carpeting.

In other parts of the country it is a very different story, with houses much harder to sell. Here regional sales managers have to allow their sales teams to offer incentives. Without this local decision-making, the builder may offer unnecessary incentives in Edinburgh or fail to sell houses in other areas.

### Advantages of place/territory grouping:

- Local offices with local knowledge can cater for local clients' needs.

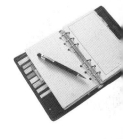

*BUSINESS DECISION AREAS*

- Local offices can overcome problems caused by language and cultural differences in other countries.

- The local office can be held accountable for success/failure in that area.

- Customer loyalty can be built up through a local personal service.

- The local office is more responsive to changes in customer needs.

### Disadvantages of place/territory groupings:

- Administration can be time-consuming.

- If the staff change, then continuity of personal contact is lost.

- Duplication of personnel and resources.

## *Technology grouping*

Here activities are grouped around the technological requirements of the product, mostly in its manufacture or in its delivery process to the customer.

In the manufacturing industry there are often distinct processes or stages which a product has to pass through on its way to completion. Each of these stages requires different technical input, and it may make sense for the manufacturer to organise their business around each of these technical processes.

### Info Point

In car production there are separate processes that a car has to pass through to reach the end of the production line. Modern cars have many layers of paint and protection from rust. The technologies involved there are very different from those involved in installing the braking system. Both are very important and complicated in terms of the technology.

It makes sense that the car manufacturer should group around these processes as there are a number of benefits in doing so. Workers in the paint area are highly skilled and able to make sure that defects in the finish or quality are kept to a minimum. There is no need for them to be involved in learning other processes, and so the work that they do can be kept as simple as possible, making it easier to train new staff and adapt to changes.

### Advantages of technological grouping:

- Using this grouping you can increase the degree of specialisation in the production process.

- Problems with the technology can be easily identified.

### Disadvantages of technological grouping:

- A high degree of specialised training of the staff is required.

- These industries tend to be very capital-intensive, which is expensive.

## Line/staff grouping

The activities of the business can be separated into two types: **core** activities and **support** activities. Core activities are those that are the main purpose of the business.

> ### Info Point
>
> A car manufacturer such as Ford would regard car production and sales as core activities. These are the activities that bring in money to the business and so allow them to earn profits.

Support activities are those needed to make sure that the businesses operate properly.

> ### Info Point
>
> Each Ford factory throughout the world has a human resources department. The department itself contributes nothing to the revenue the firm makes from sales, but without it there would be problems in the recruitment and training of staff, and in maintaining good industrial relations.

The core activities are carried out by **line** departments. They are directly involved in the production of the goods or services that the organisation provides. These would be operations departments, involved in the processes that lead to manufacture of the final product.

The support activities such as human resources, finance, research and development, are called **staff** departments. They provide specialist support and advice to the line departments, to help them with their operations. They will typically be much smaller than the line departments, with a few highly specialist staff providing support and advice to the whole organisation. For example, the human resources department would be responsible for advising on employment legislation. This is a complicated and highly specialised area and it would be unreasonable to expect line managers to have a great deal of knowledge of current legislation.

How these departments work with each other will be looked at in greater detail later in this chapter. However, it is important at this stage to understand that using this grouping means that there have to be formal relationships between departments. Who is in charge of what decisions?

The finance department has a lot of influence on what the operational departments can do. For example, they may ask that a production department change its supplier of raw materials to reduce the cost of production. This would be described as **staff authority**; the relationship here is that the finance department has direct authority over that production department. At other times, the finance department will simply advise and inform the production department, and this would be described as a **staff relationship**.

**Line relationships** describe the relationship between a superior and his or her subordinates. The superior is in charge of the subordinates and has responsibility for ensuring that their work is satisfactory. This line relationship or authority is spread throughout the organisation. At the top of the organisation there will typically be a board of directors who have responsibility and authority over the whole organisation. The line of authority will then work

BUSINESS DECISION AREAS

its way down through the organisation from the top to the bottom, from senior managers in charge of middle managers, who will then be in charge of junior managers, etc.

# **Topic** Functional activities of organisations

Although these are covered in detail elsewhere in the book, it is helpful at this stage to understand what specialist knowledge and skills are shared within these departments, and what the key tasks are.

## *Marketing*

Marketing is a key function of all businesses. They must sell their goods or services in order to survive. How they do this depends on the type of business, but there are some main tasks which all marketing departments carry out.

Marketing is the communication between the business and its customer. The marketing department is most concerned with the needs of the customer.

They will first of all find out what consumers want, both now and in the future. For example, it can take up to five years to develop a new model of car, so they must have some idea of what the customer will want in the future. They will then decide how to satisfy those wants, bearing in mind that they must make profits. Market research is the tool used to gather this information.

They then decide upon the correct **marketing mix** for the organisation. The marketing mix is made up of the four Ps:

- product
- price
- place
- promotion.

The **product** will be designed to do what the consumers think it should do, both in terms of performance and overall quality.

The **price** has to be one that consumers are willing to pay, and still allows the business to make acceptable profits.

The **place** is concerned with getting the product to the market in the right place at the right time in the right quantities.

The **promotion** will communicate with consumers to tell them all about the product.

## *Human resources*

Staff are major stakeholders in an organisation. They are resources, which on one hand should be exploited for their full potential like all the other resources, but unlike the others they are *people*, individuals who respond in different ways to their treatment and environment.

The human resource department manages the staffing of the business. They organise recruitment, staff training and staff appraisal, keep employee records and are concerned with staff welfare. They help employees to develop, and deal with issues such as negotiations on pay and conditions.

They have to be experts in employment law, making sure that the business meets all the legal requirements.

## Finance

This is also a function of all businesses. The finance department is responsible for keeping all the financial records of the business, controlling money flowing in and out of the organisation, and making sure that the business can pay its debts to keep on trading. It will find the best sources of borrowing when required, and create the best conditions for the business.

They provide senior management with the information needed to make decisions by forecasting the financial outcome of different courses of action, and preparing budgets.

They are also responsible for drawing up the reports and accounts of how the business has done over the financial period.

## Operations

Operations is concerned with the production of the goods or services, although this forms only one part of its main tasks. It is also responsible for selecting the best suppliers of materials needed for the business, and will be involved in the finished product in terms of storage, delivery and distribution to the customer.

This is fairly easily seen in a manufacturing business such as an ice cream producer, but more difficult in a service industry such as banking. In banking operations organise the resources such as bank branches, ATMs, cheque books and cards, keep the accounts accurate and up to date, and provide the services that the customer wants.

Whether it is a good or a service which is provided, the same model applies of:

INPUT → PROCESS → OUTPUT

## Administration

Administration is responsible for how the information that the business uses flows around, and in and out of the business. The administration department provides all the office support and information systems for the business. With the increase in the use of electronic communication such as email, fax, video-conferencing, and internet, this area of the business has become more and more important.

They are also concerned with health and safety issues, and the layout and design of the business.

## Research and development

The size of this department really depends on the type of business. Research and development has to work closely with marketing to ensure that customers will have the products they want

**BUSINESS DECISION AREAS**

in the future. They are constantly looking for ways to produce new products or improve existing products.

### Info Point

The size of the research and development department will again depend on the type of business. Medical companies such as Welcome and electronic companies such as Sony spend huge amounts of money on research and development, in trying to bring new products to the market. On the other hand, a national car dealer such as Arnold Clark will expect the car manufacturers and finance companies to provide new products for their consumers. However, they will spend time and money on researching ways to encourage more customers to buy from them, and what other services they could offer.

# Topic Forms of Organisational Structure

## Hierarchical structure

The line relationships that have been described form what we call a **hierarchy** with the organisation. When studying an organisation's structure, we can first look at who is in charge of who and what. Obviously the higher up the structure you are, then the more authority and responsibility you will have, and the higher or better the pay and conditions (you would hope).

A senior manager has a lot of responsibility and makes a lot of important decisions, but he or she cannot make all the decisions for the part of the business under their control. Middle managers may therefore be appointed and given the authority to take charge of some of the areas of the senior manager's responsibility. Middle managers then have junior managers, who may have the authority to make some of the decisions in the area controlled by that middle manager. Junior managers may then have supervisors, appointed to make some decisions.

Each of these levels of management represents a layer of authority. The further up the organisation, the fewer the number of staff at that layer; the further down the organisation, the higher the number of staff on that layer. If we look at the structure on a chart, we can see that it forms a pyramid shape. This is what we call a **hierarchical** or **pyramid structure**.

Within this type of structure, there is a great deal of control. The important decisions are made at the top of the organisation and then passed down through the various levels, along with the instructions on what is to be done. Each level of management has certain decision-making powers which they can then pass down the structure to their subordinates. The information that is needed to make those decisions will flow back up the chain of command through the hierarchical structure.

**Top management personnel**
Managing Director
General Manager
Senior Executives
Company Secretary

**Middle management personnel**
Subordinate managers e.g. Personnel, Marketing, Financial and Production Managers, Foremen and Supervisors

**Employees**

Because of the way this structure operates with clearly defined line relationships, it is possible to give each person within the structure clearly defined roles and tasks to be performed, and also clearly defined procedures for carrying out those tasks. Each member of staff has someone who will supervise their work, and so a great deal of control can be exercised over the whole organisation.

The tasks each member performs are often highly specialised. That is to say, that they will only be expected to carry out a limited number of tasks, and so should become expert in the performance of those tasks. Because they are specialists in a particular function or area of the business, this allows the organisation to be grouped around the main functions of the organisation, and so a hierarchical organisation structures itself around the functional departments.

For example, one member of staff may prepare invoices for a number of the business's customers. It makes sense for them to be placed with other staff that prepare invoices, as they will all use the same information and resources of the organisation (e.g. price lists, discounts, VAT details). Their supervisor(s) will probably report to the finance manager, and so they will be grouped with other workers who also report to the finance manager. It then makes sense for these other finance workers to be in the same place or area as the finance manager, and so a finance department is created. As they are all using similar resources and are now all working together, the business can save money by having only one set of resources for these workers to use, rather than having them duplicated throughout the organisation where finance staff are working. These savings are called **economies of scale**. By having one big finance department, they may save money.

The main problem with the hierarchical structure is that it is designed for close control of the organisation or business, rather than what the business needs to do. Although some decisions can be made quickly by senior managers, decisions which require information from the various levels can take a long time. Communication can also be slow, as the information makes a stop at each level on the way up and down the hierarchy.

Most businesses nowadays need to be much more customer-orientated. The set roles and procedures within this structure do not allow it to adapt or change very quickly. If their customers want something even slightly different from the organisation, then the business can often find it difficult to respond to the customers' request, and so they lose that custom.

This inability to change quickly also makes the business vulnerable to changes in the market in which they operate. Nowadays change is constant, and most markets do not stay the same from year to year. This is because of changes in competitors' actions, legislation, socio-cultural trends, the economy, and in technology.

All organisations to a greater or lesser extent have some hierarchy within them. Someone has to be the boss, someone has to make decisions. The bigger the organisation, the more people you need to make decisions, and they all have to know what they can make decisions about. However, most businesses in the profit-making private sector have moved away from the pyramid structure to one that best suits their market.

In other sectors the hierarchical structure is still very common, particularly in areas where close control of the whole organisation or individuals within it is very important. Government-run or government-funded organisations have to be seen to be taking great care in how taxpayers' money is spent, so the pyramid structure with its close control makes sure that everything is accounted for, and it is quick and easy to spot problems. Large organisations like the civil service departments, local health trusts and education departments have many layers of authority.

## *Flat structure*

In response to the fast-changing markets in which they operated, and their lack of ability to change quickly, many businesses have started to look at ways of being more responsive to

their consumers and the competition in their markets. One way was to abandon the pyramid structure and re-organise into either one (or more likely a combination) of the groupings previously mentioned. Another was to reduce the levels of management within their organisation. This process is called **de-layering**.

De-layering means stripping out levels of management, thereby flattening the organisation. This has a number of effects:

- Firstly, the number of layers that information has to pass through is reduced, making it much quicker for information to flow up and down the organisation.

- Secondly, because there are fewer layers, gathering information and consulting staff takes less time, and so some decisions can be made more quickly.

- The removal of management or supervision levels means that there is less control throughout the organisation.

The **span of control**, the number of workers one manager has responsibility for, is increased. Work is checked less often, so the workers must be reliable. In order for it to be successful, workers must be given more powers to make decisions, and trusted to make the right decisions. This is called **empowerment.**

In flat structures there are few levels of management. Smaller organisations tend to have few levels. With a flat structure you do not get the same problems with communication, decision-making and slow reaction to changes in the market.

This sort of structure helps make the whole business a more effective team. Rivalry between departments is less likely, and as this teamwork allows the business to respond to changes in the market more quickly, the business has a much better chance of surviving and being profitable.

## Matrix structures

These structures tend to be used when the business is involved in a number of large projects, such as a construction firm who may build bridges, new schools, hospitals etc, or where the business has a few large customers, such as suppliers to the oil industry. They both have reasonably long-term contracts with their customers to produce goods or services. Teams are formed with staff from all or most of the functional departments.

Each member of the team has their own specialist skills, and is responsible for their own particular expertise. For example, the accountant for the team will deal with all the financing for the project, and staff from the engineering department will provide all technical support.

However, because they are attached to the team rather than a department, there will be an opportunity to become involved in areas out with their normal expertise. This is called **multi-skilling**, where employees are given the opportunity to develop skills and expertise in other areas, while still being highly skilled in their functional area.

The matrix structure allows more freedom for individuals to use their talents effectively. There may be a team leader, but generally the team has no hierarchy, with each member having the same level of authority and responsibility.

Staff may be moved during or at the end of the contract to another team. This means they will work on a variety of projects over time. In some businesses staff may be involved in two or more projects at the same time, and this allows for staff development, increased job satisfaction and motivation.

The problem with this is that it is an expensive way of organising, with each team needing to have its own support services and staff. They will often work away from the organisation.

## Info Point

Oil suppliers usually work in the oil company's building, and require their own computers and administration staff. This leads to duplication of resources across the business, and so they lose the economies of scale that are available in the pyramid structure.

## Entrepreneurial structure

Small businesses tend to have only one or two main decision-makers, usually the owner(s). Other staff may be consulted, but will often have little input into the decision-making process. For example, a shop with an owner/manager and six members of staff, will rely wholly on the owner's expertise. If one of the staff members has a great deal of experience, then they may be involved in some decision-making, and be given some authority and responsibility. All decisions will be made centrally by these key workers.

Some larger businesses also adopt this structure. The editors of daily newspapers have to make decisions quickly and rely very much on their own expertise on what should appear in that day's edition. They may discuss this with one or two assistants, but again all decisions are made centrally. It is also common in areas of the banking industry where large amounts of money are moved between different markets throughout the day.

The problem with this type of structure is that it relies very heavily on these key decision-makers. If they are unavailable, then the decisions cannot be made. Also, it places a very heavy workload on these few individuals. The stresses involved often mean that the decision-makers can only work effectively for a relatively short period of time with that workload.

As small businesses grow it is likely that they will change their structure, employing more key staff so that the workload can be shared, and the stresses reduced.

## Centralised structures

Like the entrepreneurial structure, centralised structures rely heavily on a number of key individuals who make most of the decisions within the organisation. There may be more of them, but all control of the organisation is held by these key members of the organisation. Normally they are the senior managers or directors of the business, but they could also be the owners.

Hierarchical structures are often highly centralised in terms of decision-making, and they share many of the same advantages. Economies of scale are available through centralised purchasing.

## Info Point

McDonald's restaurants throughout the UK and much of Europe are supplied by a small number of suppliers. McCain's supply all their fries, and purchasing from one supplier allows the contracts to be so large than they can negotiate lower prices and good credit terms. Also, McCain's have to make their fries to an exact specification, using a specified type of potato. This means that all the fries take exactly the same time to cook in McDonald's fryers, and will taste exactly the same, no matter where you are. The advantage of this is that there is very little waste, and few customer complaints.

Although McDonald's have created divisions to cater for different parts of the world, leadership at the top of the organisation and the divisions is very strong, with senior managers having control over all aspects of the business, even the franchises. These decisions are made for the whole organisation or division rather than for individual restaurants. These senior managers are very experienced and so the decisions made should be better.

McDonald's have a worldwide corporate image that they can maintain through their centralised structure. All restaurants have similar or identical decor, staff wear the same uniform, products have the same name, and the service should be identical throughout the world or the division. The double arches are recognisable worldwide and no matter what country you are in, you will already know and trust what the products will look like and taste like.

## Decentralised structures

Most businesses now try to find customers wherever they can, and in any part of the world. The internet and the worldwide web have opened up foreign markets for many Scottish businesses as they can now market their products around the world. In addition, the removal of trade barriers and the movement towards global free trade have removed many of the restrictions which would have previously prevented them from trading in many of the world's countries. While this has created many new opportunities, it has also created new threats in that foreign businesses now find it much easier to sell their products in Scotland.

This process is called **globalisation**, and it has meant that in order to survive, Scottish companies must be much more able to quickly change what they do, and how they do it.

This level of flexibility is not available with highly centralised formal structures, and so there has been a move towards much more decentralised structures.

These decentralised structures offer many of the benefits of flat structures, while still retaining a good level of overall management control. More of the decision-making is left to middle and lower management levels. In particular, most of the operational decisions and some of the tactical decisions can be delegated by senior managers, allowing them to

concentrate on more important decision-making. This means that lower management levels have more power, but the overall responsibility still lies with senior management.

There are distinct advantages with decentralisation:

- It allows the organisation to be more responsive to changes in the market or environment in which they operate. This is because decision-making can be quicker as there is no need to refer matters up the chain of command.

- Secondly, the people now making the decisions are much closer to their customers and have a far better knowledge of their customers' needs, and will also have a better knowledge of what is possible within their departments. The quality of decisions should therefore improve.

- Delegation and empowerment of staff allows them to develop their professional skills and gives them greater opportunity to display their own abilities. Being trusted to make decisions can make the staff feel more wanted and appreciated, which in turn increases their motivation to work harder.

- Having the power to make decisions means that staff who are aware of their customers and market can prepare for possible changes in advance. This reduces the amount of negative impact on the organisation. Part of this process would include building in flexible practices such as multi-skilling, where workers can take on a number of roles within the organisation.

## *Factors affecting the internal structure of an organisation*

### Size

As a business grows, it becomes harder to control all the staff within the organisation. In order to keep control and supervision, managers are appointed to look after groups of workers. As these groups grow, departments are formed and the number of levels of management increases.

The bigger the organisation, the more organised it will have to be, so large businesses tend to have tall organisational structures. Small businesses need less organisation and so tend to have flat structures.

### Technology

The introduction of new technology can change the structure of a business. For example, a new information technology system could reduce the need for a large administration department.

There are now more employees working from home than ever before. This is because modern communication technology allows the worker to keep in touch with the office throughout the day, and information can be transferred easily over telephone lines by downloading completed work. The departments that they previously worked for may disappear.

Greater use of the internet may change how the sales department is organised.

### Product

Having a small number of large customers for your product means that a flat structure using teams may be more appropriate. For example, a building firm will have only a few large jobs on at any one time, so the staff will be split between each of these jobs.

### Market

If the market is small and local, the organisation will be small. For example, a hairdressing business market will normally be the local community, so a flat structure with few employees is all that is needed.

If the market is big and widespread, the organisation may be large and organised around the geographical areas it covers. For example, a national double glazing company will have a head office, and a number of regional sales teams for different parts of the country.

# Topic  Aspects of organisational structure

## *Organisation charts*

Where there are a large number of employees within an organisation, it is often useful to show the staff employed in a diagram, indicating where they work, what position they hold in the organisation, who they are responsible to and who they are responsible for.

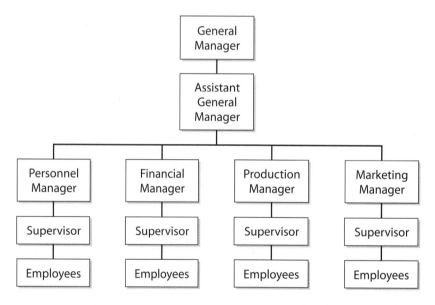

They are particularly useful for new employees, customers, suppliers, and senior management. However, in very large organisations they would be useful to all employees, as they could see who to contact about specific matters.

They are useful because:

- New members of staff can immediately see who they are responsible to, and identify other members of their department.

- Each member of staff is included, showing which department they work in, their job title, and who they are responsible to and for. It could also include telephone or room numbers, and in some cases photographs may be used to identify key individuals.

- Customers or suppliers can easily identify the various functional departments, and identify who to contact in that department.

- Senior managers can have an overview of the whole organisation, identifying where problems with communications may occur either up and down the hierarchy or between

departments. They will also be able to see the number of employees each manager has immediate responsibility for (span of control). This will allow them to identify possible problems with control, and appoint assistants if necessary.

Organisation charts can only give a very general overview of the organisation. In practice, other lines of communication between individuals and between departments may have been established. For example, teams made up of members of different departments could not be shown on the chart along with the functional structure.

## Span of control

The span of control is the number of people which a manager or supervisor has working directly for him or her. In the example below we can see the production line supervisor has a span of control of three. There are three production assistants who report directly to the production line supervisor.

The size of the span of control is important, because the bigger the span, the less supervision or control can take place. Flat organisations tend to have a wide span of control for managers; highly centralised organisations might have small spans of control. The correct size depends on the amount of control required and the abilities and skills of the manager and staff involved.

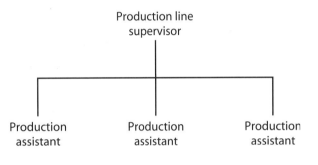

Where the tasks that are being worked upon are very important or require a great deal of technical understanding, the span would be quite small.

## Info Point

In a hospital operating theatre, the span would be very small because of the importance of the task and technical skills involved. Even in the wards, many hospitals adopt a system of double-checking. For example, when a patient is being weighed, two nurses are required in case one misreads the measurement on the scale. It is very important, because the amount of drugs given to the patient depends on their body weight. If the weight reading is wrong then the dosage will be wrong, which in some cases could prove fatal. So although weighing a patient is a minor routine task, it is also very important and one nurse has to supervise another.

In schools some departments have one teacher while others may have seven or more. The size of the department or the amount of work they have to do decides the span of control. A principal teacher of English may have a span of control of six or seven, whereas a principal teacher of RME may have a span of control of one.

The individual manager or supervisor has a certain level of interpersonal and leadership skills. Where the level is high, the span of control can be high as staff will be highly motivated to work without supervision. Where the level of skill of the manager is low, the span of control should be low.

It is also dependent on the skills and abilities of staff. Where staff are skilled and highly motivated they need less supervision, so the span of control can be high. Where there is a lack of skilled motivated workers, more supervision will be needed so the span of control will be lower.

## *Formal relationships*

### Line relationships

Where a member of staff is in charge of another member of staff, this is called a **line relationship**. In our organisation chart you can see a line drawn between a manager and the staff that she or he is directly responsible for. This line represents the relationship which the manager has with the member or members of staff. It is a vertical line which shows who is responsible for who, and who reports to who.

For example, one of the assistant headteachers in a school would have responsibility for the English department; the principal teacher of the English department would have a line relationship with that assistant head teacher.

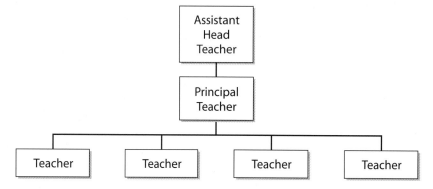

### Functional relationships

The relationship between members of staff on the same level of responsibility is called a **functional relationship**. The managers of the various departments within an organisation have a functional relationship. On an organisation chart they would appear as a horizontal line.

For example, in a college the head of the computing department would have a functional relationship with the head of the engineering department. Each is responsible for what happens within their department, but some courses would require that students spend time in both departments. The two heads of department have to work together to organise these courses for the students, and this would be part of their functional relationship.

### Staff relationships

In many organisations there are individuals, or in some cases groups of individuals, who do not fit neatly into an organisation chart because of what they do for the business. They are specialists in a particular field and provide a level of expertise and advice that support the organisation as a whole, rather than individual departments. These individuals would be described as having a **staff relationship** within the organisation. Company lawyers or ICT specialists are examples of individuals who have a staff relationship within the organisation. They do not have formal line or functional relationship with the business.

## Informal structures

Although not all organisations actually draw up an organisation chart, the chart describes the formal structure of the business. It shows the formal relationships between staff, and the formal lines of communication within the organisation. However, organisations are made up of individuals who will establish friendships and good working relationships outside of these formal lines. This could be for a number of different reasons. For example, an assistant within the accounts department may play badminton with the manager of the sales department. There is no direct line or staff relationship between them, but as they know each other well they may discuss business matters outside work, or even contact each other directly in the workplace to discuss customers' accounts, as this would be quicker than using the formal structure.

Some management theorists argue that organisation charts are a mistake because they do not reflect what a business actually does, and are therefore misleading.

It could be that the formal structure is not good enough and that staff create informal structures simply to get the job done. For example, if there are bottlenecks in the flow of information where unacceptable delays take place, staff will go around the bottleneck. If, as in the previous example, the sales manager needs urgent information for a customer, he may contact an appropriate member of the accounts department that he or she knows direct, rather than use a written request to the accounts manager, in order to keep the customer happy.

These informal communication structures within the organisation should be of concern to the senior management. The individuals involved may form close relationships and share some information only between themselves, excluding others. For those involved, there is an added feeling of belonging and an additional layer of support for them as individuals. For those not involved, there is a feeling of isolation and dislike of what they see as a clique. They may form other informal groups to avoid what they see as a potential threat to their position within the organisation. This can lead to hostility between members of staff and the destruction of teamwork. It can also lead to the informal groups working against the decisions, aims and objectives of the organisation. Senior management need to be aware of these informal groups, and work to ensure that as far as possible they remain only social groups; they need to maintain good working relationships and effective teamwork.

These informal lines of communication are often described as 'the grapevine'. The information that flows through the grapevine is often outside of the management's control, and can be incorrect or misleading. Senior management must ensure that staff are kept informed of developments within the organisation to counteract any possible misinformation flowing through the grapevine. They may also use the grapevine in addition to the formal lines of communication, to pass information quickly throughout the organisation.

## Organisational (corporate) culture

Any social group of people form their own culture. For example, a group of friends, whether they are aware of it or not, will behave towards each other in particular ways. They may have acceptable forms of dress; they will talk to each other in a way that assumes a set of beliefs about each other and their environment, which can make it difficult for an outsider to join in their conversations; they will socialise in their own particular favourite places.

Organisations are made up of individuals who form their own culture, given enough time. Management can influence this culture, for the benefit of the organisation in its dealing with customers and for the establishment of good practice and teamwork within the organisation.

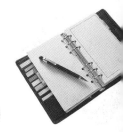

To do this, managers must understand what will influence the culture within the organisation. As with the group of friends above, it will be about behaviour, attitudes, values and their environment.

All new members of staff want to 'fit in' as quickly as possible. To do this, they take their lead about how to act or behave in the workplace from those around them. If management puts in place appropriate policies, e.g. about how to deal with customers, then this will influence the behaviour of all staff.

The attitude of staff can be influenced by the actions and motivation of management. A positive leadership style should quickly lead to a positive attitude by the staff. On the other hand, any negative signals from management will also be quickly picked up by staff.

The values of the organisation as a whole are dictated by the actions and communications of the management. For example, the business's mission statement sets out what the business expects to achieve, and what its goals are in terms of the goods and services it provides. A mission statement which states that the organisation wants to achieve 100 per cent customer satisfaction should lead the staff to value their customers more, and regard customer satisfaction as a measure of how successful they are in their career.

The physical environment in which staff work affects how staff behave. For example, an open plan office where staff are visible to each other and movement is unrestricted, should lead to an openness between staff with few barriers in terms of communication or social or work interaction. Having an individual office, on the other hand, creates physical barriers between that member of staff and others, which in turn makes them appear less approachable for both social and work interaction.

Managers who adopt an 'open door' policy towards staff can overcome these barriers through simply leaving the door open, and letting staff know that they should feel free to come and see them. This overcomes the problem of work interaction, but also keeps unnecessary social interaction to a minimum.

Other environmental factors that could influence the organisation's culture could be dress code or the use of a staff uniform which identifies individuals as belonging to that organisation, satisfying their emotional need to belong or fit in. Many shops use uniforms to give all the employees an identity belonging to the organisation. When they put that uniform on, they are mentally 'at work'. It also promotes a single corporate identity to customers, who see a member of that organisation rather than just another individual.

The type of corporate culture which the organisation creates is dependant on the organisational structure. If the organisation is centralised and hierarchical in nature, the culture will be much more formal, whereas in a decentralised flat structure, staff tend to be less formal. In either case, a management-inspired organisational culture can be a very positive force for motivation, and for accepting the organisation's goals and objectives as personal for each member of staff.

Corporate culture can be defined as the values, beliefs and norms relating to the organisation that are instilled in all staff and shared by them. It brings a number of advantages:

- Employees have a greater sense of belonging to the organisation, and new employees can settle in more quickly.

- If successful, there will be increased motivation for staff and greater job satisfaction, which should lead to improvements in production.

- Relationships between employees are improved, with increased teamwork.

- Staff will be more loyal to the organisation meaning lower staff turnover, more co-operation and fewer disputes.

- The goals of the organisation are shared among all staff, with the original ideas and principles of the firm carried throughout all branches and offices of the organisation.

---

### Info Point

**Corporate Principles**

Our Corporate Principles have been developed to create and deliver consistently superior value to our:

- shareholders
- customers
- employees
- communities.

Our core beliefs and values are based on the following principles:

- We will be open and honest.

- We take ownership and hold ourselves accountable (for all our actions).

- We expect teamwork and collaboration across our organisation for the benefit of all stakeholders.

- We treat everyone with fairness and respect.

- We value speed, simplicity and efficient execution of our promises.

And we do not have room for people who do not live these principles.

*Source:* www.cbonline.co.uk

---

## Changes in structures

We have already seen why organisations have been forced to move away from traditional hierarchical single structures. The increasing rate of change in the business environment has forced organisations to reorganise so that they can be much more responsive to these changes.

In addition to the speed of change, Scotland's manufacturing industries have declined over the past 30 years or so. Much of this has been a natural development for a mature economy as it goes through the process of what is called **de-industrialisation**. During this time, service industries such as banking and insurance, have become very successful in Scotland and have seen an increase in output.

Many foreign multi-national companies have opened centres in Scotland. Their management structures and organisational operations are very different to the traditional hierarchical structures. In order to do business with these multi-nationals, Scottish organisations were forced to change their operations to match those of their new customers.

The global marketplace where many Scottish businesses find themselves demands greater efficiency and quality from the goods and services that are offered. In order to compete in the global market, Scottish businesses had to adapt.

Traditional structures:

- have direct lines of responsibility

- employ people to do as they are told

- pay people for the position they hold

- dictate that all decisions are made by management, and management must be allowed to manage.

Scottish production needed to be revolutionised, as just becoming more efficient was not enough. To gain competitive advantage, Scottish businesses must be innovative and imaginative in their approach to management.

Industries in western economies have tried a number of approaches to make their businesses more competitive. One of the first approaches used was **Total Quality Management** (TQM). Total Quality Management is a comprehensive and structured approach to organisational management that seeks to improve the quality of products and services through ongoing refinements in response to continuous feedback. However, TQM brought problems of its own.

- A number of organisations were unable to introduce TQM successfully, for a number of reasons.

- Others found that in order to achieve TQM, they had to change their operations significantly.

- Many organisations found that the cost was too high, despite the potential long-term benefits.

- For others there was simply not the will among management and staff to achieve TQM successfully.

Some of these organisations had to either change significantly or cease to exist. For others, TQM was only the first step on a long hard road to achieve competitive advantage, and so remain ahead in world markets.

Modern management issues centre around change, quality, cost but most importantly survival. Some of the more successful management strategies for survival are:

- business/corporate re-engineering

- empowerment

- outsourcing

- down-sizing

- de-layering

- lean production.

## Re-engineering

This is the most radical step which management can take. It involves a complete change in the way the firm operates, in order to be the best it possibly can be. The whole organisation is changed. Departments may disappear completely to be replaced by project or customer teams.

## Empowerment

This is more than just the delegation of some decision-making powers to employees. It also involves a fundamental change in management attitude to employees at all levels if it is to be successful.

Employees must be given the power to make decisions that affect their part of the organisation, and be trusted to do so. There has to be an acceptance that errors will be made until the worker becomes fully competent.

Empowerment comes with de-layering, where the supervision of activities is reduced. This can increase the motivation of workers.

## Outsourcing

This is where part of the operations of the organisation is passed or 'outsourced' to a specialist, who may be able to do the job better than the organisation itself.

For example, many firms used to have their own in-house ICT specialists. The cost involved in recruiting and keeping these staff was high due to skills shortages, which meant that there were always better opportunities for the best employees elsewhere. A solution is to employ a specialist ICT consultancy, who then carries out the work for a fee and deals with the problems involved in training and retaining ICT personnel.

Outsourcing allows firms to reduce their direct obligations to the payment for resources, and passes the burden to other companies. The cost of employing staff is far greater than simply their wage or salary. The firm also has to pay to equip the worker and provide accommodation. If these costs are being paid for by someone else, the organisation simply pays for what it needs when it needs it, and can more readily increase the demands on outside contractors than it could on its own employees.

The ability of the management of the organisation to focus on its core activities increases, allowing them to deal more effectively with changes in their markets, increased production levels, or even rush orders.

The specialist firm may have more specialist equipment or staff which can produce the function with higher quality and lower cost.

Some firms prefer not to outsource because they then become dependant on them. They lose some of the control of the function, and the specialist firm may let them down in terms of delivery or quality. There are also questions over the confidentiality of sharing business information. The specialist company needs to have some detailed information, which they could potentially share with competitors.

In order for it to be successful, the communications between the two organisations needs to be very good. This may involve staff from each other's organisations working alongside each other, or staff being moved between the organisations.

## Info Point

The Aberdeen Met Office supplied weather information to Shell in the North Sea in order that they could ensure the safety of their employees and contractors working there. The Shell deal to provide forecasting services for its North Sea operations was thought to have been worth £1 million.

Shell have now given the contract to a rival supplier as they require a service that covers their entire north-west European E&P operations, not just the UK.

## Activity

Discuss why it is better for Shell to outsource weather forecasting to a specialist company, rather than do it themselves.

## Downsizing

Downsizing involves reducing the operating costs of the organisation by looking for what it does not need to spend money on. This could include:

- reducing the scale of operations to meet actual market demand
- removing excess capacity within the organisation
- consolidating complementary operations under one function
- reducing the resources of the organisation following increases in productivity
- focusing only on core operations.

This has the effect of reducing the costs for the organisation, making them more efficient and competitive.

During recessions, organisations need to look very closely at ways of reducing costs in order to survive. Many find that their productive capacity exceeds the actual or planned demand for their product. Even after coming out of recession, the demand for their products may continue to be less than it had been before.

For some organisations, downsizing means the closure of factories or productive units. For others it means the merging of two or more separate operations being brought under the one management umbrella. For some it simply means the scaling down of their productive capacity.

Duplication occurs not only in production and management, but also in areas such as sales, research and administration. For example, having two separate sales forces for different product ranges is an expensive luxury which may have been sustainable and even profitable in the past. However, with ever increasing competition, many organisations find that the additional cost makes them uncompetitive.

Downsizing leads to unemployment, but the level of unemployment is much lower than if the company itself had failed.

There will inevitably be a loss of knowledgeable and experienced staff, and with uncertainty about the security of their jobs, staff morale will decrease until it becomes clear who will be made unemployed and what redundancy packages are available. It is important that the

organisation keeps staff informed so as to keep any possible conflict to a minimum; however, once downsizing has been completed, the remaining staff will feel that their importance has been recognised. They may also find that they have far greater power than before.

## De-layering

De-layering is the removal of levels of management or supervision for the organisation. For example, changing from a tall structure to a flat structure would involve the removal of layers of management from the hierarchy.

Some management levels in the organisation exist just to supervise the work of other staff. The cost of employing these managers or supervisors has to be weighed against the cost of any mistakes that employees make in their work. If the cost involved is higher, then continuing to employ these managers does not make economic sense.

In addition, organisations have to weigh the cost of their employment against the costs of additional or continuing training for these members of staff, to ensure minimum errors. Again, if the cost is higher then their continued employment does not make economic sense.

When fully trained, the staff will be more aware than any supervisor or manager of what operational (or in some cases, tactical) decisions should be made. If the staff are then empowered to make these decisions, there is no longer a necessity to employ the manager/supervisor.

As we have already seen, additional levels of management slow down the communication process and consequently its ability to change quickly in response to changes in their market.

Many middle managers lost their jobs in the 1990s due to the process of de-layering. Whether this process was successful for the individual organisation depended on whether it was simply trying to cut staffing costs, or whether it was genuinely trying to reorganise itself to better meet its customer needs. In the majority of cases they went too far and then found themselves having to re-employ managers.

All of these approaches can be used in an attempt to make the organisation more responsive to change and therefore more competitive. However, the main function of the structure of the organisation is to meet its strategic aims, and it is management's responsibility to make sure that this is the case.

One of the main problems with changing the structure is the resistance to change among the staff employed by the organisation. Any change has to be managed properly. This includes planning within a realistic timescale; keeping staff informed and updated about the changes including reasons for the change; and monitoring the impact of changes as they take place, with adjustments as necessary.

If management fails to convince staff of the benefits of change, the outcome will be worse than if the change did not take place at all.

The consequences of de-layering include the following:

- Each manager has a wider span of control.
- Decision-making can be quicker, allowing the organisation to respond better to changes in their markets.
- It empowers staff as they have increased responsibility.
- It allows greater opportunity for delegation.
- It reduces the cost of salaries for the organisation.

- It prepares staff for promotion as they have more decision-making powers.
- It also reduces the opportunities for promotion.

### Lean production

Lean production is used in mass production where unit production costs are kept to a minimum.

However, it can always be improved upon. The Japanese adopted a 'total approach' to eliminating waste, removing anything that did not add value to the final product.

# End of chapter revision questions

1   Explain why schools need principal teachers in charge of individual departments.

2   What decisions can they make for their departments?

3   A supermarket will have very different departments from those in a school. What will their departments be?

4   Identify one organisation which would have a large human resources department, and justify your choice.

5   Describe what you understand by functional grouping.

6   What are the main advantages and disadvantages of a functional grouping?

7   Identify the main functional activities of organisations, and briefly describe what they do.

8   Explain how each of the functional departments interacts with and depends upon each other.

9   The Virgin group provides a wide variety of goods and services. Identify as many of their products as you can, and then describe what advantages and disadvantages Virgin has in grouping this way.

10   Insurance companies group their organisation around the different categories of customers they have, such as life assurance, motor insurance, house insurance, etc. Describe why insurance companies do this, and what the drawbacks of such a grouping would be.

11   Shell exploration and production has facilities all around the world. Explain why they would group geographically, describing the benefits and drawbacks of such a grouping.

12   WH Smith organises its activities around three areas: wholesale operations, retail operations, and internet sales. Explain why WH Smith could be described as grouping around different technologies used in different processes.

13   Within your school/college, identify those activities which could be described as core, and those which could be described as support.

14   Describe what you understand by a hierarchical structure.

15   Identify the advantages and disadvantages of this type of structure.

16   Describe what you understand by a flat structure.

17 Identify the advantages and disadvantages of this type of structure.

18 Explain the meaning of the terms empowerment and de-layering.

19 Describe what you understand by a matrix structure.

20 Identify the advantages and disadvantages of this type of structure.

21 Explain the meaning of the term multi-skilling.

22 Describe what you understand by a entrepreneurial structure.

23 Identify the advantages and disadvantages of this type of structure.

24 Describe what you understand by a centralised structure.

25 Identify the advantages and disadvantages of this type of structure.

26 Describe what you understand by a decentralised structure.

27 Identify the advantages and disadvantages of this type of structure.

28 Look at the following examples and then decide what type of structure would best suit them. Describe the factors that made this the best choice.

a) a national supermarket chain

b) a supplier of drilling equipment to a single oil company in Aberdeen

c) a small graphic design business.

29 Explain why organisation charts can be useful.

30 Explain what you understand by the term span of control.

31 Look at the list of organisational relationships below and then explain whether they are line, functional, or staff. (NB some of the examples may be of more than one type.)

a) a personnel department of a large oil company

b) an expert on the European Union appointed to a company trading with France for the first time

c) a lawyer working full-time for a national newspaper

d) a foreman mechanic working in a local garage

e) a sales manager for a double glazing company

f) the Marketing Department of a supermarket chain.

32 All organisations develop a corporate culture, whether it is intended by management or not. Your school or college has its own corporate culture, part of which is decided by the management of the school/college, and part of it by the students.

a) Describe the corporate culture of your school/college as you see it, and identify those areas which are decided by the management, and those decided upon by the students.

b) The role of the school/college is to provide a caring atmosphere in which students can learn. What parts of the corporate culture work towards this aim, and what parts work against it?

c) Describe action which the management of the school/college could take to improve the corporate culture.

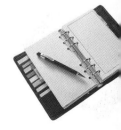

d) Using the answers to the previous questions as a guide, explain why the management of a new medium-sized electronics company may wish to introduce its own corporate culture as soon as possible.

33 Explain why organisations may feel they have to change.

34 Describe what you understand by the term outsourcing.

35 Why would trade unions work against attempts to downsize an engineering business?

## Chapter Summary

At the end of this chapter you should be able to:

★ identify and describe the main functional activities of an organisation including marketing, human resources management, finance, operations, and research and development

★ identify and analyse the factors that influence the internal structure of an organisation

★ describe the main forms of organisational structure such as hierarchical, flat, formal and informal, matrix, entrepreneurial, centralised and decentralised

★ describe with examples the different grouping of activities including functional, product/service, customer, place/territory, technology, and line/staff

★ identify and describe various aspects of organisational structure, including the use of organisation charts, and span of control

★ show awareness and understanding of organisational culture, changes in structure including downsizing and de-layering, and the role and responsibility of management.

# Glossary

| | |
|---|---|
| **ACAS** | Arbitration, Conciliation and Advisory Service. See www.acas.org.uk for more information. |
| **Appraisal** | Evaluation of staff performance and identification of training needs. |
| **Aptitude testing** | Tests carried out to assess a candidate's suitability for a position. |
| **Arbitration** | Where two opposing parties meet with an independent third party and agree to abide by the decision of the third party. |
| **Articles of Association** | This legal document applies to limited companies and lays out the terms of business for the company. |
| **Automation** | The use of machines and technology in production. |
| **Bar codes** | A series of black and white vertical lines used to identify different products. |
| **Batch production** | Where identical products are produced in batches, followed by a batch of a different product. |
| **Benchmarking** | Used in the area of quality control to establish an accepted standard. |
| **Brainstorming** | A method used to generate new ideas by taking note of all kinds of ideas at a meeting no matter how outlandish. |
| **Branding** | A method of attaching a 'persona' to a product based on an established make. |
| **CAD** | Computer Aided Design – the use of computers and computer software in the design process. |
| **CAM** | Computer Aided Manufacture – the use of computers in the manufacturing process. |
| **Capital** | Money invested in business by the owners(s) at the commencement of the business. |
| **Capital intensive production** | Where the cost of capital is greater than the cost of labour. |
| **Cash flow management** | Ensuring the organisation has sufficient funds to meet its objectives |
| **CBI** | Confederation of British Industry. |
| **Centralised structures** | Businesses where the main functions are to be found in one central location. |
| **Channel of distribution** | The method by which the product produced by the manufacturer reaches the consumer or end user. |
| **Collective bargaining** | A system whereby negotiations are carried out on behalf of several parties instead of negotiating separately. |
| **Consultation** | A process of seeking and gathering information from interested parties. |

GLOSSARY

| | |
|---|---|
| **Consumer trends** | The general fashion that is followed by the general public at any point in time. |
| **Core activities** | The main commercial activities of a business. |
| **Corporate culture** | A phrase used to describe the atmosphere or feel of a business. |
| **Customer grouping** | Where an organisation organises itself around the different types of customers it has. |
| **Cycle of business** | The identification and satisfaction of consumer needs, only for more needs to be created. |
| **Data protection** | Legislation on how information must be handled by organisations. |
| **De-layering** | The removal of layers of management to flatten the organisations structure. |
| **Delegation** | The transfer of responsibilities from a manager to a subordinate. |
| **Demand-oriented pricing** | This occurs when the price of a product is set according to the level of demand. |
| **Demographics** | The study of how households are made up, births, deaths, etc. |
| **Desk research** | Research that is carried out solely from a desk relying on information to hand e.g. in books and journals rather than collecting it from the field. |
| **Destroyer pricing** | This occurs when a business sets the price of a product so low that it destroys the market share of a similar product produced by a rival company. |
| **Differentiated marketing** | Offering different products to different groups of consumers in the market. |
| **Disciplinary procedures** | A set of actions that are followed when a member of staff breaks the accepted code of conduct. |
| **Discrimination** | Making a distinction on the basis of unjust grounds. |
| **Diversification** | Organisations targeting new markets or moving into the production of new goods or services. |
| **Downsizing** | Changing the size and focus of a business to a smaller scale. |
| **Durable goods** | Goods which can be used again and again. |
| **E-commerce** | Conducting business and accepting and making payments using the Internet. |
| **Economic stock level** | The level at which there is no excess or shortage of stock. |
| **Emotional selling proposition** | When consumers trust a brand or business, and so will return to buy again and again. |
| **Employee relations** | Referring to the relationship that exists between employer and employees. |
| **Employment protection** | Legislation which exists to protect the rights of workers. |

| | |
|---|---|
| **Employment tribunals** | A legal hearing heard by the Employment Tribunal Service for employees who have raised an employment law issue against their employer. |
| **Empowerment** | Creating a sense of worth and responsibility amongst employees. |
| **Entrepreneur** | The person who has the idea and takes the risk in combining the factors of production to provide a good or service. |
| **Entrepreneurial structures** | Structures which are based around one or two key decision makers. |
| **Equal opportunities** | Employers must provide the same opportunities to all employees and potential employees regardless of gender and race. |
| **Extension strategies** | Ways in which an organisation can extend the life cycle of a product. |
| **Factors of production** | Land, labour, capital, and enterprise which are required for the production of goods or services to take place. |
| **Field research** | Research that is carried out away from the office. |
| **Flat structure** | An organisation where there are few levels of authority. |
| **Flexi-time** | Flexibility in working hours meaning that employees can start and finish work at different times so long as they complete a set number of hours each week. |
| **Flow production** | Constant production of identical items moving through separate processes on a production line. |
| **Franchises** | A business that is operated under the name of a parent business and the 'owner' effectively rents the name to trade under e.g. McDonalds and The Body Shop. |
| **Fringe benefits** | Extra benefits that employees receive from their employer or as a result of their employment over and above their salary. |
| **Functional relationships** | Relationships between the functional departments of the organisation. |
| **Generic advertising** | Advertising which promotes a whole industry such as the beef industry rather than individual producers' products. |
| **Goods** | Items which are produced by manufacturers. |
| **Government-funded Service providers** | Bodies which are set up and funded by the government. |
| **Grievance procedures** | A set of rules and regulations set up in a business to govern breakdowns in employee and employer relations. |
| **Health and Safety** | The protection of employees from risks through unsafe working environments. |
| **Hierarchical structure** | Relating to the structure of a business where it resembles a pyramid with those at the top (fewer) having more authority and in charge of those at the bottom (more). |
| **Hierarchy of needs** | The different needs employees need to have satisfied through their employment. |

| | |
|---|---|
| **Hot-desks** | Work areas for staff who do not need space all the time. |
| **Induction training** | Orientation training for new employees usually carried out before they start work. |
| **Industrial action** | Action taken by employees who are in dispute with their employer. |
| **Informative advertising** | Advertising that conveys useful information instead of trying to convince you to buy a product or service. |
| **Inputs** | The factors of production which are put into the production process. |
| **Integration** | Organisations taking over or merging with other organisations. |
| **JIT – Just in Time operations** | Operations set up to minimise stock and production levels to meet actual demand. |
| **Job analysis** | The process of identifying what vacancy might exist within an organisation. |
| **Job enlargement** | Creating extra tasks and responsibilities for employees. |
| **Job enrichment** | Allowing the job holder to develop their own specialist expertise. |
| **Job production** | A single unit of production completed to customers specifications. |
| **Job rotation** | Allowing workers to carry out a variety of different tasks. |
| **Job specification** | Details of what a vacancy will involve for the candidates in terms of tasks to be undertaken, responsibilities, etc. |
| **Kanban** | Stock record card system used in Just-in-Time production. |
| **Labour** | The mental and physical effort of the employees of the organisation. |
| **Labour-intensive production** | Production where the cost of labour exceeds the cost of capital. |
| **Land** | The natural resources used in production, including all things grown on and extracted from the land, sea, and atmosphere. |
| **Lead time** | The time taken between placing an order for supplies and the supplies arriving. |
| **Limited liability** | Where the owners/shareholders of the organisation are only liable for the amount they invested in the business. |
| **Line relationships** | The relationship between superiors and subordinates whithin the organisation. |
| **Line/staff grouping** | Line employees are the core workers of the business, and staff are the employees that support the core activities of the organisation. |
| **Local authorities** | Local government bodies/the local council. |
| **Market growth** | When the sales and customers within a market increase. |

| | |
|---|---|
| **Market orientation** | When organisations base their operations on market research, finding what customers want, and then supplying it. |
| **Market segmentation** | Where organisations split the whole market into different groups who have similar wants and needs. |
| **Market share** | The share of the whole market (sales/customers) that one organisation has. |
| **Memorandum of Association** | A legal document required when setting up a limited company. |
| **Merchandising** | Methods of encouraging customers to buy at point of sale such as displays, posters, etc. |
| **Minimum stock level** | The least amount of stock a firm can hold without production having to be stopped before new stock arrives. |
| **Mission statement** | A document issued by an organisation detailing their strategic aims and objectives. |
| **Motivation** | The management skill involved in getting workers to work harder and/or better. |
| **Multi-Skilling** | The development of a number of different skills amongst workers to enable them to perform a variety of jobs. |
| **Negotiation** | The process of coming to an agreement between employers and employees. |
| **Non-durable goods** | Goods which are used only once or twice and then have to be replaced e.g. food. |
| **Off-the-job training** | Training which takes place away from the workstation. |
| **On-the-job-training** | Where workers are trained while they are doing the job. |
| **Operational decisions** | Routine decisions on the day to day running of the company. |
| **Organisation charts** | Diagrams which show the place of employees within the organisation in terms of their department, their level of authority, and their immediate superiors and subordinates. |
| **Output** | The product or service which the organisation produces. |
| **Outsourcing** | Arranging for outside suppliers to provide support functions which are not core to the business e.g. printing. |
| **Overtime** | Working beyond the normal contracted hours, usually attracting higher rates of pay. |
| **Parent companies** | A firm which owns all the shares in another firm. |
| **Pay and conditions** | The details which are contained in the contract of employment including rate of pay, hours to be worked, etc. |
| **Payment systems** | The different methods of paying production workers. |
| **Penetration pricing** | A low-price pricing strategy to allow a new product to the market to gain sales and market share. |
| **Performance-related pay** | Paying workers according to how well they work or rewarding them for achieving targets. |

| | |
|---|---|
| **Person specification** | Drawn up during the selection process to identify the qualities and skills the ideal candidate for the job should have. |
| **Personality tests** | Tests carried out during selection to establish the personality type of a candidate for a job, and how they would react in different situations. |
| **Persuasive advertising** | Advertising which attempts to persuade the customer to buy the product |
| **PEST analysis** | Analysis of the external environment in which the organisation operates (Political – Economic – Socio-cultural – Technological). |
| **Piecework** | Where employees are paid by how many items they produce. |
| **Place/territory grouping** | Where the organisation is organised around the different areas of the country or the world where they operate. |
| **Primary sector** | Industry which is based around the exploitation of natural resources including farming, fishing, mineral extraction, etc. |
| **Product differentiation** | Where businesses use factors such as a brand name to make their product appear different to similar products on the market in the minds of consumers. |
| **Product life cycle** | The various stages a product will go through from introduction to growth to maturity to decline. |
| **Product line** | A range of similar products produced by an organisation with slight differences to appeal to different tastes and markets. |
| **Product mix (range)** | A range of different products produced by the same organisation at different stages in their life cycle, to spread risk, maintain profit levels, and to provided investment for new products. |
| **Product orientation** | Where an organisation concentrates on the production of new products rather than carrying out research to see what consumers want. |
| **Product portfolio** | *see Product mix.* |
| **Product/service grouping** | Where the organisation is grouped or organised around the different products or services that it provides. |
| **Production planning** | The process of establishing what is required in terms of land, labour and capital to meet consumer demand. |
| **Production systems** | The methods available to the organisation to produce goods and services. |
| **Profit-sharing** | Where employees are rewarded with a share of the organisation's profits when they exceed certain levels. |
| **Promotional pricing** | A short term pricing strategy to lower price in order to boost sales. |
| **Promotions into the pipeline** | Promotions offered to companies to encourage them to buy more of a product for sale. |

| | |
|---|---|
| **Promotions out of the pipeline** | Promotions offered to consumers to encourage them to buy more of a product. |
| **Psychometric testing** | A tool used during the recruitment process to establish how each of the candidates thinks. |
| **Public relations** | The communications tool of the organisation when dealing with those outside the organisation including customers, the media, and the government. |
| **Public sector** | Here the organisations are owned by the government on behalf of the people. |
| **Publicity** | Planned or unplanned discussion in the media about the organisation. |
| **Purchasing mix** | Finding the best supplier in terms of price, reliability, quality, etc. |
| **Pyramid structures** | Organisational structures with few people at the top of the organisation and many at the bottom (hierarchical structure). |
| **Quality circles** | Groups of workers meeting to solve production problems and improve standards. |
| **Quota sampling** | A method of selecting the number and type of consumer to carry out market research on. |
| **Random sampling** | Random sampling involves producing a random list of individuals to survey. |
| **Ratio analysis** | A financial tool for calculating performance between one year and another and between firms. |
| **Recruitment** | The process of attracting the right applicants to apply for a vacancy. |
| **Re-order stock level** | The point at which new stock should be ordered to ensure that the stock level does not fall below the minimum stock quantity. |
| **Re-order stock quantity** | The amount of stock needed to bring the stock level back to the economic stock level. |
| **Sampling** | The process of selecting who and how many consumers should be selected for market research. |
| **Scheduling** | Ensuring that all parts of the operation process work smoothly and that delivery times are met. |
| **Secondary** | Organisations who are primarily involved in the manufacture of goods or semi-finished goods. |
| **Selection** | The process of deciding on the right candidate for a job. |
| **Services** | Things that are done for consumers for a price such as banking, hairdressing, etc. |
| **Shareholders** | Private individuals who own a part or a share in a limited company. |
| **Shortage/bottle necks** | Problems in production when too few or too many items move from one part of the production process to the next. |
| **Skimming** | A short term high pricing strategy used when there is little competition in the market. |

| | |
|---|---|
| **Sole traders** | One person businesses where the owner takes all the profits and makes all the decisions. |
| **Span of control** | The number of subordinates a person has working directly for them in the organisation. |
| **Staff authority** | Areas where the staff or support departments have the right to tell the core departments what to do, e.g. human resources ordering health and safety checks. |
| **Staff relationships** | How the staff departments interact with the core departments. |
| **Staff welfare** | The responsibility of the human resources department to look after the employees within the organisation. |
| **Stock control** | The function in operations where the levels of stock are maintained in the most economic and efficient way. |
| **Strategic decisions** | The long term goals or aims of the organisation. |
| **Subsidiary companies** | Businesses which are wholly owned by another business. |
| **SWOT analysis** | A tool used in decision making to look at the internal and external environment of the business. |
| **Tactical decisions** | Decisions about how the resources of the organisation are to be organised and used to achieve their goals or aims. |
| **Target markets** | Where organisations market their products or services at specific parts of the market rather than the whole market. |
| **Tele-working** | Information and communication technology used to allow employees to keep in contact with the organisation whilst away from the workplace. |
| **Tertiary/service sector** | The sector of industry which provides services to the consumer such as retailing, banking and insurance, etc. |
| **Test marketing** | A tool used in marketing where the product is released in one small market to gauge consumers reactions to it prior to the full market launch. |
| **TUC** | The Trade Unions Council is the parent body of all trade unions. |
| **Undifferentiated (mass) marketing** | Marketing directed towards all consumers in the market rather than targeting specific groups. |
| **Unique selling proposition** | Something about a product that makes it different in the consumers mind from similar products, e.g. the brand name. |
| **VAT** | Value added tax is a tax placed on the purchase of most goods or services. |
| **Voluntary sector** | This includes organisations such as charities who are not owned by government or private individuals. |
| **Wealth creation** | The process whereby the activity of organisations creates wealth for the whole economy. |
| **Works councils** | A group of representatives from the workforce who have the legal right to access information from management, and have joint decision-making powers on most matters relating to employees. |

# Index

The arrangement is word-by-word. Bold page numbers indicate a glossary entry.

INDEX

INDEX